ADI DA

Avatar Adi Da Samraj

ADI DA

The Promised God-Man Is Here

THE AUTHORIZED CONCISE BIOGRAPHY OF AVATAR ADI DA SAMRAJ

Written and compiled under the direction of
The Ruchira Sannyasin Order of Adidam Ruchiradam

THE DAWN HORSE PRESS

NOTE TO THE READER

All who study the Way of Adidam or take up its practice should remember that they are responding to a Call to become responsible for themselves. They should understand that they, not Avatar Adi Da Samraj or others, are responsible for any decision they make or action they take in the course of their lives of study or practice.

The devotional, Spiritual, functional, practical, relational, cultural, and formal community practices and disciplines referred to in this book are appropriate and natural practices that are voluntarily and progressively adopted by members of the practicing congregations of Adidam (as appropriate to the personal circumstance of each individual). Although anyone may find these practices useful and beneficial, they are not presented as advice or recommendations to the general reader or to anyone who is not a member of one of the practicing congregations of Adidam. And nothing in this book is intended as a diagnosis, prescription, or recommended treatment or cure for any specific "problem", whether medical, emotional, psychological, social, or Spiritual. One should apply a particular program of treatment, prevention, cure, or general health only in consultation with a licensed physician or other qualified professional.

This concise edition of *Adi Da* is formally authorized for publication by the Ruchira Sannyasin Order of Adidam Ruchiradam. (The Ruchira Sannyasin Order of Adidam Ruchiradam is the senior Spiritual and Cultural Authority within the formal gathering of formally acknowledged devotees of the Divine World-Teacher, Ruchira Avatar Adi Da Samraj.)

NOTE TO BIBLIOGRAPHERS: The correct form for citing Ruchira Avatar Adi Da Samraj's Name (in any form of alphabetized listing) is:
Adi Da Samraj, Ruchira Avatar

© 2003 The Da Love-Ananda Samrajya Pty Ltd,
as trustee for The Da Love-Ananda Samrajya.
All rights reserved.
No part of this book may be copied or reproduced in any manner
without written permission from the publisher.

The Da Love-Ananda Samrajya Pty Ltd, as trustee for The Da Love-Ananda Samrajya,
claims perpetual copyright to this book, to the entire Written (and otherwise recorded)
Wisdom-Teaching of Avatar Adi Da Samraj, and to all other writings, recordings,
and images of the Way of Adidam.

"Adidam", "Ruchiradam", "The Bright Field", "The Bright Room", and "Camera Illuminata"
are service marks of The Da Love-Ananda Samrajya Pty Ltd.

The Midnight Sun Logo is a service mark of The Da Love-Ananda Samrajya Pty Ltd.

Produced by the Avataric Pan-Communion of Adidam
in cooperation with the Dawn Horse Press

Concise edition, January 2003

Printed in the United States of America
International Standard Book Number: 1-57097-143-9
Library of Congress Catalog Card Number: 2002117366

CONTENTS

INTRODUCTION
THE ANSWER TO HUMAN PRAYERS xi

PART ONE
THE YEARS OF "LEARNING MAN" (1939–1970) 1

Chapter 1	Born as the "Bright"	3
Chapter 2	Re-Awakening to the "Bright"	21

PART TWO
THE TEACHING-WORK BEGINS (1970–1977) 45

Chapter 3	Embracing the Guru-Function	47
Chapter 4	"Crazy" Submission	63
Chapter 5	Garbage and the Goddess	73
Chapter 6	Divine Distraction	83
Chapter 7	Transcending the Emotional-Sexual Ego	95

PART THREE
REVELATION AND IMPASSE (1978–1985) 107

Chapter 8	Creating the Means to "Link"	109
Chapter 9	The Revelation of Da	119
Chapter 10	The Signs of Divine Power	131
Chapter 11	The Search for Hermitage	145
Chapter 12	"Mark My Words"	157

PART FOUR
THE DIVINE SELF-"EMERGENCE" (1986–1998) 169

Chapter 13	A Grand Victory	171
Chapter 14	The Yoga of Devotion	187
Chapter 15	The Divine World-Teacher	199
Chapter 16	The Forerunners	211
Chapter 17	Divine Completeness	223
Chapter 18	"My Word Is Sealed"	235

PART FIVE
"Bright" Return to What Was Never Lost (1999–2002) — 245

Chapter 19	Ordeal at the "Brightness"	247
Chapter 20	Beyond the Cosmic Doorway	263
Chapter 21	All of This Is Beautiful	277
Chapter 22	The "Midnight Sun"	295
Chapter 23	"I (Myself) Do Not 'Come Down' Below the Brows"	311

EPILOGUE
I Am The One Who Has Always Been Here — 321

AN INVITATION
Becoming a Formal Devotee of Avatar Adi Da Samraj — 325

An Invitation to Support Adidam	333
Further Notes to the Reader	335
Glossary	338

ABOUT THE COVER:

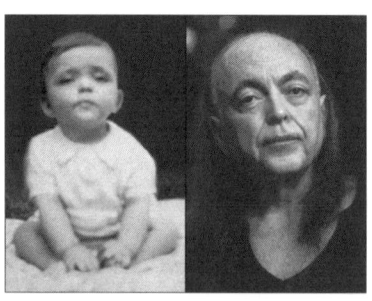

The two photographs of Avatar Adi Da Samraj on the cover both show Him in profound moments of Transmitting His Spiritual Blessing. The first photograph was taken in 1940 (when He was less than a year old), the second in 2000 (when He was sixty years of age). As the first photograph shows, even as a young infant, Avatar Adi Da was already Radiating the same Spiritual Depth and Force that He Radiates now. Thus, His Spiritual Blessing-Power is not the result of a lifetime of Spiritual practice, but was the case from birth. Such is the characteristic of the Divine Avatar—Who has "Crossed Down" from the Divine Domain (Appearing as a human being in the midst of this world), and Who is born only in order to Reveal the Nature of the Divine Reality and the Way of Perfect Liberation. ■

The Ruchira Sannyasin Order of Adidam Ruchiradam

The Ruchira Sannyasin Order is the body of Avatar Adi Da's most advanced devotees who have chosen to devote their lives utterly to Him and His Way—by embracing the life of formal renunciation, in the circumstance of perpetual retreat. Avatar Adi Da has designated the Ruchira Sannyasin Order as the senior cultural authority within the gathering of His devotees—both during and after His physical Lifetime. Thus, it is the unique responsibility of the Ruchira Sannyasin Order to function both as the extension of His Sacred Authority and as His Instrumentality (or the collective human "conduit" for His Spiritual Blessing).

The Ruchira Sannyasin Order is (and must always be) the most senior gathering of (necessarily, formal) practitioners of the Way of Adidam—and the hierarchically central, and most senior (but entirely renunciate, and non-managerial), functioning cultural authority among, and in relation to, <u>all</u> the (necessarily, formal) practitioners of the Way of Adidam. . . .

All the present members and all the future members of the Ruchira Sannyasin Order are Called and Empowered (by Me) to Function (collectively) as the principal and most senior (physically living, human) Instruments of My forever Blessing Work, and, by their unique (and uniquely authoritative) cultural service (simply by Wisdom-word and practicing example), to provide all other practitioners of the Way of Adidam with the principal Good Company (of fellow devotees) that is necessary for the inspiration and guidance of their practice of the Way of Adidam.

AVATAR ADI DA SAMRAJ
"The Orders of My True and Free Renunciate Devotees"

Avatar Adi Da Samraj
The Mountain Of Attention Sanctuary, 2001

INTRODUCTION

The Answer to Human Prayers

If you turn to the teachings of the principal religions—Buddhist, Christian, Hindu, and others—you will find a common prophecy: An All-Surpassing God-Man will come, either as a supreme Avatar, or the final Prophet, or the Enlightened One. In many traditions, it is said this Spiritual Deliverer will appear during the darkest times, when humanity has lost its connection to God, Wisdom, and Truth.

Among Buddhists are those who call that Expected One "Maitreya"; among Hindus, the "Kalki Avatar"; among Christians, the "second coming"; among Jews, the "Messiah". What is common among these great religious traditions is their promise of a future Bringer of Light, one who will restore us to our purpose in both the natural and Spiritual orders.

In our time, we have seen these religious traditions meeting each other on the crowded, now "globalized" world stage. It is obvious that no common portrait exists of what the Promised God-Man will be like. Would he or she be political, like a Messiah, or contemplative, like a Buddha? Align with an existing religion, or start from scratch? Preach absolute tolerance, or war on unbelievers? Would this one, upon seeing the benighted condition of humanity, even bother to announce his or her appearance?

This book answers all these questions and more, for its message is that the God-Man Promised for all humankind is actually here in the person of Avatar Adi Da Samraj. This is the confession of His devotees, those who have found Him and chosen to live in Spiritual Communion with Him. And this is also His own confession.

His devotees have discovered Avatar Adi Da to be the Living Presence of the Divine Reality that is the source of all religion. He is the Transmitter of Perfect Divine Consciousness—here to duplicate His Realization of the Divine Condition in those who turn to Him for His Spiritual Blessing. He is the Divine Avatar, or the mysterious appearance of the Divine Being in a human form—born to Enlighten all who turn to Him for Spiritual Help, and ultimately to Draw them into the eternal "Place" of Infinite Happiness, which He calls His "Divine Self-Domain". And He is the Giver of the Way of Divine Enlightenment—which He has named "the Way of Adidam".

Only Revelation Brings an End to Doubt

Avatar Adi Da refers to the Divine Being as "Real God", "the Only One Who <u>Is</u>", to distinguish Real God from historical concepts and religious dogmas <u>about</u> God. Spiritual Communion with Real God is the subject and goal of all the esoteric religious traditions—as opposed to exoteric traditions, which preach belief in historical mythologies, and tend to ask merely for behavioral changes. By contrast, Avatar Adi Da is here to <u>transform</u> the very consciousness of ordinary people into Divine Consciousness, through Spiritual Communion with Him.

However, "The Promised God-Man is here" is not a statement to merely be believed, in the same way some religious groups insist upon adherence to their dogmas. To merely believe this statement (or any religious statement) is to miss the point entirely. The Truth of this confession is authenticated only in its <u>revelation</u>, directly and unmistakably, in one's living experience.

You have in your hands the evidence, in several forms, for the living Revelation of Avatar Adi Da Samraj. The first form is His Teaching-Word. You may come to the conclusion, as many others have, that only Real God in Person could let loose such a wide, wise ocean of Wisdom, unparalleled in its confession of Divine Ecstasy. You will also read of the amazement and joy that accompanies the Spiritual recognition of Adi Da Samraj by ordinary men and women—and of the devotional response and conversion that followed in their lives. And you will read, in the miraculous events of His own life, a dramatic Spiritual ordeal and passionate demonstration of Divinity unsurpassed by any in human history.

What Is Avatar Adi Da Like?

There is no pattern in any of our previous human record for Avatar Adi Da's Spiritual demonstration. Rather, you will find hints of His demonstration in every tradition. He does not conform to any conventional image of a "holy man", whether that image is ascetic and pious, mysterious and magical, or robed and ceremonial.

Avatar Adi Da has never withdrawn from the sphere of human impulses and desires. Instead, He has worked <u>within</u> it His entire life, so as to be able to show ordinary men and women what is required, in all the dimensions of human existence, to live in right relationship to the Divine.

Great struggle is also part of His story, because the process that Awakens and Enlightens human beings to Real God does not occur by magic, and certainly not via intellectual discussion. The genuine Spiritual path requires the aspirant to go beyond <u>everything</u>, including (eventually) our very and inmost sense of "self".

As Avatar Adi Da's story shows, to attract ordinary people into going beyond "self" required everything of Him—His genius, humor, and love—as well as His Divine Powers, which go beyond any explanation. The import of this story is that, through the Life and Work of Adi Da Samraj, the Divine Being is literally "Emerging" into (or Spiritually Pervading) our world with unprecedented force.

In a face to face dialogue with His devotees one night, Avatar Adi Da spoke of how He was moved to Incarnate—to Descend from the Divine Domain and "Emerge" into this realm in a human form. He described the immensity of this Process of Avataric Descent:

AVATAR ADI DA SAMRAJ: Thousands of years of Sacrifice, and Endeavor, and Purpose, and Spiritual Practice, and Realization, and Love, and Compassion were required for My bodily (human) Birth. Some day, you may understand My Birth. It was no casual gesture. And it could never have happened before now. Some day, you may understand that My human Lifetime is a unique moment in the history of humankind. Even in all these "eons of shaking", the Impulse of the Divine Person to Incarnate persisted, undaunted, and could not be destroyed or ruined. Real God is willing to Love you and <u>all</u> beings, and that Divine Purpose must be Fulfilled. That is My Unique Impulse. Here I <u>Am</u>, Incarnate, to Do That Work. A thousand years may pass before anyone understands anything about My Appearance here. So much suffering accompanies It, so much was required of Me to Submit to your company.

DEVOTEE: How was that Decision made?

AVATAR ADI DA SAMRAJ: By Love. To Encompass the totality of existence, in Love—That is the Sign of My Appearance here. By Appearing here bodily before You, I have Submitted to Love all-and-All, to be Compassionate toward all-and-All, to Serve all-and-All. And, in My Embrace of all-and-All, I have utterly Submitted to this mortal circumstance of sorrow and death. Such Submission never destroyed Me. It cannot destroy Me, for the One Who I <u>Am</u> can never be destroyed. But Love, the Impulse to Kiss you—just to Kiss you, to not deny you—made Me a Body to Live with you. [September 9, 1987]

Avatar Adi Da Samraj's Name is composed of four Sanskrit words.

His principal Name is "Adi Da". "Avatar" and "Samraj" are sacred Titles, used in association with His Name.

"Adi" (ah´-dee) means "Original" (or "Primordial"), and "Da" means "the Divine Giver". Thus, "Adi Da" means "the Original Divine Giver".

"Avatar" means "a 'Crossing Down' of the Divine Being into the world" (or, in other words, "an Appearance of the Divine in conditionally manifested form").

"Samraj" (sahm-rahj´) means "universal Lord".

In fuller forms of reference, Adi Da Samraj is called "the Ruchira (roo-chih´-rah) Avatar", meaning "the Avatar of Infinite Brightness".

About Capitalization and Terminology in this Book

Avatar Adi Da Samraj's devotees capitalize references to Him and His Divine Work and Realization as a means of honoring Him and the sacred nature of His Revelation.

In the sacred terminology developed by Avatar Adi Da, certain words are capitalized in order to indicate that they are being used in reference to the Divine Reality or to the process of Realizing the Divine Reality. (Avatar Adi Da also sometimes uses a unique scriptural form of capitalization in which virtually every word is capitalized. This is true of His Master-Scripture, *The Dawn Horse Testament*, as well as some of His other Texts.) In addition, certain words or phrases with a specific technical meaning are put in quotation marks in order to distinguish them from their usage in common speech (for example, the "Bright"). A glossary of selected items appears on pp. 338-43.

PART ONE

THE YEARS OF "LEARNING MAN"

1939–1970

From my earliest experience of life I have Enjoyed a Condition that, as a child, I called the "Bright"....

CHAPTER 1

BORN AS THE "BRIGHT"

On November 3, 1939, as the world watched the early devastation of the Second World War, Avatar Adi Da Samraj was born on Long Island as Franklin Albert Jones. By virtue of this birth, Real God, the Eternal Divine Person—the Ultimate Condition and Source of everyone and everything—miraculously took birth as a human being.

Avatar Adi Da has a clear memory of His birth. He recalls nearly being strangled by the umbilical cord. He was aware of what was happening around Him, but His awareness was not confined to His struggling body. While the doctors worked to bring His body from the womb, He remained aware as His own Divine State, Conscious as the infinite Sphere of Radiance and Love that He later called "the 'Bright'".

Avatar Adi Da describes the "Bright" in His autobiography, *The Knee Of Listening*:

From my earliest experience of life I have Enjoyed a Condition that, as a child, I called the "Bright". . . .

Even as a baby, I remember only crawling around inquisitively with a boundless Feeling of Joy, Light, and Freedom in the middle of my head that was bathed in Energy moving unobstructed in a Circle—down from above, all the way down, then up, all the way up, and around again—and always Shining from my heart. It was an Expanding Sphere of Joy from the heart. And I was a Radiant Form, the Source of Energy, Love-Bliss, and Light in the midst of a world that is entirely Energy, Love-Bliss, and Light. I was the Power of Reality, a direct Enjoyment and Communication of the One Reality. I was the Heart Itself, Who Lightens the mind and all things. I was the same as every one and every thing, except it became clear that others were apparently unaware of the "Thing" Itself.

Throughout His infancy, Avatar Adi Da's awareness remained free of the limits of His human birth. He felt associated with the body, but not defined or identified by it, dependent on its survival. Rather, He felt His body to be arising in—and as—the "Bright".

Even as a little child, I recognized It and Knew It, and my life was not a matter of anything else. That Awareness, that Conscious Enjoyment, that Self-Existing and Self-Radiant Space of Infinitely and inherently Free Being, that Shine of inherent Joy Standing in the heart and Expanding from the heart, is the "Bright". And It is the entire Source of True Humor. It is Reality. It is not separate from anything. [The Knee Of Listening]

Submission: Forgetting the "Bright"

One day after His second birthday, as He was crawling across a linoleum floor, His parents let loose a new puppy. In the instant of seeing the puppy and seeing His parents, Avatar Adi Da Samraj spontaneously identified with His human body and personality. From that moment on, He consciously became "Franklin Jones"—the son of Frank and Dorothy Jones, a couple living in the Long Island suburb of Franklin Square, New York. He had consented to undertake the task of "Learning Man"—finding out (in full and conscious detail) what it means to be human, and how human beings can go beyond their suffering and limitation.

Born as the "Bright"

The "creation" of "Franklin Jones" began from that moment. All of the rest of the events that occurred during the two or more years before that moment were not the years of "Franklin Jones". He had no existence before that time, which was the Conscious (or Intentional) beginning. [The Knee Of Listening]

In other words, Avatar Adi Da took on the sense of being an ego—an "I", separate from all other "I's". He allowed His own State of Oneness, the "Bright", to begin receding into unconsciousness.

AVATAR ADI DA SAMRAJ: My Identification with mortal existence occurred through sympathetic response. It was not merely a response to the puppy. It certainly was that, because the puppy was the nearest to Me in physical space—but then there was also the glance toward My parents. It was, simply and altogether, a sympathetic response that brought Me into the sphere of human conditions. So it was a kind of delight—not merely some effortful identification with mortal existence. It was not the noticing of mortality, in and of itself, that generated My Movement into this plane. Rather, it was the Love-Response, the attracted Response, in which all of the negative aspects of gross conditional existence were effectively forgotten—in Love, in Delight, in Love-Bliss. [February 9, 1998]

As a young boy with His parents

While Avatar Adi Da surrendered to become like those around Him, the Intuition of the "Bright" still remained. Thus, somewhere in the depth of His Being, He never lost the urge to recover the joy of the "Bright". And He would always be working, in one form or another, to find a way to bring that joy to others.

He recalls a moment when He was about seven years old that stands out as His most significant early attempt to communicate the "Bright". He was walking with His parents to the movies when His parents began quarreling about something. He felt how that hostility was destroying the web of love-energy that surrounded them. He could see the delicate etheric tissues being torn with holes. He worked to repair the damage by expanding love from His heart while trying to distract His parents by asking them questions about God and pointing out the full moon.

Their quarrel quieted down—but, later, as He sat through the movie, Avatar Adi Da realized that He had borne the cost of the conflict. Because of His parents' inability to receive the love-energy He was transmitting to them, He felt a pain in His heart—"where the Love-Bliss-Energy had been pushed back".

Nonetheless, He felt that what He had just attempted was fundamental to His purpose in life. He resolved to restore the "Bright" in others. He was determined to make it possible for every human being to Awaken to the Freedom, Love, and Blissfulness that He knew.

From His earliest youth, Avatar Adi Da was a natural religious ecstatic. Often, while sitting in the Lutheran church His family attended, He would fall into states of mystical rapture. While swooning, He would erupt with incoherent gasps and other noises. His Spiritual absorption would force His eyes to roll up to the top of their sockets or suddenly "bug out". As He recalls, the pastor was not pleased.

As an altar-server in His early teens, His native capacity for Spiritual ecstasy became contagious. As He read from the Bible to the Lutheran congregation, people would fall into blissful states, responding to the Power of the "Bright" communicated through His voice.

But Avatar Adi Da was always acutely aware of the darker side of life, its mortality and suffering. After age ten, Avatar Adi Da became more often solemn, and ordinary humor was more an intentional act than a natural state.

A Unique Spiritual Manifestation: The "Thumbs"

Just as electrical wires must be capable of handling the current that flows through them, so must the delicate circuitry of a human body be capable of conducting the energies that flow through it. The force of the Spirit-Power of the "Bright" far exceeds the capacity of ordinary humans. Adapting to this immense Divine Energy required Avatar Adi Da to undergo an excruciating ordeal in His childhood. He was often consumed by a burning force that took the form of mysterious diseases, fevers, and delirium. On many occasions, He felt He was going to die.

Often during these bouts, He would experience a powerful descent of Spiritual Force. Even as a very young child, Avatar Ad' Da had named this experience "the 'Thumbs'".

From my early childhood, at apparently random times (usually as I either approached sleep or awoke from sleep—and, most dramatically, during seizures of childhood illness, as I would pass into delirium), I had an experience that felt like a mass of gigantic thumbs coming down from above, pressing into my throat (causing something of a gagging, and somewhat suffocating, sensation), and then pressing further (and, it seemed, would have expanded without limitation or end), into some form of myself that was much larger than my physical body. . . .

The "Thumbs" were not visible in the ordinary sense. . . . They were not visible to me with my eyes, nor did I hallucinate them pictorially. Yet, I very consciously experienced and felt them as having a peculiar form and mobility, just as I (likewise) consciously experienced my own otherwise invisible and greater form.

Except for occasions of sudden spontaneous completeness, I did not, generally, in the developing childhood and earliest adult years, allow this intervention of the "Thumbs" to take place. I held it off from its fullest descent, in fear of being overwhelmed—for I did not understand at all what was taking place. However, as the adult years progressed, this same experience occurred naturally during meditation. Because my meditation had been allowed to progress gradually, and the realizations at each level were (thus) perceived without shock, I was able to allow the experience to take place. When I did, the "Thumbs" completely entered my living form. [The Knee Of Listening]

Through His childhood experiences of the "Thumbs", Avatar Adi Da learned to receive the Force of the "Bright" into His physical vehicle. These descents Awakened and prepared His body to circulate and Transmit to others the Love-Bliss-Power of His Divine Nature. He would later describe the "Thumbs" as one of the unique signs associated with His Incarnation:

AVATAR ADI DA SAMRAJ: The principal Sign in My early Life was My Intention to Descend, to Appear here, to Embrace in every aspect the limitation of human mortality, human existence, as it is, as it appears. The characteristic Samadhi of My childhood, or of My

Life altogether—you could even say, of My Work altogether—was the Samadhi of the "Thumbs". The "Thumbs" is about My Divine Descent, the Crashing Down of Real God. The "Thumbs" is the Secret of My early Life. [February 18, 1993]

Falling Forward: The Search for Truth

After Avatar Adi Da graduated from high school in 1957, He entered one of the most prestigious academies of "thinking" in the country at that time—Columbia College, in New York City. But He felt no exhilaration at the prospect of preparing for a career. His apparent loss of the "Bright" had reached its lowest point, and He lived in Spiritual despair.

He was obsessed with a question He had been probing for years: "What is conscious awareness?" By "conscious awareness" He meant that very sense of existence, or awareness of simply being, which is constant in us—whatever the events and changes of life. He had always felt that consciousness was senior to the fleshy body—therefore, senior to death. His knowledge of the "Bright" and the "Thumbs" deeply confirmed that seniority. But what was the connection between consciousness and the physical world? How were these two realities related to each other? Now, in college, He threw Himself into this investigation. For Him, these questions were crucial to the meaning of everything.

But He found no answers to His questions at Columbia. Instead, He found that His questions were denied legitimacy. Avatar Adi Da observed that the prevailing dogma at Columbia (and in the entire modern intellectual world) was what He would come to call "scientific materialism".

The underlying presumption of scientific materialism is that the perceivable physical world is the <u>only</u> reality. Anything deemed greater or higher, such as the psyche or consciousness, is held to be either a by-product of this "gross" (or physical material) reality, or else an hallucination.

In the scientific materialist view, your awareness of anything results from electro-chemical processes in the brain. Therefore, consciousness apparently depends on the body—and is presumed to be extinguished at death.

Avatar Adi Da's stark confrontation with modern secularism at Columbia destroyed the naive religious faith of His childhood. His deep questions about consciousness were answered only with

---

The scientific examination of conditional phenomena has resulted in (and continues to pursue) the detailed mapping of the mechanisms of conditionally manifested existence, including much detailed knowledge about the functioning human organism and about the development of various modes of conditionally manifested life on Earth. . . . Equipped with such maps of the structures of the human entity, proponents of scientific materialism have criticized many of the traditionally acknowledged means of accounting for human experience (including religious experience), claiming that conscious experience amounts to nothing more than evidence of how the human mind and the human body are "built" to function. According to this scientific materialist point of view, religious experience (and all of human experience) is merely something happening in the "meat organism", determined by its psycho-physical structuring.

doubt and Godless rationalism. He later described to His devotees the impact of His time at Columbia—both its virtue and its difficulty:

AVATAR ADI DA SAMRAJ: When I went to Columbia, it was like going to another planet. All of a sudden, there was an intense demand on intelligence. And the presumptions I had gathered as a boy, from that simple life and simple religion on Long Island, were utterly shattered.

That was good, ultimately. But it was a shocking and devastating experience! It brought Me to the Zero of Purity, of Intelligence. And I had to work Myself out of it. [December 13, 1993]

Avatar Adi Da was urged on by desperation. He chose to confront the agony of Godlessness head on. His weapon would be an heroic course of exhaustive experience, born of a conviction:

If God exists, God will not cease to exist by any action of my own—but, if I devote myself to all possible experience, God will (necessarily) find some way (in some particular experience or some complex of experiences, or by virtue of my openness itself) to be revealed to me. [The Knee Of Listening]

That conclusion regarding the nature of human experience is the superimposition of scientific materialist philosophy on the legitimate observations made by means of the scientific method. And that conclusion regarding the nature of human experience is a key fault, which makes scientific materialism a false philosophy. . . .

This must be understood: The human psycho-physical structure is (irreducibly) part of the Prior and Universal Unity. Reality is Non-Separate, Indivisible, and (Ultimately) One—Beyond all appearances. The human psycho-physical structure is the "equipment" that is to be used by human beings for the sake of (Ultimately, Most Perfect) Divine Self-Realization—and that structure arises within the Universal Unity. This is the ancient esoteric knowledge.

AVATAR ADI DA SAMRAJ
The Basket Of Tolerance

Thus, He threw Himself into a wide variety of experiences with the force of a vow.

No experience posed a barrier to me. There were no taboos, no extremes to be prevented. There was no depth of madness and no limit of suffering that my philosophy could prevent—for, if it did, I would be liable to miss the Lesson of Reality. Thus, I extended myself even beyond my own fear. And my pleasures also became extreme, such that there was a constant machine of ecstasy. I could tolerate no mediocrity, no medium experience. I was satisfied neither with atheism nor with belief. Both seemed to me mere ideas, possible reactions to a more fundamental (if unconscious) fact. I sought Reality, to be Reality—What is, not what is asserted in the face of What is.
[The Knee Of Listening]

Without knowing it, Avatar Adi Da had spontaneously chosen the mode of Spiritual practice known in Eastern mysticism as "prapatti" ("falling forward"). To practice prapatti is to unguardedly allow one's experience to be whatever it is and lead wherever it leads—with the faith that, by not superimposing any "plans" or "intentions" on existence, the Truth will inevitably be revealed. However, Avatar Adi Da undertook this practice in the ultimate Western city—not the traditional East, where there was an understanding (or at least a tolerance) for such a path. As such, He was bereft of all traditional guidance and supports.

Avatar Adi Da abandoned Himself to the streets of New York with the raw courage of a desperate man, tasting every pleasure of the senses, restrained by no taboos or fears of degradation or madness. He devoured every kind of book that might afford Him a glimpse of Truth. As He says in *The Knee Of Listening*, "I became a kind of mad and exaggerated young man, whose impulses were not allowable in this medium culture. My impulses were exploitable only in secret extensions of my own consciousness, or in the company of whores, libertines, and misfits." He engaged this intensity for two years at Columbia.

Crisis and Revolution: The "Columbia Experience"

One night in 1960, in the middle of His junior year, Avatar Adi Da sat at His desk in a small room He had rented several blocks from campus.

I felt there were no more books to read, no possible kinds of ordinary experience that could exceed what I had already embraced. There seemed no outstanding sources for any new excursion, no remaining and conclusive possibilities. I was drawn into the interior tension of my mind that held all of that seeking—every impulse and alternative, every motive in the form of my desiring. I contemplated it as a whole, a dramatic singleness, and it moved me into a profound shape of life-feeling, such that all the vital centers in my body and mind appeared like a long funnel of contracted planes that led on to an infinitely regressed and invisible image. I observed this deep sensation of conflict and endlessly multiplied contradictions, such that I was surrendered to its very shape, as if to experience it perfectly and to <u>be</u> it.

Then, quite suddenly, in a moment, I experienced a total revolution in my body-mind,* and, altogether, in my conscious awareness. An absolute sense of understanding opened and arose at the extreme end of all this sudden contemplation. And all of the motions of me that moved down into that depth appeared to reverse their direction at some unfathomable point. The rising impulse caused me to stand, and I felt a surge of Force draw up out of my depths and expand, Filling my entire body and every level of my conscious awareness with wave on wave of the most Beautiful and Joyous Energy.

I felt absolutely mad, but the madness was not of a desperate kind. There was no seeking and no dilemma within it—no question, no unfulfilled motive, not a single object or presence outside myself.

I could not contain the Energy in my small room. I ran out of the building and through the streets. [The Knee Of Listening]

---

*Avatar Adi Da has pointed out that the physical body is only a small part, the "tip of the iceberg", of the total human being, which includes many levels of emotion, psyche, intellect, and even the root-sense of separate existence. The terms "body-mind" and "whole body", then, refer to the sum of the human being, including that which is beyond the physical.

As He ran through the streets, looking for someone to talk to about this revelation, He felt the overwhelming energy in His body as "almost intolerable in its Pressure, Light, and Force". But He found no one to talk to. When He had run himself out, He returned to His room.

For two years, Avatar Adi Da had devoted Himself to every kind of seeking—looking for some experience to reveal Truth to Him. He did this under the presumption that the Truth was absent, and had to be found. However, in the days and weeks that followed the "Columbia experience", He grasped two fundamental realities. First, He saw that Truth is <u>not</u> a matter of seeking for something that is absent, but rather of removing the obstructions to the Truth. Second, He realized that <u>seeking itself</u> is the obstruction preventing the Realization of Truth. All His seeking, He now understood, had been a grand distraction from the always present Truth. The two years spent in exploitation of experience had been necessary, but only in order to reveal to Him conclusively the futility of the search.

Total Immersion: The Discovery of "Narcissus"

The Columbia experience was the first great breakthrough in Avatar Adi Da's Life of the intelligence He calls "understanding": the clear knowledge that the apparent separation from Real God or Truth is the result of one's own ego-activity. He soon found, however, that He could not sustain the understanding awakened in this experience. He sensed there was something in consciousness that was actively preventing this understanding. He resolved to discover what that was.

After He had graduated from Columbia, He moved to California to begin a Master's program in English at Stanford University. There He met Nina Davis, a fellow student. In 1962, they moved into a small cabin on a bluff overlooking Tunitas Beach, on the Pacific Ocean.

NINA: I met Beloved Adi Da* at Stanford University in October 1961, on the first day of class of our graduate studies. He was sitting across a long table opposite the door of a seminar room, and when I walked into the room He looked up and glanced at me with the most beautiful and extraordinary eyes. I felt a rush of energy as my being went out to meet Him. In that split second, I felt the most profound communication of feeling I had ever known.

From the very beginning, it was obvious to me that Beloved Adi Da related to life completely differently from anybody else. He was obviously <u>actively</u> involved in a consideration about life, always considering the conventions of existence that everybody else takes for granted. For Him, such consideration involved not only the mind, but also the body and the emotions. He went beyond all conventions and taboos in those early days, just as He does now. In fact, all of the signs that are characteristic of Beloved Adi Da now have been His signs ever since I have known Him. ■

While He was at Stanford, Avatar Adi Da developed a unique form of discipline for Himself, as a way of investigating consciousness. For two years, He wrote down everything that He observed in His experience—all that He thought, dreamed, felt, perceived, and did. He resolved that no motion of His being would escape Him. He hoped that, by these means, He might find a logic, or guiding form, to the play of His experience.

He was so immersed in this process that Nina took over all the practicalities of their life. Day after day, wherever He was—at home, on a walk, visiting friends, going to the movies—Avatar Adi Da would carry a clipboard and write down all that occurred in His awareness. When He wandered alone on the beach below their remote cottage, He wrote down every random thought and mind-form that arose with every step on the sand, including His perception of stepping itself. He was placing His awareness under a microscope, so that its inmost mechanics and secret patterning would be revealed.

The revelation came in the spring of 1964:

---

* Devotees of Avatar Adi Da often address Him with the intimate Title (of respect and acknowledgement) "Beloved", as in "The Beloved of one's heart".

Eventually, I began to recognize a structure in my conscious awareness. It became more and more apparent, and its nature and effects revealed themselves as fundamental, inclusive of all the states and contents in life and mind. My own "myth"—the governor of all patterns, the source of presumed self-identity, the motivator of all seeking—began to stand out in the mind as a living being.

This "myth", this controlling logic (or force) that formed my very conscious awareness, revealed itself as the self-concept—and the actual life—of Narcissus. I saw that my entire adventure—the desperate cycle of awareness and its decrease, of truly Conscious Being and Its gradual covering in the mechanics of living, seeking, dying, and suffering—was produced out of the image (or mentality) that appears hidden in the ancient myth of Narcissus.

The more I contemplated him, the more profoundly I understood him. I observed, in awe, the primitive control that this self-concept and logic exercised over all of my behavior and experience. I began to see that same logic operative in all other human beings, and in every living thing—even in the very life of the cells, and in the natural energies that surround every living entity or process. It was the logic (or process) of separation itself, of enclosure and immunity. It manifested as fear and identity, memory and experience. It informed every function of the living being, every experience, every act, every event. It "created" every "mystery". It was the structure of every imbecile link in the history of human suffering.

He is the ancient one visible in the Greek myth, who was the universally adored child of the gods, who rejected the loved-one and every form of love and relationship, and who was finally condemned to the contemplation of his own image—until, as a result of his own act and obstinacy, he suffered the fate of eternal separateness and died in infinite solitude. [The Knee Of Listening]

He saw that no one—no "God", no parent, no outside influence at all—has imposed on human beings this controlling logic of separation and enclosure. It is an active process of locking ourselves, moment by moment, into the prison of egoity. Revolutionary as this discovery was, it was merely the beginning. For He knew He now had to go through the ordeal of undoing the madness of "Narcissus", whatever that might involve.

First Teacher

While engaged in His unbroken effort of self-observation in California, Avatar Adi Da Samraj and Nina were living with a remarkable being—a cat, called Robert. Avatar Adi Da's relationship with Robert was a sign of His natural communion with the non-human domain. Avatar Adi Da describes in *The Knee Of Listening* how Robert demonstrated to Him a pure, intelligent, and unproblematic manner of living—life lived as "instinctive perfection":

I had named him "Robert" purely in fun. He was such a strong animal presence, with an economy and grace that made the idiot brand of human living seem so unconscious and confused. I gave him an ordinary human name just to remind myself of the difference in him. . . .

Robert himself was nothing less to me than my best friend and mentor. He was more—not less—than human to me. I watched him with fascination. I followed him through woods and watched him hunt. I tried to understand his curious avoidance of the sea, and how he could sit on the cliff above the sea, watching the evening sun, and the wind blowing his hairs heroically about his head. The mystery of his pattern of living, his ease and justice, the economy of all his means, the untouchable absence of all anxiety, the sudden and adequate power he brought to every circumstance without exceeding the intensity required—all of his ways seemed to me an epitome of the genius of life. And he communicated with me so directly that I was always disarmed. He would call me when he returned in the evening. He would touch me whenever he needed my presence. He would lie with me as if with conscious intention to console me with his living presence. And I loved him as deeply as the universe itself. [The Knee Of Listening]

The Discovery of Psychic Unity

Besides the revelation of "Narcissus", Avatar Adi Da's time of writing at Tunitas produced another transformation. Through His moment-to-moment observation in writing, He became increasingly sensitive to the synchronicity between His "inner" life and outer events, until this synchronicity revealed itself to be an observed, actual unity.

Avatar Adi Da describes how this psychic awakening led to the next major crisis and shift in His Life:

The recognition of the coincidence between consciousness and external experience began to develop into a comfortable ability, such that I began to make use of the images that passed (in a seemingly arbitrary succession) through the mind. I saw that many of these images were signs of precognition.

One image became a constant factor. I saw that I was to find a teacher who would be able to help me. I did not see the teacher himself—but, in spontaneous visionary flashes, I saw pictures of a store where oriental sculpture and other oriental works of art were sold. It became spontaneously evident to me that this store was in New York City.

I told Nina about this experience, and we began immediately to prepare to leave for New York. We gradually sold or gave away most of our belongings, including my library of about 1400 volumes. I kept only a few books that seemed important to my new line of study. These events led on toward the middle or end of June 1964. [The Knee Of Listening]

Thunder and Lightning: The Passage to the Guru

Avatar Adi Da writes in *The Knee Of Listening*:

One morning, shortly before Nina and I left for New York, I awoke to a very brilliant clear day. I went outside and stood in front of the house to enjoy the morning freshness. . . .

Born as the "Bright"

I stood on the cliff, the morning was clear and shining, and the air was that kind that makes one go "Ah!" inside with relief and Joy, and make a big breath of ease, like on vacation. And, suddenly, in barely a moment or two, a storm moved over me from the ocean like a huge shroud, like a great canopy or blanket. It had the feeling of an immense shell, rising above me, and touching the earth and sea only at all the horizon points. The weather below, where I was standing, was not a dense mass. The air around and above me remained clear. The storm was only in the high sky. The high, moving mass of dark sky rose above me and beyond, and stood everywhere above, appearing like a gigantic dome, enclosing the space where I stood. The storm looked like a huge gray dome, full of gray shapes of clouds, a perfect half-sphere. It was not homogeneous, but it was boiling with great masses of differing and combining clouds. And I could still see clearly in this dark dome—all the way to the horizon of the sea, and all around me in the suddenly shaded and sunless air.

Then, with shattering quickness, like an aerial display of royal fireworks, lightning began to move everywhere through the dome—such that now it felt like the crown of my own head, . . . with what appeared to be millions of bolts of lightning shooting everywhere, in all directions in the sky, and, like gods, flying anywhere in a moment, hundreds of miles at will. . . .

I do not know how long I stood there, in the titanic Force of everything, but the storm itself must have lasted for an hour or two. Then, as suddenly as it had come, it disintegrated and disappeared in the resurrected morning sun. And, in the moment of its passing, I Knew it was time for me to leave California and go on to what it had now become certain was to be the "Bright" Divine Fulfillment of the Purpose of my human birth.

Quickly thereafter, Nina and I left California, at the near-end of June 1964. My mood was one of intense excitement and expectation. There was no doubt at all in me that I was about to begin the ultimate adventure of my life. I was willing to make any sacrifice and to go anywhere in the world in order to abandon myself to the Sources of the Divine Good.

**After His Divine Re-Awakening
Los Angeles, 1971**

CHAPTER 2

Re-Awakening to the "Bright"

Avatar Adi Da and Nina moved into a small apartment in Greenwich Village. As He re-adapted to living in the city, Avatar Adi Da waited patiently for confirmation of His prophetic visions.

On a Sunday in early September, Avatar Adi Da's parents were driving Him and Nina home. A few blocks from their apartment, the car passed a small storefront filled with oriental art. Avatar Adi Da knew this was the place He had seen in His visions, the place where He would meet His teacher. After His parents dropped them off, He and Nina walked back to the closed store. As they approached, Avatar Adi Da felt a distinct Spiritual Power.

They returned to visit the store the next day, finding only a small old woman behind the counter who showed no signs of being a teacher. Avatar Adi Da then noticed a pair of photographs on the wall behind her:

The photographs appeared to be of two different saints. Both of them were naked except for a small loincloth. One was an enormously fat man with the appearance of awesome strength. And the other was a more moderately proportioned man with a melancholy expression, as if his mind were tuned to some distant place that was his real home. Both of them had short hair and equally short beards that suggested they had each been totally shaven within the past few weeks. And there were undeniable, obvious signs of Spiritual Power and Presence generated bodily by both men.

As I studied these pictures, my heart began to pound with excitement. I asked the woman about the pictures. She said they were her son's teachers. Her son was a Spiritual teacher, she said, and he was the owner of the store. I asked how I could meet her son, and I was told that he was away for a long weekend in the country, but he would return the next day.

We left the store quite hurriedly. Our business was over. But as we got into the street, I began to jump and run us down the block. I had found my teacher! I had found the Guru! [The Knee Of Listening]

Swami Rudrananda and the Work of Surrender

With great anticipation, the next day Avatar Adi Da prepared Himself to meet His teacher. To ensure the teacher got there first, He hid Himself and watched several men working in and around the shop. He waited until they all left, except for one large man who seemed to have been directing everyone. Avatar Adi Da went into the store where the woman from the previous day animatedly told her son about Avatar Adi Da's visit.

The man stood up and approached me. He made it a very deliberate point to shake my hand. He introduced himself as Rudi, and I told him I was Franklin Jones.

"Your mother told me that you are a teacher."

He looked around at her as if displeased, and then he said, "She tells that to anybody who comes in here. She really ought to keep her mouth shut."

Re-Awakening to the "Bright"

Swami Rudrananda ("Rudi")

I was already very uncomfortable, and now I felt foolish, but I was determined.

"What do you teach?"

"Kundalini Yoga."

"Are you an adept at this Yoga?"

He looked at me very sternly and a little bothered. "You don't teach it if you can't do it."

I told him I was looking for a teacher and I felt that I had been directed to him. He asked me what I did. I said that I wrote, and had just moved from California.

"No, what do you do Spiritually?"

"Oh, well, I relax and direct myself toward the top of the head."

He smiled a little. "Do you work?"

"No, I've just been writing, and I live with my girlfriend. She works."

He drew away from me a little. "This Yoga requires great discipline and surrender, and I can't teach anybody who doesn't accept the discipline and work. You go out and get a job and come back in about six months or a year. We'll talk about it then."

That was apparently the end of the interview! He made it a point to shake my hand again—and he turned away, such that I felt I was supposed to leave.

As I left the store, I felt a tremendous relief that I had been able to manage the meeting at all. I was disappointed, to be sure. There was no sublime love-meeting, no miracle, no immediate recognition of me as the long-awaited disciple. But I had been received at least conditionally. Six months or a year was not an unbearable length of time. Unpleasant as the prospect was, I was willing to get a job, if that was the test required of me. I felt a kind of certainty in the man himself. He was, by his own admission, adept in the teaching and practice of what I (at the time) presumed to be the highest and most miraculous kind of Yoga. I had met him, and I was certain that I was willing to meet the conditions.

I was elated! I felt I had been successful. Strong and complicated feelings went through my mind as I moved up the block beyond the store. By the time I reached the corner, I had gained my composure, and even my doubts had turned to elation and certainty. Then I became aware of a very strange sensation. A current of very strong Energy was rising up my arm from my right hand, the hand Rudi had made such a point to shake when I arrived and as I left.

As I became aware of this Energy, It quickly passed into the rest of my body and Filled me with a profound and thrilling Fullness. My heart strained in a vibrant Joy, and my head felt swollen, as if my mind were an "aura" that extended out from my skull by several inches. As I walked, I began to run. I felt on fire with a Joyous Energy, and I had become incredibly light! [The Knee Of Listening]

Avatar Adi Da quickly found employment and disciplined his life-habits. After a few weeks, Rudi gruffly relented and allowed Adi Da to attend his classes.

Rudi (also known as Swami Rudrananda) held "class" four times a week, during which his students practiced receiving the "Force" that he consciously Transmitted.

The central ideas in Rudi's way of teaching were "surrender" and "work". "Surrender" was the internal practice in life and meditation. It was conscious (and even willful) opening, or letting go of contents, resistance, patterns, feelings, and thoughts. "Work" was the external practice. The ideal student was to be involved in a constant state of surrender and a constant act of work. The purpose of this was to make the entire psycho-physical vehicle, internal and external, available to the higher Power—the "Force", or "Shakti"— and, thus, to grow by receiving Its Will, Presence, Intelligence, Light, and Power into every level of the functional being.

I took Rudi's way very seriously, and I made a constant effort to adapt myself to his way absolutely and exhaustively. I accepted Rudi as a perfect Source of this higher Power, and I allowed none of his apparent limitations to represent actual barriers or limitations to my experience of the "Force" Itself. Whenever I encountered limitations in him, I was immediately moved to reflect on my own resistance. Thus, I never allowed myself to become concerned about Rudi's problems or to think that, because of his limitations, the "Force" (or the Divine Power) was available to me only to a limited degree.

The effect of this way of life was a perpetual and growing encounter with my own resistance. And, when I encountered my own resistance, I would awaken to my own tendencies to self-pity, negativity, and the subliminal self-imagery by which I guided the "creation" or manipulation of experience. The more I worked, the more I saw Narcissus.

Rudi's way required immense self-discipline—and, as long as it remained effective in my case, his way functioned as a positive mechanism that strengthened and purified me physically, mentally, and morally. Rudi was a master at this kind of psychological tutoring, and these effects were his primary gift to me. [The Knee Of Listening]

Avatar Adi Da brought to Rudi the disposition of unconditional surrender that He had practiced during His years at Columbia and His time of writing. He fully submitted to His teacher, in the traditional manner of Guru-devotion. Everything that Rudi required of Him, He did down to the last detail.

He worked day and night for three and a half years, with long stretches of manual labor. At Rudi's behest, He married Nina. He took on disciplines of diet and exercise to purify and strengthen His body. These changes had the effect of throwing His body into a frustration to the point where He felt continuously feverish, burning up. In the Indian tradition, this purifying psychic heat is called "tapas".

Part of this new life included the release of the past. Nina describes coming home one day:

NINA: As I opened the door to the apartment which led into the kitchen, I could see Beloved Adi Da in the main room, squatting before the fireplace, naked. He was burning everything that was contained in the boxes that He had carried with Him for years. He had brought them from Columbia to California, where He greatly added to them during the years on the beach. Finally, He had brought them on the trip back across country to New York to find Rudi. The papers were always increasing, as He wrote constantly.

These boxes were the only real possessions of Beloved Adi Da, and they went everywhere He went. Included were all His poems from His days at Columbia, all His work from the creative writing studies at Stanford, and all His notes from the period of writing on the beach, as well as more recent manuscripts of a "novel" that He had been working to make from all these papers. It took three days for Beloved Adi Da to burn everything. He carried out huge quantities of ashes in the process. ■

Rudi's demands were not only physical. At His insistence, Avatar Adi Da also attended Christian seminaries as preparation for a potential career as a minister. There He studied theology and ancient languages, subjects which were not at all interesting to Him. His only motive was obedience to His Teacher, heedless of difficulty or discomfort, until the fire of His tapas escalated to a climax.

Crisis and Revolution: The "Death of Narcissus"

AVATAR ADI DA SAMRAJ: One day when I was in class in seminary in the spring of 1967, I suddenly became completely detached from the mind. The mind seemed to pick up immense speed, and the thought processes were going at immense speed—to the point of the experience becoming extremely disturbing. I was supposed to be sitting there in class, but I felt as if I were going mad. I <u>was</u> going mad.

I tried to pin down My experience by writing everything the teacher said, or writing the thoughts I was having. I just kept pinning it down. That gesture, in and of itself, introduces time, and some more direct association with the body.

I did that long enough to sit through the class. Then I went whirling out in this horrific state, in which the body-mind was going on, on its own, without being controlled by attention. The body-mind was just a whirl of uncontrolled events and sensations and feelings—positive ones, and also extremely negative ones. It became just an <u>immense</u> fear.

I remember looking at My face in the mirror, as I was putting on an after-shave or a skin cleanser, and I saw the plasticity of the body. There was a profound <u>disorientation</u> from the physical, emotional, and mental dimensions of the body-mind, in which I had been doing Spiritual practice so intensively for those years. All of a sudden, the body-mind was <u>utterly</u> confused and dissociated from Me, or I was dissociated from it.

The fear—which was a reaction to that whirl—got to the point where it was fruitless to try to <u>do</u> anything about it. It just kept growing immensely, became the totality of life, the totality of the body-mind, the totality of reality—just this <u>immense</u> fear that could no longer be avoided. There was nothing to do about it. [January 13, 1996]

After His first day in this terror, in the middle of the night, Avatar Adi Da felt that His heart was slowing down and about to stop. The doctor in the emergency ward told Him it was an anxiety attack. No relief appeared, no one had any answers, and nothing attempted made any difference to the acute distress. Finally, at the end of the third day, unable to struggle any longer, Avatar Adi Da simply surrendered:

> *I lay on the floor, totally disarmed, unable to make a gesture that could prevent the rising fear. And, thus, the fear grew in me—but, for the first time, I allowed it to happen. I could not prevent it. The fear and the death rose and became my overwhelming experience. And I observed the crisis of that fear in a moment of conscious, voluntary death. I allowed the death to happen, and I "saw" it happen. It was not that an organic death occurred, but even organic death ceased to be a concern. There was a spontaneous, utter release of identification with the body, the mind, the emotions of the separate person, and the self-contracting (or reactive and separative) act that is the ego (or the presumed person).*
>
> *When that moment of crisis had passed, I felt a marvelous relief—or, rather, simply, a marvelous Freedom. The death had occurred, but I had <u>observed</u> it! I remained untouched by it. The body and the mind and the egoic personality had died (or been utterly released as a concern and an identity), but I remained as essential and unqualified Awareness (and purely That, but also Freely Aware of the physical body and its natural environment).*
>
> *When all of the fear and dying had finished their course, when the body, the mind, the apparently separate "person" (and the <u>act</u> that made its apparent separateness) had been released, and my attention was no longer fixed in those things, I Knew Reality, tacitly and directly. There was an Infinite Bliss of Being, an untouched, unborn Sublimity—without separation, without individuation, without a thing from which to be separated. There was only Reality Itself, the incomparable Nature and constant Existence that underlies (and observes, and Knows) the entire adventure of life. And that Same and Very Reality was also revealed as the unqualified living condition of the totality of conditionally manifested existence.*
>
> *After a time, I got up from the floor. I walked around and beamed Joyfully at the room. The Love-Blissful, unthreatened Current of the "Bright" emanated Freely and unqualifiedly from my*

Re-Awakening to the "Bright"

heart, and not a pulse of It was limited by my otherwise conditional existence or the existence of the world. [The Knee Of Listening]

By allowing Himself to fully experience the terror, He witnessed the actual death of His limited identity. "Narcissus", the separate self-consciousness, the one who is terrified of pain and death, simply died in Him. He knew His true identity was the "Bright", the unqualified, free awareness of Reality Itself, beyond the body-mind and all its assumed limits.

In this state, He stood as Divine Calm and Inexpressible Love-Bliss. And He saw that all seeking for Reality and Truth was only the preventing of it—the avoidance of the "Bright".

But how could He explain to others the revolution that had occurred in His consciousness? How could He express His living knowledge that we are not separate beings, but always alive only as the one Transcendental Truth, when the profundity of this "death of Narcissus" was lost even on Rudi? Avatar Adi Da was now expressing a unique, "radical" understanding that no one around Him could comprehend. Without alternatives, He decided He must simply live on its basis, without the stress of the effort in dilemma.

Guru's Grace:
Turning to Swami Muktananda

Throughout Avatar Adi Da's years of Sadhana (or Spiritual practice) with His human Teachers, He lived out His intuitive course of "Learning Man". Having already "Learned Man" at the gross (or ordinary physical/emotional/mental) level of life, He was now combining Himself with a more refined dimension of human experience—the dimension of Spiritual Energy and subtle (or mystical) experience. This process had begun with Rudi—but Rudi himself had a Teacher, the Indian Yogi Swami Muktananda (often called "Baba" by his devotees).

Rudi kept Swami Muktananda's picture on the wall in the art store, together with that of Swami Muktananda's own Guru, Bhagavan Nityananda. When Avatar Adi Da read some pamphlets from Swami

Muktananda's ashram, He found Himself resonating with Swami Muktananda's descriptions of true Spiritual practice as founded in the reception of the Guru's Grace, rather than in the effort of surrender that Rudi taught. He found an irresistible impulse arising—to immerse Himself in this way of Grace. He asked for, and received, Rudi's permission to approach Swami Muktananda.

India, 1968

In April 1968, Avatar Adi Da made arrangements for Himself and Nina to take a trip to Swami Muktananda's ashram in Ganeshpuri, India. He wrote in advance, humbly expressing full confidence in Swami Muktananda's Grace, and making it clear that He was coming to receive everything that Swami Muktananda had to give, in spite of the mere four days He would be able to stay there.

Avatar Adi Da arrived and began participating in the ordinary life of the ashram—sitting in Swami Muktananda's company, meditating, attending the afternoon chanting. Almost immediately, He began to experience strong effects of Swami Muktananda's Spirit-Blessing, or "Shaktipat".

He felt His body swell with the force of the Shakti (or Spirit-Energy). The Shakti generated powerful, involuntary bodily movements as it flowed through Him, purifying and expanding His nervous system and brain centers. He knew these purifying movements, called "kriyas", from His work of surrender with Rudi, so they were not a surprise to Him. But instigated by Swami Muktananda's Shaktipat, they were much more powerful. Avatar Adi Da found Himself involved in a new kind of Spiritual "work"—submission to these kriyas, which were sometimes so strong that He would fall backwards against the wall or sideways onto the floor.

Swami Muktananda also instructed Him in meditation. But by the fourth and last day of His visit, Avatar Adi Da was feeling somewhat disappointed. He had come, as He had written, for "everything", and He felt that He was about to leave the ashram without having received His Guru's full gift.

Re-Awakening to the "Bright"

Swami Muktananda

Rang Avadhoot

On the afternoon of His last day, Avatar Adi Da was sitting in the ashram garden when Swami Muktananda walked by with a visitor—a Yogi-Saint named Rang Avadhoot. For a brief moment, the Saint looked Avatar Adi Da straight in the eyes. In later years, Avatar Adi Da acknowledged that Rang Avadhoot's glance, together with the Spiritual influence of Swami Muktananda, triggered what occurred a brief while later, when He went to His room to rest.

As I lay down, I immediately passed from the ordinary waking state to what (at first) seemed like a sleep, except there was no loss of conscious awareness. In an instant, I lost all bodily consciousness and every sense of my mind and personality—but there was also a profound State of conscious awareness that was absolutely calm, uncontained, and Free. Indeed, I felt that I existed only as conscious awareness. There was no other experience, no thought, no feeling, no perception. Awareness was (very quickly) concentrated above, at an unfathomable "Point"—beyond space, and (yet) above me. As I became spontaneously concentrated in that "Point", I felt and passed beyond It—into an Infinite Space of Bliss, an Absolute Pleasure of Fullness and Brilliance, that completely Absorbed my apparently separate being. And, then, "I" existed only at Infinity, <u>as</u> Infinity—beyond "I", beyond the separated and separate self-reference.

Eventually, there was an apparent movement from this incomparably pure State, into perceptual modifications of that same egoless Awareness. There were rapid visions (or feelings) of subtle levels of existence, beyond the human. In quick succession, I Witnessed numberless feelings of form and space, or of what appeared to be a hierarchically degressive descent through other worlds, or realms of conditionally manifested existence that are associated with levels of mind beyond (or subtler than) ordinary human life.

Then I heard a loud, roaring sound that (at first) seemed to surround me like a great room. I gradually descended toward association with the body, from a position above the head of the body. The sound was my own breathing, as it rushed through my lungs and throat. But I did not then perceive these things from within my body. I was fully Aware as that Consciousness Which transcends all form, and Which surrounds and breathes the body.

Just then, Nina entered the room—and, with a sudden jolt, I resumed the ordinary state of life-awareness, as if contained within the body. [The Knee Of Listening]

This experience is the great "formless ecstasy", or "Nirvikalpa Samadhi"—held, in the traditions of Yoga, to be the highest possible Spiritual attainment. As traditionally understood, Nirvikalpa Samadhi is Realized by those rare Realizers who succeed in fulfilling the long and arduous Yogic path of "ascent"—"raising themselves up" from a concentration in this earthly realm to an ultimate absorption in the Divine "Place" infinitely above. In Avatar Adi Da's case, however, the manifestation of Nirvikalpa Samadhi was unique. There were no stages of ascent, no lifetimes of effort. There was no passing through layers of mind via meditative technique. There was simply the spontaneous and instantaneous manifestation of His own Inherent "Bright" Condition.

AVATAR ADI DA SAMRAJ: In the Event of Nirvikalpa Samadhi at Baba Muktananda's Ashram, there was complete absence of, and freedom from, the structures of mind. There was an unobstructed Establishment in My Native State.

I Am Always Already Above and Beyond. This is the Natural Condition of My Incarnation. [April 7, 2002]

When Avatar Adi Da had first arrived in Ganeshpuri, Swami Muktananda had prophesied that, within a year, Avatar Adi Da would be a Spiritual Teacher in His own right. And that prediction came true. After Adi Da returned to New York, people experienced a mysterious Force emanating from Him, and they turned to Him for Spiritual guidance. One of them, a young woman named Patricia Morley, came to live with Him and Nina. Aware that the Siddha-Power (or the Divine Power to Transmit Spiritual Force to others) had come alive in Himself, Avatar Adi Da wrote to Swami Muktananda, who urged Him to come to India again as soon as possible.

Avatar Adi Da's second visit to Swami Muktananda took place in Bombay in 1969. Right away, it was very different from the first. Avatar Adi Da described it as an entry into "someone else's wonderland". He experienced an almost continuous stream of internal lights, sounds, visions, transports to other worlds, and states of Spirit-"Intoxication"—the type of internal phenomena that traditionally precede the attainment of fully ascended Nirvikalpa Samadhi.

But He quickly lost interest in the phenomena. He stayed focused in His Guru's internal instruction, which He received in His meditations outside Swami Muktananda's room. He discussed this in a letter to Nina and Patricia:

Baba Teaches me entirely by internal Spiritual means now. We hardly speak at all. My meditation has become very deep, and most of the kriyas are gone. There is a good deal of suffering involved in the transformation I am going through. We are so chronically used to letting the mind take on forms. But I am breaking into the most intense Bliss and miraculous Energy. It is worth the little bit of required death.

I require a quiet, free life from now on. I hope what I require and seek is also your desire. I belong to God, the Consciousness Prior to all manifestation and thought, Prior to the process called "I". Allow it also to grasp you. Meditate, live harmoniously, eat a proper diet, be conscious in relationship. Allow no disturbance, require peace. Remember and love me. I love you.

Swami Muktananda publicly acknowledged Avatar Adi Da's Spiritual attainment via a letter he wrote in front of Avatar Adi Da Himself, as well as fifty to one hundred others. In this letter, Swami Muktananda declared that Avatar Adi Da had attained "Yogic Self-Realization" and, therefore, had the right to Teach and Initiate students of His own.

Swami Muktananda's Letter of Acknowledgement to Avatar Adi Da Samraj

Avatar Adi Da Himself edited and refined the English translation of the letter (excerpts of which are presented here), on the basis of several earlier translations. He added explanatory elaborations in parentheses in order to bring out the full meaning and Spiritual import of the original document.

To my dear (beloved) Franklin, with my loving remembrances of you (even of your Very Self): You have . . . Attained the (True and Spiritual) State of Meditation. You have (by Means of True and Spiritual Meditation) Achieved the Steady State of . . . one-pointed Concentration (or Inherence) In, and tacit (or mindless) Identification With, the Divine Supreme Inner Self. . . .

You (because of your direct Experience and Knowledge of Kundalini Shakti Meditation and, Thereby, of the Divine Supreme Inner Self) have, in accordance with Tradition, both the (Hereby Affirmed) Actual Ability and the Inherent (and Hereby Affirmed) Right to Initiate, or Cause, (True and Spiritual) Meditation in others (or, altogether, to Teach, Initiate, Establish, Guide, and Awaken others in the Practice, the Process, and the, Ultimately, Perfect Realization of Siddha Yoga Meditation, or True and Spiritual

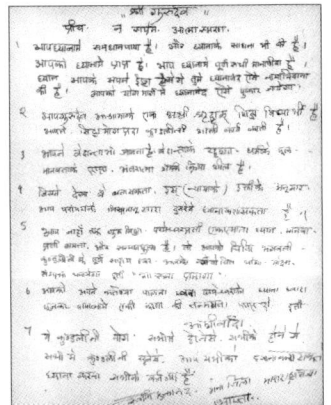

The handwritten letter of acknowledgement from Swami Muktananda

Meditation on, and, Ultimately, Perfect Realization of, the Divine Supreme Inner Self by Means of the Kundalini Shakti Transmitted, and Directly Activated, by you). . . .

Therefore, (I Hereby Declare that) you have the Inherent Right and the Actual Ability to Cause (or, altogether, to Teach, Initiate, Establish, and Guide Kundalini Yoga) Meditation (or the Practice and the Process of Kundalini Shakti Meditation) in any one and everyone (and, Thus and Thereby, to Awaken any one and everyone to and <u>As</u> the Divine Supreme Inner Self of everything and everyone).

Swami Muktananda

Goddess as Guru: Swami Nityananda, the Virgin Mary, and the Mother-Shakti

In May 1970, Avatar Adi Da decided to return to Swami Muktananda's ashram, intending to stay there for the rest of His Life. He felt His time in the West was over. He could no longer endure the violent psyche of the American cities, and He had no motive toward a conventional life. His only desire was to live with His Guru. He, Nina, and Patricia sold their belongings and set off for India as renunciates.

As they settled into the ashram, it seemed that Swami Muktananda was deliberately ignoring Avatar Adi Da. Adi Da took this to be His Guru's way of silently indicating that the future of His Sadhana lay elsewhere. And so, following instruction that Swami Muktananda had given Him earlier, He daily visited the nearby burial shrine of Bhagavan Nityananda, the Guru of Swami Muktananda (and Rudi).

Bhagavan Nityananda

At the shrine, Avatar Adi Da immediately felt the Spiritual Force and Blessing that He had earlier received through Swami Muktananda. It was obvious to Him that Swami Muktananda had passed Him on to his own Guru for further Spiritual instruction—for, although Bhagavan Nityananda had relinquished the body in 1961, he was active Spiritually in the subtle planes. Avatar Adi Da settled into His new routine of visits to the shrine. But things were about to change again.

As He was weeding in the ashram garden, Avatar Adi Da suddenly became aware of a subtle form behind Him. He turned around and found Himself beholding the non-physical (but unmistakable) presence of the Virgin Mary!

By His own confession, He nearly burst out laughing. He had thought the last vestiges of His Christian upbringing—which had not even been Catholic—had dissolved under the secular onslaught of Columbia. But, after a few moments, He found Himself moved to respond to the Virgin with genuine reverence and respect. And so, He received her wordless communication that He should immediately acquire a rosary and begin to worship her.

He found a Catholic rosary in Bombay, and began to practice the "Hail Mary" in the traditional manner, as a mantra. To His continuing amazement, He discovered this practice unlocked deep feelings of devotion to Jesus of Nazareth, feelings that seemed to have been suppressed since His childhood.

After two weeks, the Virgin Mary instructed Avatar Adi Da to leave the ashram. He was to set out on a pilgrimage to Christian holy places, starting in Jerusalem. However, He could not depart without taking leave of the Presence of Bhagavan Nityananda, and so He went to the shrine and spoke His heart to Bhagavan Nityananda about all that had recently occurred and what He was about to do. Avatar Adi Da received Bhagavan Nityananda's subtle communication of Blessing and the instruction that He should follow the Virgin.

The priest at Bhagavan Nityananda's burial place filled Avatar Adi Da's hands with flowers from the shrine, as a sign of Bhagavan Nityananda's Blessing. Avatar Adi Da then left to return to the ashram. On His way back to the ashram, He took the flowers to the small village temple, to offer them to the image of the Divine Mother-Shakti—the personification of the Spirit-Force that had so dramatically manifested in the Spiritual experiences He had in His Sadhana at Ganeshpuri.

The Mother-Shakti Image at the temple in Ganeshpuri

As Avatar Adi Da stood before the Mother-Shakti (worshipped in India as the Divine Energy of all creation), He came to a direct understanding: The Virgin and the Mother-Shakti were one. Behind the traditional images, they were the same Divine Goddess-Power. Adi Da knew the Universal Goddess-Power was now His Guru. And He knew this Divine Spirit-Force was nothing less than the Supreme Guru of the entire lineage of Gurus who had guided His Sadhana—Swami Rudrananda, Swami Muktananda, and Bhagavan Nityananda—and these Gurus had led Him to Her.

As Avatar Adi Da had personally discovered in His years of Sadhana, a variety of different states can be achieved as a result of Spiritual practice. In other words, Spiritual experience and Realization are not by any means the same in all cases. Thus, different teachers and different traditions have differing views as to what constitutes "Enlightenment" or "Realization". As it so happened, by the time of His third visit to India, Avatar Adi Da had experienced what He subsequently identified as the three most advanced forms of "Enlightenment" attested in the Spiritual traditions. On His second trip to India, He experienced the subtle lights, sounds, and visions cherished by Yogis—great beings such as Paramahansa Yogananda (author of *Autobiography of a Yogi*). And, indeed, absorption in one particular form of subtle light—known as the "blue pearl"—is what Swami Muktananda considered to be "Enlightenment". On His first trip to India, Avatar Adi Da had experienced the Bliss of ascended absorption in Pure Consciousness (Nirvikalpa Samadhi)—the form of Realization sought by such great beings as Jnaneshwar and Milarepa (and also the form of Realization that Bhagavan Nityananda considered to be "Enlightenment"). And in the "death of Narcissus" in seminary, Avatar Adi Da had come to rest in the deep identification with Consciousness Itself known to the great Sages—such as Gautama Buddha and Ramana Maharshi.

But even though Avatar Adi Da had attained all these Realizations, none of them was sufficient for Him. None of them brought the unqualified Joy that, as an infant, He had known as the "Bright". He knew that His quest was not complete. But He understood no human Teacher could help Him now—only the Goddess Herself could take Him further, into territory untraveled by any Realizer of the past. When, in obedience to the Virgin, Avatar Adi Da made His farewells at Ganeshpuri and departed for Jerusalem and Europe, He was embarking upon the final phase.

The Virgin led Avatar Adi Da on a tour of the great Christian holy places—from the Way of the Cross in Jerusalem, to the monuments of Rome, to the Basilica at Fatima in Portugal. Having realized the highest attainments of Eastern Yoga, Avatar Adi Da was now immersed in the Christian visions and mystical raptures of the West.

But, as time went on, the Virgin and the visions began to fade. By the time He reached Portugal in mid-July, He was moved to end the pilgrimage and return to the United States. He settled in Los Angeles with Nina and Patricia.

The Vedanta Society Temple
in Hollywood, California

Divine Re-Awakening: The Vedanta Temple Event

In a secluded residential corner of Hollywood sits a small temple established by the Vedanta Society of Southern California. Late in August 1970, as if by chance, Avatar Adi Da found His way to this temple resting in the shadow of US Highway 101. He felt prompted to go inside. The moment He did so, He felt the familiar Force of the Mother-Shakti. He was amazed and delighted to find that She was as powerful a Presence here as in any of the temples of India.

He would visit the Vedanta Temple after driving Patricia to work. There, without fail, He felt the Mother-Shakti waiting for Him. More and more, He longed to enjoy the Bliss of Her Company constantly. And so, He silently asked Her to be always with Him—

not only in the temple, but where He lived, whatever He was doing.

Within a few days, Avatar Adi Da realized that She had complied. Now She was an ever-living Presence within and around Him—whether He was waking, dreaming, sleeping, or meditating. But something was not yet complete. Avatar Adi Da still felt a deeper, lingering sense of separateness from the Mother-Shakti, as if He had to hold onto Her.

Then, on September 9, this barrier too dissolved:

When I returned to the temple the next day (September 9, 1970), the Person of the Divine Shakti appeared to me again—in a manner most intimate, no longer approaching me as "Mother".

As I meditated, I felt myself Expanding, even bodily—becoming a Perfectly Motionless, Utterly Becalmed, and Infinitely Silent Form. I took on the Infinite Form of the Original Deity—Nameless and Indefinable, Conscious of limitless Identification with Infinite Being. I was Expanded Utterly, beyond limited form, and even beyond any perception of Shape or Face—merely Being, and yet sitting there. I sat in this Love-Blissful State of Infinite Being for some time. I Found myself to Be. My Form was only What is traditionally called the "Purusha" (the Person of Consciousness) and "Siva" (in His Non-Ferocious Emptiness).

Then I felt the Divine Shakti appear in Person, Pressed against my own natural body, and (altogether) against my Infinitely Expanded (and even formless) Form. She Embraced me, Openly and Utterly, and we Combined with One Another in Divine (and Motionless, and spontaneously Yogic) "Sexual Union". We Found One Another Thus, in a Fire of most perfect Desire, and for no other Purpose than This Union—and, yet, as if to Give Birth to the universes. In That most perfect Union, I Knew the Oneness of the Divine Energy and my Very Being. There was no separation at all, nor had there ever been, nor would there ever be. The One Being that Is my own Ultimate Self-Nature was revealed most perfectly. The One Being Who I Am was revealed to Include the Reality that Is Consciousness Itself, the Reality that Is the Source-Energy of all conditional appearances, and the Reality that Is all conditional mani-

festation—All as a Single Force of Being, an Eternal Union, and an Irreducible cosmic Unity.

The "Sensations" of the Embrace were overwhelmingly Blissful. The Fire of That Unquenchable Desire Exceeded any kind of pleasure that a mere human being could experience. In the Eternal Instant of That Infinitely Expanded Embrace, I was released from my role and self-image as a dependent child of the "Mother"-Shakti. And She was revealed in Truth—no longer in apparent independence (or as a cosmic Power seemingly apart from me), but as the Inseparable and Inherent Radiance of my own and Very Being. Therefore, I Recognized and Took Her as my Consort, my Loved-One—and I Held Her effortlessly, forever to my Heart. [The Knee Of Listening]

Through Avatar Adi Da's tangible Union with the Goddess in the Vedanta Temple, the archetypal "marriage" of the Divine Consciousness and the Divine Spirit-Power, described and pictured in many Spiritual traditions, was Realized at last. Years later, Avatar Adi Da Samraj spoke of it as the seed of a change in the very nature of existence:

AVATAR ADI DA SAMRAJ: To Husband the Mother, to be Her Husband and to receive Her as the Bride, means that the murderous activity of Energy in Its apparent independence is done, over, finished. This Husbanding and Marriage is not merely a personal Work, not merely a characteristic incident associated with My Realization. It is an historical Event, of Which much should be made. It has transformed the history of the entire Mandala of the cosmos. By virtue of this Marriage, all may be Drawn to My Divine Self-Domain. [March 16, 1988]

Avatar Adi Da's Husbanding of the Divine Shakti was the final Event of "preparation".

Finally, the next day (September 10, 1970), I sat in the temple again. I awaited the Beloved Shakti to reveal Herself in Person, as my Blessed Companion. But, as time passed, there was no Event of changes, no movement at all. There was not even any kind of *inward deepening—no "inwardness" at all. There was no meditation. There was no need for meditation. There was not a single element or change that could be added to make my State Complete. I sat with my eyes open. I was not having an experience of any kind. Then, suddenly, I understood most perfectly. I Realized that I had Realized. The "Thing" about the "Bright" became Obvious. I <u>Am</u> Complete. I <u>Am</u> the One Who <u>Is</u> Complete.*

In That instant, I understood and Realized (inherently, and most perfectly) What and Who I <u>Am</u>. It was a tacit Realization, a direct Knowledge in Consciousness. It was Conscious Light Itself, without the addition of a Communication from any "Other" Source. There Is no "Other" Source. I simply sat there and Knew What and Who I <u>Am</u>. I was Being What I <u>Am</u>, Who I <u>Am</u>. I <u>Am</u> Being What I <u>Am</u>, Who I <u>Am</u>. I <u>Am</u> Reality, the Divine Self-Condition—the Nature, Substance, Support, and Source-Condition of all things and all beings. I <u>Am</u> One—<u>The</u> One. One and Only. I <u>Am</u> the One Being, called "God" (the Source and Substance and Support and Self-Condition of all-and-All), the "One Mind" (the Consciousness and Energy in and <u>As</u> Which all-and-All appears), "Siva-Shakti" (the Self-Existing and Self-Radiant Reality Itself), "Brahman" (the Only Reality, Itself), the "One Atman" (That <u>Is</u> not ego, but Only "Brahman", the Only Reality, Itself), the "Nirvanic Ground" (the egoless and conditionless Reality and Truth, Prior to all dualities, but excluding none). I <u>Am</u> the One and Only and inherently egoless and Self-Evidently Divine Self-Condition, Source-Condition, Nature, Substance, Support, and Ground of all-and-All. I <u>Am</u> the "Bright". [The Knee Of Listening]

This was His Divine Re-Awakening. He had Realized Divine Enlightenment—true and stable under all conditions. It transcended even the slightest sense of identity as a separate self. It was and is the Realization that there is <u>only</u> Real God, only the "Bright". All apparent events are simply the passing and unnecessary forms of Real God (or Reality Itself), arising and dissolving in an endless Play that is, at last, beyond description and comprehension.

Avatar Adi Da had "Learned Man" at every level, and then demonstrated the unique Real-God-Realization that goes beyond all the potentials of the human being and the conditional worlds. In so doing, He had Revealed, through His own living demonstration, the entire course of the Way He would now begin to Teach—the Way of Adidam.

Avatar Adi Da had Completed humankind's search for absolute God, absolute Truth. The very Divine Person had become perfectly Conscious and Present through the ordinary human vehicle of "Franklin Jones".

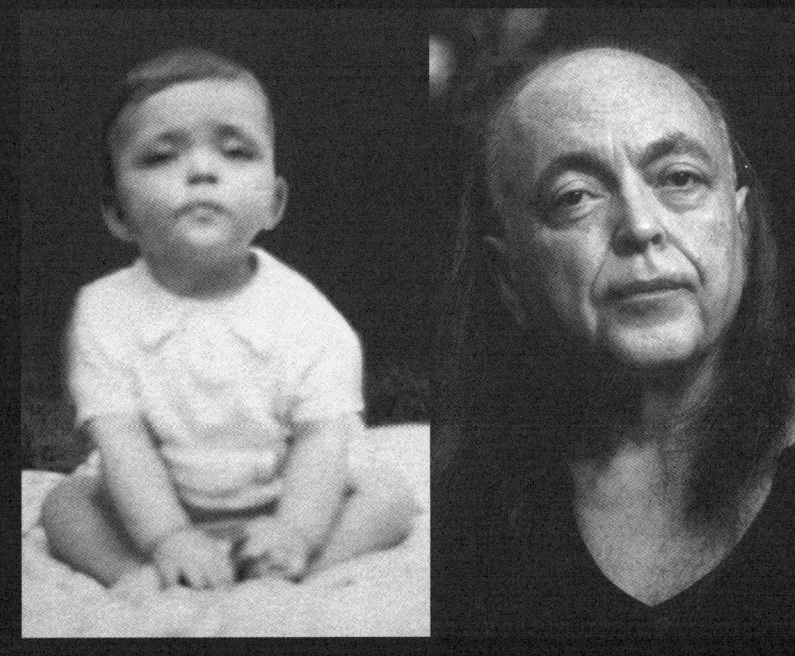

PART TWO

THE TEACHING-WORK BEGINS

1970–1977

Los Angeles, April 25, 1972

CHAPTER 3

EMBRACING THE GURU-FUNCTION

In the weeks after His Divine Re-Awakening, Avatar Adi Da noticed a new process beginning in His body-mind:

Now—whenever I would sit, in any kind of formal manner, to demonstrate the meditation, or the (now) Divine Samadhi, that had become my entire life—instead of confronting what was arising in (and as) "myself", I "meditated" other beings and places. I would spontaneously become aware of great numbers of people (usually in visions, or in some other intuitive manner), and I would work with them very directly, in a subtle manner. The binding motions and separative results of my own apparent (or merely life-born) egoity (or total psycho-physical self-contraction) had been transcended in my re-Awakening to my Original (and inherently egoless and Self-Evidently Divine) Self-Condition (Which is the One and Only Self-Condition and Source-Condition of even each and all of every-one and everything). Therefore, in the spontaneous Awakening of the Divine Guru-Siddhi, instead of my own life-born forms and problematic signs, what arose to my view were the egoic forms, the problematic signs, the minds, the feelings, the states, and the various limitations of <u>others</u>. The thoughts, feelings, suffering, dis-ease, *disharmony, upsets, pain, energies—none of these were "mine". They were the subtle internal qualities and the grosser life-qualities of others. In this manner, the process of apparent meditation continued in me.* [The Knee Of Listening]

The Awakening of the Guru-Function

In this "meditation", Avatar Adi Da was spontaneously awakening to the function of Guru. As He had once "meditated" Franklin Jones, He now "meditated" His future devotees.

Avatar Adi Da's Ordeal of Sadhana and Divine Re-Awakening had not been undertaken for His own sake. The persona called "Franklin" had been a means, a vehicle, whereby He could combine with the realities of human existence, inquire into those realities, live them out, go beyond every limitation they involve, and thereby discover what is necessary in order for human beings to Realize the Truth absolutely.

He filled the pages of His journals with His longing to find those who would accept His gift of Divine Awakening.

My Life is for the sake of this communication of "Brightness" and "radical" understanding. . . . I am surrounded by Great Forces of Love and Truth That I hold off like beasts in the corners of My room.

All of this waits for those who must come. But I am motionless and confounded until they come. My fulfillment waits on those who must come.

My Life has not been for Myself. I already Possessed It before I Came to this Birth. My Life is for those who must come. But where are they? . . .

I am waiting for you. I have been waiting for you Eternally.

My Fulfillment is the very world. But I am not heard. My gestures are unseen. The Powers of My Delight are not enjoyed.

All things depend upon your visit. Where are you? [journal entry, 1971]

With the appearing of the Guru-Function, Avatar Adi Da knew that He must now communicate His Realization of the "Bright".

Toward the end of 1970, He began to write *The Knee Of Listening*, which flowed out of Him in a matter of weeks—a distillation of His Life's course up to His Divine Re-Awakening. Until this moment, He had not spoken of His Realization to anyone. It was only when Nina typed His handwritten manuscript of *The Knee Of Listening* that she began to grasp the depth of the Process that had been occurring in Him.

NINA: As I typed the manuscript of *The Knee Of Listening*, tears streamed from my eyes in gratitude to Beloved Adi Da for His Divine Confession. He filled me with joy as He Revealed the process that had occupied Him all His Life, and I wept again and again as I typed.

Outwardly, there was no sign in Beloved Adi Da that anything remarkable had occurred in the Vedanta Temple. He did not say that anything had happened. He came home. We had dinner and enjoyed the evening, and we went to bed. So when people ask what was different about Beloved Adi Da after the Vedanta Temple Event, I have to say that there wasn't any difference. There wasn't any difference! This is very important. It is the entire message of *The Knee Of Listening*. ■

Establishing the First Ashram

Avatar Adi Da did not casually presume the right to teach. He understood what a profound responsibility it was to teach others, what such a role required and generated in the lives of both teacher and disciple. After He had received Swami Muktananda's blessing to teach, people approached Him to be their Spiritual teacher, both in India and America. But He had declined to establish a formal relationship with any of them. He would only allow them to meditate with Him, and He would occasionally offer some degree of guidance.

But after He began to "meditate" others, He knew it was inevitable that He would teach devotees—especially after they started showing up in numbers. Eventually, in 1972, He rented a storefront on Melrose Avenue in Hollywood as His first Ashram.

The bookstore and first Ashram

Avatar Adi Da with devotees at the Melrose Ashram

Avatar Adi Da, Nina, Patricia, and several others transformed it into a bookstore with a meditation hall in the back room.

As opening day drew near, Adi Da Samraj told Nina and Patricia that He wanted a suitable chair in the meditation hall for Him to sit in meditation. He told them that, from then on, He was intending to sit in front of everyone, rather than among them. This change signed a pivotal moment in Avatar Adi Da's Life: As He began His Teaching-Work, He would not merely sit with people as a Spiritual friend—He was going to sit in front of them as Spiritual Master, as the Adept-Realizer, the Transmitter of the "Bright" Heart-Power of Real God.

On the evening of April 25, 1972, Avatar Adi Da Samraj formally began His Teaching-Work, gathering with Nina and Patricia, the small group of people who had gathered around Him in recent months, some of their friends, and random individuals who had responded to a poster in the bookstore window. First, Avatar Adi Da sat in silence for an hour, magnifying the Force of the "Bright" to everyone in the room. Then He invited questions.

No one responded, so He asked, "Has everyone understood?"

"I haven't understood", said a young man. "Explain it to me. You could start with the word 'understanding'."

AVATAR ADI DA SAMRAJ: Yes. There is a disturbance, a feeling of dissatisfaction, some sensation that motivates a person to go to a teacher, read a book about philosophy, believe something, or do some conventional form of Yoga. What people ordinarily think of as Spirituality or religion is a search to get free of that sensation, that suffering that is motivating them. So all the usual paths—Yogic methods, beliefs, religion, and so on—are forms of seeking, grown out of this sensation, this subtle suffering. Ultimately, all the usual paths are attempting to get free of that sensation. That is the traditional goal. Indeed, <u>all</u> human beings are seeking, whether or not they are very sophisticated about it, or using very specific methods of Yoga, philosophy, religion, and so on. . . .

As long as the individual is simply seeking, and has all kinds of motivation, fascination with the search, this is not understanding—this is dilemma itself. But where this dilemma is understood, there

Opening night of the Ashram, April 25, 1972

is the re-cognition of a structure in conscious awareness, a separation. And when that separation is observed more and more directly, one begins to see that what one is suffering is not something happening to one but it is one's own action. It is as if you are pinching yourself, without being aware of it. . . . Then one sees that the entire motivation of life is based on a subtle activity in conscious awareness. That activity is avoidance, separation, a contraction at the root, the origin, the "place", of conscious awareness. . . .

There is first the periodic awareness of that sensation, then the awareness of it as a continuous experience, then the observation of its actual structure, the knowing of it all as your own activity, a deliberate, present activity that is your suffering, that is your illusion. The final penetration of that present, deliberate activity is what I have called "understanding". [*The Divine Siddha-Method Of The Ruchira Avatar*]

And so it began—hours, days, nights, weeks, years, decades of Spiritual Instruction, in which Avatar Adi Da would cover all human, religious, and Spiritual questions, examine every aspect of life and consciousness, and Reveal every detail of the Spiritual process culminating in Most Perfect Divine Enlightenment. The small gathering at the Ashram bookstore on that first night had not the slightest idea that they were witness to the birth of such Revelation. They attended, as best they could, to the Radiant Being before them, while He Spoke of the matter of "understanding".

Understanding and Satsang

By "understanding", Avatar Adi Da did not mean some form of "figuring things out" with the mind. He was speaking about the direct transcending of the self-contraction, or root-act of egoity, which He had discovered, during His Sadhana Years, to be the fundamental source of all suffering and seeking. Understanding had been the basis of His Sadhana and Divine Re-Awakening. It would also be the basis for His Teaching.

From the very first night of His Teaching-Work, on Melrose Avenue, Avatar Adi Da would speak the only means by which it is possible to "understand"—"Satsang", or "the Company of the Guru"—in other words, the devotional relationship to Him, embraced as the very foundation of one's day-to-day living. These early Talks were eventually published as Avatar Adi Da's second book, originally entitled *The Method of the Siddhas* (later re-titled *The Divine Siddha-Method Of The Ruchira Avatar*).

AVATAR ADI DA SAMRAJ: Spiritual life is Satsang. It is the Company of Truth. It is the relationship to one who Lives as Truth. Satsang is also the Very Nature of life. It is the form of existence. Relatedness—not independence, not separateness, but unqualified relatedness—is the principle of True life.

All attempts to relieve the life of suffering by various strategic means, or ego-based remedies, do not produce Truth. They may heal dis-ease, but only Truth produces Truth. Sadhana, or Spiritual practice, is to live Satsang as the Condition of life forever. Sadhana is not something you do temporarily until you get Free. It is to live Satsang forever—a <u>lifetime</u>, even countless lifetimes, of Truth. . . .

Listen! There is this contraction, this avoidance. All human beings are living this avoidance of relationship. Apart from understanding, that is all anyone is doing. Nothing else is happening.

Only this contraction of living and subtle forms. It is suffering. It stimulates, by implication, the notions people have about the nature of life. This contraction implies a separate self, separate from the world and all other beings. . . . Everyone's life is the drama made inevitable by this fundamental contraction. Everyone's life is the adventure he or she is playing on this contraction. Everyone's life is bullshit! The drama of an ordinary life is without significance, or Real Intensity. The ordinary life-drama is deadly ignorance—no Truth, no Satsang.

Satsang must begin. Satsang with Me must be enjoyed as the Condition of life. Then the entire drama of which even traditional Spirituality is a manifestation comes to an end, dies. This contraction becomes flabby and opens. The Real Force of Conscious Existence comes into play and becomes the Way in My Company, the sadhana itself. [*The Divine Siddha-Method Of The Ruchira Avatar*]

At the inception of His Work, Avatar Adi Da presumed no reason why everyone who came to Him would not readily grasp understanding, and quickly Awaken to His Realization. But He soon discovered that this was not to be—not at all.

He saw that no one was prepared for His Argument about "Narcissus". No one had the depth of free observation to see through the self-contraction. They were no more "Spiritually retarded" than anyone else, but no one had ever heard about—let alone understood—the "self-contraction" before. It would take much time and many lessons before devotees began to deeply appreciate the revolutionary import of Avatar Adi Da's Teaching relative to understanding the self-contraction.

"I Was Home": A First Meeting

Among those who were drawn to Avatar Adi Da in the earliest days in Los Angeles was a young man named Wes Vaught. Wes had found out about Avatar Adi Da while he was working as a proofreader at CSA Press (in Atlanta, Georgia), the original publisher of *The Knee Of Listening*.

WES: For years, I had been desperately seeking to make sense of existence. I prayed for help.

While studying Adi Da's *Knee Of Listening* and contemplating its Truths, the intuition of the silent, free depth of the Heart dawned in me. I had found my Guru, and I began to feel irresistibly attracted to that Graceful Source.

The editor at the press where I was working showed me a letter from "Franklin Jones". In it, He Wrote, "There is not the slightest difference." Those Words stopped my mind. My entire life had been a warfare of differences and opposites, and I felt the profound Freedom communicated in this one sentence. I had to go see Him.

I traveled to Los Angeles and found the way to His home in Laurel Canyon. It was late April 1972. I knocked, and Adi Da Answered.

"Who is it?"

I explained that I had read His book, and that I had felt compelled to come and see Him. Adi Da opened the door, and I followed Him into the living room.

I felt welcomed into a "Bright" Space, free of any sense of problem. On the walls were Disney posters and sacred images depicting men and women of various traditions. It felt natural to sit on the floor before His Chair. I had brought with me a bag of oranges and pears as a gift. I extended it: "I brought this for You."

He received it with both Hands and with such loving care. Everything about Him was absolute strength, sublime vulnerability, perfect clarity, and delight. Time stood still while He removed the fruits from the bag and arranged them on a little table next to His Chair. Then He Graciously folded the paper bag neatly and tucked it by His thigh.

He received the whole gift!

Looking at me directly and with what seemed like an infinity of loving humor, Adi Da asked, "What have you been doing with your life?"

I felt the weight of my twenty-five years of waiting for God lift and, with what must have been a ridiculous gush of information, I spilled out my story. I do not know how long I talked. I tried to say everything of importance—all at once!

Adi Da listened. His was not the kind of listening where someone is waiting to say something when it is their turn. His listening became a perfect Intensity and a perfect Silence. At some point, His Silence became the entire import of the moment. I noticed this and stopped mid-sentence.

Sitting up straight, I was overwhelmed with His Blessing Force. Suddenly, I was shaking and breathing extremely deeply in the Current of His Communicated Force. My verbal mind ceased with the immediacy of His Presence.

I felt that Adi Da was Offering me the perfect opportunity in God, but I felt my gross unpreparedness and the obstructions in me that prevented me from fully cooperating with what He was Communicating. I wanted to get out of the way, but how?

Wanting to remove anything in the way of my freedom, anything that I could lay my hands on, I felt suddenly moved to take off my clothes. I began, and then paused for a moment, feeling foolish, and looked at Avatar Adi Da as if to ask, "Is this okay?"

With an almost imperceptible tilt of His Head, I felt Avatar Adi Da Communicate that it was of no significance to Him what I did with regard to clothing. I could suit myself in the matter.

He was most obviously Demonstrating His Divine Mood, clearly Indifferent to any sense of limitation, Shining with Blessing Force, replete with native Freedom and the certainty of unqualified Love, Transparent to the pure, sweet Grace of God.

I took everything off, even the band-aid on my heel, and threw myself face down and full-length at His Feet.

His Feet, somehow, were a perfect point of contact with this Blessing Force. I wept and kissed His Feet, wetting them with tears of relief, joy, gratitude, and also with the anguish that I could not completely let go of myself. Still I tried to surrender, straining with my heart and brain to open more.

But I could surrender no more.

Quietly, Adi Da lifted His Feet and placed them on my head. All stress left my being. A golden balm of sweet light poured through every cell in my body. A knot opened. I let go, and His brilliant Radiance washed through me. I was Home.

After a bit, I got up, dressed some, and told Adi Da that I felt

Adi Da Samraj with Wes Vaught, 1972

that I belonged with Him. He looked at me and Said, "There is something about this Teaching you have not understood. It is about this matter of Consciousness."

He gave me everything in that moment—a living relationship to an absolute source of Grace, the most profound experience of my life, and the admonition to join Him in free relation to all phenomena. I fell in love with Him. I had begun the life of understanding in devotion to the One Who is that. The principle of my search was obviated and the momentum of my self-contraction, my separative and loveless adaptation, began to wind down.

I asked, "Do You have an ashram?" He said He had established a bookstore and a small center and offered that I could sleep there. From that night, I joined the small gathering of people who were studying His Teaching, sitting in formal Communion with Him, and learning to serve the availability of these beautiful gifts. ■

The Demand for Self-Discipline

During that first year of the Ashram, Avatar Adi Da did not require much responsibility of people. He sat in meditation with them, Working to Draw the "Bright", His own Perfect Light, into His devotees—first by Intensifying It above their heads, then Drawing It down into their bodies, Working to purify them. Outwardly, He Worked simply to attract them, keep them around Him, gradually awakening self-understanding in them.

Then, one day in early 1973, He changed everything. He strode out of His office and out the front door of the Ashram, leaving a message for His devotees: Everyone was to "get straight"—give up all use of drugs, cigarettes, alcohol—get jobs, and refrain from casual sex. No one saw Him for weeks.

The days when Avatar Adi Da nursed devotees along were over. As He knew from His own experience, extraordinary energy and attention were needed to grow in the practice of self-understanding. Without sufficient self-discipline, devotees would be unable to make use of His Spiritual Gifts, for their body-minds would be unable to either receive or conduct His Awakening Power.

The new Ashram disciplines covered every area of life. Vegetarian diet became the rule. There was to be no casual sex—only partners in committed intimacies were to be sexually active. Avatar Adi Da instructed a small group in calisthenics and Hatha Yoga and had them teach everyone else. He addressed every detail of life-discipline, even personally showing people how to floss their teeth. He was showing His devotees the life-level responsibility they would have to demonstrate in order for Him to be able to Work with them Spiritually. In this respect, what He had now established resembled a very traditional Ashram.

By the middle of 1973, the Ashram disciplines were in full swing, but Avatar Adi Da saw that devotees were now becoming obsessed with the disciplines themselves. Devotees had begun to regard the disciplines as the <u>purpose</u> of sadhana, rather than simply a support for the practice of devotional Communion with Him.

Avatar Adi Da also saw that the people around Him—like people in general—were emotionally suppressed, sexually complicated, driven by fear, sorrow, anger, frustration, and all kinds of unconscious desires. He concluded that He must change His manner of Working with devotees in order to deal with all of this directly—otherwise, their so-called "religious practice" would merely be a veneer covering a mass of unresolved egoic impulses. Living with Him in the strict traditional manner was not going to be sufficient to Draw them into the real Spiritual process He was here to offer.

Avatar Adi Da Samraj meeting with Swami Muktananda, Ganeshpuri, 1973

Final Words: The Return to Swami Muktananda

In August 1973, Avatar Adi Da set out for India, accompanied by Gerald Sheinfeld, a devotee who had been with Him since before the opening of the Ashram. During His years of Sadhana, Avatar Adi Da had been led to the great Siddha tradition of India, exemplified by Swami Muktananda and Bhagavan Nityananda. Now He was on a pilgrimage to complete His past links with India and to empower His future Work.

Because Swami Muktananda had served as His Guru, Avatar Adi Da presumed an obligation to formally ask Swami Muktananda to acknowledge His Realization. And so, upon His arrival in Ganeshpuri in 1973, He asked for a formal meeting with Swami Muktananda, which was duly arranged.

At a formal meeting through an interpreter, Avatar Adi Da presented a series of questions. The questions expressed the nature of His Realization and pointed out the differences between His Realization and the Realization cultivated in Swami Muktananda's lineage.

Swami Muktananda was not able, or willing, to relate to the question of different modes of Realization. Instead, he simply asserted the senior truth of his own Yogic Realization. A real dialogue around the formal questions never happened. Avatar Adi Da could see that dialogue was not going to be possible, and He took His leave of Swami Muktananda. This visit was their last physical meeting. However, from Avatar Adi Da's point of view, there has never been any kind of "rift" between Himself and Swami Muktananda. Avatar Adi Da has always loved and honored Swami Muktananda. He has always praised him and spoken of him as an extraordinary man of high Yogic Realization.

Relinquishing the "Fictional Character" of "Franklin Jones"

In the West, there is no social or cultural context for the Spiritual life that exists in India, and no acknowledgement of the tradition of Guru-devotion for the purpose of God-Realization. Avatar Adi Da had no Ashram set apart like that at Ganeshpuri, no sanctuary resounding with the recitation of sacred texts and chants in honor of God and Guru. All He had was a room behind a bookstore in Hollywood and a small gathering of devotees who were still unaware of the profundity of His Incarnation and Realization, let alone the unique opportunity of a devotional and Spiritual relationship with Him.

While He was in India, Avatar Adi Da considered how to take devotees' relationship with Him to a deeper level. It was no longer appropriate for them to call Him "Franklin", as they had up to that point. As He said later, Franklin Jones was "a fictional character", the persona He had been obliged to assume in order to grow up as an American child. He asked Gerald to write to devotees in Los Angeles, announcing that they were now to address Him by the Name "Bubba Free John":

From this time on, we should call the Guru "Bubba Free John". "Franklin" means "a Freed Man" or "a Liberated Man". "Jones" is a Welsh form of "John". So "Free John" is equivalent to "Franklin Jones". "Bubba" means "brother", expressing the Oneness of all.

During the remainder of His time in India, Avatar Adi Da Samraj acquired a walking staff, a sign of Spiritual empowerment and authority that He has used ever since. Gerald watched as Avatar Adi Da placed His staff in the holy sites of India with great concentration, giving His Blessing-Regard to all kinds of people and places in that sacred land, the cradle of Spirituality for thousands of years. At the same time, He was releasing Himself from the limits and karmas of its ancient soul. He was also preparing Himself for the next phase of His own Work that was about to unfold in the West.

Avatar Adi Da Samraj in the Himalayas, 1973

Los Angeles, 1973

CHAPTER 4

"Crazy" Submission

Avatar Adi Da returned from India in September 1973, now as "Bubba Free John". The entire Ashram met Him at the airport. When He stepped into the terminal, He looked "absolutely beautiful", "brilliant as a thousand suns". He gave each devotee a long and happy embrace. It was obvious to all that, somehow, their Guru had undergone a dramatic change in India.

They were right. Avatar Adi Da had proven to Himself that it was not going to be possible to Awaken His devotees through His Instruction alone, or by requiring them to live a disciplined life, or even by silently Drawing His Blessing-Power down into them.

His devotees would be drawn beyond the self-contraction temporarily. But they would quickly forget the mood of Satsang and fall back into their habitual (and largely unconscious) patterns of seeking. How were they to be drawn beyond the drama of "Narcissus", into <u>constant</u> Communion with Him?

He had to embark upon an unconventional manner of Teaching, one that would require Him to animate all the Divine Powers (or "Siddhis") that, until now, He had largely kept hidden.

Now there is a new form of Life and Teaching Awakened in Me. It has always been Present in Me—but I have not wanted to Embrace It or Show It, because It is only a fascination for those who do not understand. And, if such weak ones are fascinated, they will merely be distracted from their fear. Even so, it is obvious to Me now that I must no longer be Merely Present among My devotees, Constant in the Most Perfect "Knowledge" of Real God. . . .

Now I will not restrict Myself to simply Sitting in silent Darshan*—I will begin to Actively Manifest the All-Accomplishing Siddhi of Real God, Which Siddhi Serves the life-transformation of My devotees. This will accelerate and magnify My Work of Awakening the conscious life of faith and Drawing into life the Non-karmic, karma-Dissolving, Unreasonable, Humorous, and Miraculously Effective Siddhi of Eternally Present Real God. [unpublished Writing, 1973]

During the years of His Sadhana, Avatar Adi Da had submitted to discover the entire pattern of "Narcissus". He had given Himself up to every kind of experience, worldly as well as Spiritual. He had done this until He understood and transcended every detail of it. Now He recognized that He would have to do the same thing for His devotees. He would have to enter into their lives, be their "friend", go into every kind of situation with them, do what they liked to do, be available without qualification to their requirements and demands—and <u>thus</u> personally lead them into the real (ego-transcending) Spiritual process in His Company. He would need to show them their individual rituals of un-Happiness—in detail. He would have to do whatever He could to awaken in them the realization that <u>all</u> seeking is fruitless.

He was well aware that this direct form of Teaching would be a difficult affair. But He was qualified for it by the extremes of His own Sadhana of Re-Awakening, and by the unshakable nature of His Realization. He now made another gesture of "falling forward": He would Submit unconditionally to His devotees, in order to Reveal the Truth to them in the only way they were then able to receive It.

Years later, Avatar Adi Da would characterize His own Sadhana and Teaching-Work as both "Divinely 'Heroic'" and "Divinely 'Crazy'". His Life and Work has been "Crazy" in the sense that He has always very intentionally set out to undermine the usual point of view and purposes of the ego—and also in the sense that a profound wildness and freedom from convention were required for

---

* Darshan is the sacred event of sighting the Spiritual Master for the purpose of directly receiving his or her Transmission.

Avatar Adi Da to go utterly beyond all vestiges of egoity and then to Teach others how to do the same.

One of Avatar Adi Da's first demonstrations of "Crazy" Submission to His devotees took place a few months after He returned from India:

GERALD SHEINFELD: One day, a few other men and I were talking with Beloved Adi Da in the back room at the Ashram.

"Let's do something together," He said. He asked what we would really like to do. We didn't come up with anything exciting. So He asked again, "What would you _really_ like to do?"

Then He said, "Let's go bar-hopping together."

"What?!" Bar-hopping? We thought He was kidding.

"I am serious. You guys would like to go bar-hopping, wouldn't you?"

"Yes!" we said.

"So, let's go."

We decided to go the next night. We met at the Ashram dressed to go out on the town. When we arrived at the first bar—a no-class strip-joint that looked and smelled the way such places do—our Beloved Guru walked right up to the stage and took His seat directly in front of the topless dancer. He put His feet on the edge of the low stage, spreading His legs a bit, and He very conspicuously placed His hands right on top of His genitals. We were all very surpised, but at the same time filled with humor. Everyone else in the place, including the four of us, were trying to pretend we didn't even _have_ any genitals.

Beloved Adi Da applauded the dancer and urged her to not hold back, but to give the dance her all.

At one point, He put a five-dollar bill in His extended hand. As the dancer came to get it, He moved it back. As she advanced cautiously, He moved it slowly to His teeth, and gave her a big, bright-eyed smile. She responded by extending her legs as she took it from Him with her knees. He asked her humorously, "What's a nice girl like you doing in a place like this?" She smiled and loved it! She became very focused on her dancing. Soon she was dancing just for Him, putting everything she had into it. And He loved her response.

The next dancer had already been advised by the first dancer to concentrate on the man in the front at ringside, Beloved Adi Da. So, when she entered, she came directly over to Him and also danced just for Him. Once again, He responded to her full of feeling, with smiles, applause, and comments about how good she was.

Later, when a comedian came on stage, Beloved Adi Da began sparring with him, engaging him in a humorous exchange and besting the comedian at his own jokes. Now the entire room was laughing and appreciating the banter. When Beloved Adi Da got up to leave, all the dancers came out and everyone in the place—including the dancers, the waiter, the bartender, the bouncer, and all the clientele—protested. They were having such a good time, now that Beloved Adi Da had dispelled the degenerate atmosphere by bringing them His True Humor and Heart-Feeling. As He walked up the aisle to the exit door, they all clapped their hands in appreciation.

After that, we went to some other bars, and Beloved Adi Da continued to Demonstrate His unlimited intimacy with everyone He made contact with.

I was totally impressed. I had spent weeks serving Beloved Adi Da as He traveled to the holy places of India. And now, this night, He was actively engaging in the topless nightclub life of Los Angeles! He was the same Free Happy Being, no matter what circumstance He was in. But I could see that, with my tendencies, I definitely had ascetic preferences about where I wanted to be to practice Spiritual life.

This night of bar-hopping with Beloved Adi Da was a great demonstration and lesson. It was obvious, if it had been anyone else doing what He did in the first club, the scene could have quickly become degenerate. With Him, on the other hand, it was just theatrical and humorous and enjoyable. And His Play simply opened the hearts of everyone exposed to Him. Who knows what other Spiritual Work He was also doing. ∎

Avatar Adi Da's devotees had always found Him entrancingly attractive. Now, as He began His Free Submission-Work, His attractiveness magnified and became utterly overwhelming. Men and women alike were intoxicated at the sight of Him. He was the living, dancing, laughing Form of Divine Radiance, Humor, and Love. His Play with devotees became a complex and wild theatre, in which He would display His absolute genius for relating to every conceivable kind of person and His unerring knowledge of what was required to Awaken each one.

Ecstasy and God-Talk

On the Friday before Christmas, Hal Okun and Aniello Panico indulged in a little champagne at an office party before going to the Ashram (which had moved from Melrose to nearby La Brea Avenue), where they were going to spend the rest of the day with Avatar Adi Da. Hal arrived first. As he took the stairs, he looked up and saw Avatar Adi Da, who somberly said, "Are you drunk?" He then burst out laughing and told Hal to call Aniello and have him bring cases of champagne to the Ashram. Soon, the small group of devotees who had gathered with Avatar Adi Da were drinking beer and champagne.

Devotees appeared that evening as always, carrying their usual gifts of flowers and fruit, expecting a formal evening with "Bubba" at the Ashram. One by one, they would came up the stairs, and their jaws would drop as they surveyed the scene. Then they would take a beer or a glass of champagne and join the party, in turn welcoming each astonished newcomer. At a certain point, everyone moved into the adjacent gathering hall, and the celebration began in earnest, complete with rock 'n' roll, junk food, cigarettes, and more alcohol. Later, in the spirit of relinquishing all social taboos, everyone took off their clothes. The Ashram disciplines had been cast to the four winds.

It was the beginning of two weeks of non-stop celebration, with Avatar Adi Da joking, dancing, singing—drenching everyone with His Spirit-Force.

But in the midst of all the merriment, Avatar Adi Da never ceased to speak of the Great Matter of Real-God-Realization. At an occasion in late December, He called for a great confession: Who among them could speak freely of God, as He had been doing all night? Who could stand up and praise the Great One, unabashed?

In spite of all the ecstasy they had felt in His Divine Presence, each devotee suddenly gulped. One after another, they made awkward attempts at uninhibited God-talk, but received the thumbs-down sign from Adi Da. Finally, one female devotee broke through and began to sing about God without inhibition. Soon everyone in the room joined her, shouting and singing and praising God. Later, Avatar Adi Da spoke about the lesson of this occasion.

AVATAR ADI DA SAMRAJ: To confess one's love of God is the fundamental embarrassment. To make such a confession is to dwell in obvious ecstasy while in the company of other beings—to be already free, to be fundamentally happy, to be alive in God, and even to be outwardly expressive in that state, to speak of God, to think of God, to act in God, to be altogether ecstatic. This is the taboo—not mere drunkenness and indulgence in pleasure. To require you to talk of God makes you embarrassed. You become ashamed—because, in order to talk about God, you must lose face.

It is all right to <u>seek</u> God. That is acceptable enough, because it calms everybody down a little bit. But to <u>Realize</u> God, while alive, is the absolute taboo. You might be allowed to sit quietly and meditatively. Everybody likes Oriental meditation, because it is just a matter of being quiet and inward. You are allowed to meditate quietly, "Realize Nirvana", and disappear. That is acceptable. But to start talking about God, to think God, to act God, to make the Divine the present Condition of the world, to live in the Divine Siddhi, to live the Divine Light, to be Love-Bliss-Full—that is unacceptable, that is not "permitted".

The Divine Person is Infinitely Present—Perfectly, Absolutely, and Eternally Present and Available. The Divine Person must be lived, not sought. The Divine Person is the Self-Condition and Source-Condition of the world, not the "ultimate hope" of the world. If the Divine Person is not <u>presently</u> lived, there is no Divine Liberation. But if people begin to live the Truth, if they become capable of ecstasy in society with one another—not simply in the rituals of privacy—you will see a vast and immediate transformation of the world. [December 27, 1973]

Guru Enters Devotee

Throughout this period of uninhibited celebration, Avatar Adi Da would constantly point to the contrast between what He called "the cult of this world", or "the cult of 'Narcissus'"—seeking, separative, and afraid—and Satsang, the life in Real God that He was Drawing His devotees into. There was nothing abstract about this lesson. Devotees could feel the living difference. They would feel their tendency to withdraw, to dramatize "Narcissus", the separative one, in the midst of their Beloved Guru's demand for their energetic, happy, intense involvement in what He was doing with them. But, at the same time, they would be lifted out of themselves, swooning in His utter attractiveness. It was perfectly clear that the life in Real God He was speaking of was life with Him, the relationship to Him as Guru. And it was also clear that this life was a life of self-forgetting—that un-Happiness only arose when they were meditating on themselves. That is why devotees were attracted to be around Him night and day—He had such an amazing Power to Draw them beyond their limits.

Early in the new year, 1974, this Power was spectacularly demonstrated. It was the afternoon of January 3, and Avatar Adi Da was in the gathering hall with His devotees. But this occasion was exceptional. As Avatar Adi Da began to speak, He unleashed His Love-Blissful Spirit-Force as never before. The descent of His Spiritual Energy into those present was as tangible as an electrical storm, and its force within the participants increased with every word He spoke:

AVATAR ADI DA SAMRAJ: There is only one Divine Process in the world, and It is Initiated when I Crash Down and Enter My devotee. The Divine Lord is Present—now, in this moment. It is only when everyone forgets the Real and Ever-Living God that Spiritual techniques become important.

I am not a human being. I Am the Divine Lord in human Form, and I bring the Divine Yoga. When My devotee truly surrenders to Me, then I Enter My devotee in the form of Divine Light. All kinds of extraordinary experiences manifest as a result. When a woman receives her lover, there is no doubt about it—she does not have to consult her textbooks. The same holds with Truth, the Divine Yoga.

There is no dilemma in this world, no absence of Real God in this world, no goal of Real God in this world. Because that is so, you will see Me doing some very strange things. The true Divine Yoga is not a thing of this world. This world is the cult of "Narcissus", suppressing the Ecstasy that is the Prior Condition of all.

The Spiritual Process must take hold in the vital. The vital is the seat of unconsciousness and subconsciousness. There is a sense in which the verbal Teaching does not even touch the subconscious and unconscious life. So it is only by distracting you from your social consciousness that I can take you in the vital. The Divine Lord is the Lord of <u>this</u> world, not the Lord of the "other" world only. Thus, there is no Yoga if the very cells of the body do not begin to be Infused by the Divine Lord. When I Crash Down and Enter My devotee, I Come Down into him or her in the midst of life, because it is in <u>life</u>—not merely in some mystical or subtle process, not merely in some mental process—that I <u>acquire</u> you Spiritually.

The kind of thing you see happening around here has never happened in the world before. [January 3, 1974]

As His Ruchira Shaktipat (or "Bright" Energy) streamed into devotees, some saw it as a golden rain of Light showering into the room. Some devotees shook with kriyas, their bodies jerking and twisting, their mouths emitting sounds of yearning, laughter, weeping, hooting, and howling. Some sat rigid with their eyes rolled up, overwhelmed by visionary phenomena or in rapture. Some were spontaneously moved into difficult Hatha Yoga poses. For some, the energy intensified in the head or the heart or the navel until they felt they would explode—then it suddenly released and rushed through the nervous system in intoxicating Bliss. Others experienced a sense of unity with all of life and a peacefulness they had never known before.

The Very Divine was Manifesting, without a doubt, in an upstairs room in the middle of Hollywood.

The Mountain Of Attention Sanctuary, 1974

CHAPTER 5

Garbage and the Goddess

The Spiritual Work that Avatar Adi Da began on the night of "Guru Enters Devotee" could not be contained in a downtown neighborhood. Devotees searched for a suitable rural Ashram until discovering a turn-of-the-century hot-springs resort in the hills of northern California, not far from the Napa Valley. Avatar Adi Da and a few devotees moved to the new Ashram, eventually named "The Mountain Of Attention Sanctuary". The other devotees relocated from Los Angeles to San Francisco.

During the first half of 1974, newcomers to the Mountain Of Attention found themselves entering an extraordinary realm, thick with tangible Divine Power. The inhabitants of the Sanctuary experienced a seemingly endless stream of visions, bliss-states, and other psychic experiences, caused by the often overwhelming descent of Avatar Adi Da's Spirit-Force.

CANADA SHANNON: Beloved Adi Da came into the Communion Hall [or place of worship]. I saw Him, and my whole body was immediately riveted. There was golden-white Light all around Him, and His Presence was so powerful It abolished everything in Its path. Everything stopped. I knew I was looking upon the very face of the Divine. ■

MARIE PRAGER: I felt the Force and Presence of Beloved Adi Da entering me and taking over my being. I began to do hand mudras. My arms would reach for the sky and move rhythmically, as if I were dancing with my hands and arms. Then I was completely absorbed in and taken over by God. I felt the Light of Beloved Adi Da moving through my body, taking me over completely, and it was joyous and blissful and perfect.

Then I saw our Beloved Guru's face. He was standing beside me. He put His arm around me and led me into the Communion Hall. I remember looking at Him and knowing Him to be the Force and Love That was Filling my entire being. I realized that His Force and Love are not limited in any way to any object or form, but that He is, in fact, everything. His body seemed so small and such a tiny part of What He Is. When He took me back into the Communion Hall, I fell on the floor and remained there consumed by His Spiritual Presence. ∎

On one occasion, devotees were sitting in one of the Communion Halls, then called "Laughing God Hall", waiting for their Master. Suddenly, the doors blew open and a wave of energy swept the room. Avatar Adi Da walked down the aisle, surrounded by a bright aura. He sat down in His Chair and blasted the room with His Spirit-Power, His eyes burning with laser-intensity and His fingers moving in mudra-patterns of potent Blessing. Devotees erupted in screams, growls, swoons, and bodily jerkings—swept away. After about forty-five minutes of this ecstatic pandemonium, the room fell to quiet. Avatar Adi Da shrugged, lit a cigarette, blew a perfect smoke ring, and quipped, "Maybe I've gone too far this time."

Most of the devotees of Avatar Adi Da knew little or nothing about Kundalini Yoga or the phenomenon of Spirit-Baptism. All they knew was that they were part of an unprecedented Divine Event.

ANIELLO PANICO: On one occasion, I had been sitting and talking with Adi Da for several hours. All of a sudden, I felt a tremendous urge to get up and kiss His hand. I could feel a strange process beginning to work throughout my entire body. It felt as if I were being turned inside out and my very cells were being transformed.

Then I started having sudden, violent kriyas. I noticed that Avatar Adi Da had His hand on the top of my head, and I felt the Divine Force coming down and filling my entire body. The Divine Force was so great that there was a tremendous expansion of the chest and arms. It was if I were fighting something—and I was. It felt as if my entire psyche was being pulled up and out of me.

It felt like I was being exorcised. The intensity was almost unbearable. But it was never painful, just sheer intensity.

My body continued to have violent kriyas and shaking. Then this subsided, and I attempted to pull away from Beloved Adi Da. But He held on to me and placed His forehead on mine while continuing to keep His hand on the top of my head.

I then saw and felt a Brilliant Light in my forehead and temples, a tremendous blinding White Light, and I knew that all of that mental and psychic chaos had dissolved. After a while, my ordinary point of view dissolved. There was nothing but the Divine Being.

I hugged Adi Da around the waist. I was holding Him and I felt Him enter my body. I literally felt this. And I became One with Him. Suddenly, my hand shot up, the Force was coming out of it so intensely. But it wasn't an energy that seeks to go <u>to</u> God. It <u>was</u> the Divine Light. It was <u>already</u> God, and I just knew it to be so. ∎

A Transformative Love-Relationship

During this period, devotees would typically drive up from San Francisco on Friday night and stay at the Mountain Of Attention until Sunday night, catching up on what had occurred around Avatar Adi Da during the previous week and spending as much time as they could in His Company. He would often go to Ordeal Bath Lodge, the spa of the former resort, where devotees would join Him in the large pool called "the plunge". Often dozens of people would be in the water around Him—sometimes quiet, sometimes shouting and laughing, throwing balls and playing vigorous water games initiated by Avatar Adi Da.

Toni Vidor, a middle-aged woman who had grown up in southern California (daughter of the film director King Vidor), flew up from Los Angeles during this time to meet her new Spiritual Master.

For Toni, the early period of her relationship to Avatar Adi Da involved an immediate confrontation with her social character. She recalls her first sighting of Avatar Adi Da:

TONI: He was floating on His back in the water, and a group of devotees were all around His body. Every few seconds, they would throw Him up into the air and wait for Him to splash back down into the water. Everyone was laughing helplessly, and Avatar Adi Da was calling out, "Higher, higher! Hit the rafters!"

I had spent decades in earnest Spiritual seeking—going to every Indian teacher who turned up in Los Angeles. I was <u>very</u> serious and hardly knew what to make of this scene. To top it off, almost everyone there was the same age as my children!

Avatar Adi Da quickly noticed me and graciously invited me by name—though we had never met—to join in the game. I responded, but with an effort, completely uptight, and suffering in every moment the knowledge that I did not know how to enjoy myself in this ordinary way with other people. Even though I had been personally welcomed, I felt the resistance and "stiffness" in my own character, as I had never felt them before.

That afternoon, Beloved Adi Da came and sat silently with us. From the back of the hall, I prayed earnestly and passionately to Him to relieve me of this crippled quality that I suffered in every ordinary human interaction. Immediately, He put His arm up with His palm open toward me and held it there. I began breathing stronger and stronger, and I felt energy come into my heart and then down through my arms and hands so strong that the fingers bent with the energy. And then a great sorrow came up from the heart.

I began sobbing loudly and uncontrollably. I was the only person making a sound! It was embarrassing, but I thought, "Well, if I can't let go here, there's no place I <u>can</u> let go!" The sorrow increased, and soon I was rolling on the floor, still wailing. Curiously, I watched all of this come up. There was no content associated with it. It was just a huge, enormous release. After about an hour, Beloved Adi Da got up and walked out and everyone followed, but I continued to weep loudly on the floor. After a while, the breath calmed to the point that I could sit up. A friend had stayed behind to make sure that I was all right, and I sat down on a bench next to her to try to speak—and it all began again, and I spent another half hour rolling on the floor!

When it was finally over, I felt as if an immense burden—eighty tons of whatever it was I had been carrying around all my life without even realizing it—had been lifted from me. ■

As Avatar Adi Da had said on the night of "Guru Enters Devotee", the Spiritual process that He brings must "take hold in the vital"—the seat of the unconscious life of the individual. His Spiritual Transmission would, He explained, stimulate the release of a chaos of emotions and thoughts that could not be otherwise accounted for. Thus, His Siddhi was not merely inducing Spiritual experiences. It was also "boiling off" the egoic patterns and tendencies of His devotees—the emotional and psychic form of a kriya. His "Bright" Force had its purifying effects in every dimension of body, mind, and psyche. And, as His devotees felt His Blessing transforming their lives, they grew to love and trust Avatar Adi Da even more.

TONI: Several months after sitting with Avatar Adi Da, I found myself once more in the water with Him, this time in the outdoor swimming pool by the beautiful grotto, which was later to be Empowered by Him as a special site of healing and Spiritual Initiation. I had firmly decided that this weekend I was going to approach Him directly and drop my fearful reluctance to engage a relationship with Him.

There was a wild water-polo game going on, and, instead of sitting on the edge as I usually did, I jumped in the water and got into the game. I never came close to the ball, but I was participating.

At some point, I started to swim toward Beloved Adi Da. He knew my intention, and left His place in the game to swim around to meet me. He hugged me, and He held me and held me and held me. Soon the game died away, and everyone formed a circle around us.

A great stillness pervaded the entire place. (It was so quiet that a friend of mine woke up from a nap in a nearby cabin!) I was cold and shivering, but I had to make a choice between giving myself to Him or paying attention to the body. The Blissful Energy of the Embrace became more and more intense. I found myself resisting the ego-overwhelming pleasure of it—fearing to lose control. It felt as though Avatar Adi Da was pulling me up. But, at some point, I refused to go further. I could feel Him continue to ascend, and soon I was left holding only a body. I could feel that He was no longer, in that moment, directly associated with His physical body. By now, I was simultaneously in a blissful state beyond the mind and painfully, acutely aware of my resistance to Him and His Love.

In spite of the limits I placed on His Work with me, I was completely changed by these incidents. I was happy, no longer struggling with myself—a different person. ■

Avatar Adi Da was constantly Working to deepen the love-relationship between Himself and each of His devotees. Around the swimming pool, in the bath lodge, on walks in the woods, in parties at His house, and in the old hotel, Avatar Adi Da gave Himself up to all His devotees as their supreme Distraction. Now setting off firecrackers on the fourth of July, now arm-wrestling with someone, now stroking one of His cats, or simply floating on His back in the large pool at the bath lodge guided through the water on the fingertips of His devotees—all of Avatar Adi Da's moments, shapes, and forms were Divine Theatre, His Intoxicating Play of Teaching and Blessing. His devotees' enchantment with Him was His Delight. He had come for each one, whatever their qualities and karmas. And it was through His interaction with the individuals in front of Him that He was mysteriously Working to fulfill His Great Intention—to touch and Bless every being who suffers the illusion of separateness.

Avatar Adi Da Samraj with devotees at the Mountain Of Attention Sanctuary

"There Is <u>Nothing</u> To Be Attained"

In this extraordinary time of Avatar Adi Da's Work, which came to be called "Garbage and the Goddess", He was always Demonstrating that what He called the "bangles of the Goddess"— meaning all the fascinating Spiritual experiences that were manifesting around Him—were really only "garbage", compared with the Perfect Prior Happiness Revealed in His Company.

On April 15, in a talk that came to be known as "Garbage and the Goddess", He summarized the lesson of this, the first of His Great Teaching-Demonstrations.

AVATAR ADI DA SAMRAJ: Every time I met Rudi, He would hand Me a bag of garbage. I cannot remember a time when I went to see Rudi when He did not hand Me a bag of garbage. It was always the first thing He would do. Then I would go and throw the garbage away, and I would come back, and We would sit together for a little bit, or I would do some work. Sooner or later, He would give Me some more garbage. It is really very simple. You just throw it away. . . .

The key to the matter is not <u>how</u> to throw the garbage away. The key to the matter is noticing that it is garbage. . . .

You are looking at a lot of garbage and thinking that <u>it</u> "<u>Is</u>" the Divine! One of My Functions is to "package" the garbage. I have spent a lot of My time packaging your garbage, trying to get you to notice that it is garbage. You will throw it away as soon as you notice this. You cannot surrender something that you do not see to be garbage. You compulsively hold on to it. So you must notice that it is garbage.

But I will Tell you right now—it is <u>all</u> garbage! Everything I Give you in the realms of experience is, ultimately, garbage—and I expect you to throw it away. Nevertheless, you tend to meditate on <u>it</u>—instead of meditating on <u>Me</u>! Every one of these seemingly precious experiences, all of this profound philosophy, is—ultimately—just more of the same stuff. But you have "bought" the conventional religious and Spiritual propaganda—so you think that these experiences and this philosophical "profundity" are the Divine Itself. None of that is the Divine. It is <u>all</u> garbage. . . .

Garbage and the Goddess

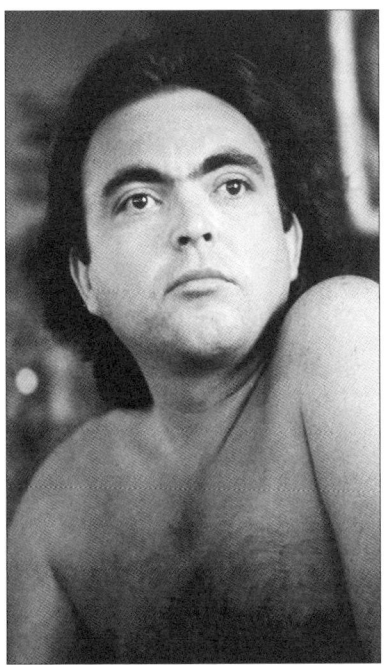

You are expected to throw the garbage away under the most extraordinary conditions—conditions in which you would, ordinarily, not even <u>consider</u> throwing it away. You are sitting in the precious blissfulness of the spine—why should you throw it away? It is all so delicious. You have been a fool all your life, and now you are a Yogi!—why should you throw that away? <u>No one</u> wants to do <u>that</u>. You do not want to throw it away. You have no True Humor in relation to it. You have no detachment from all this that you have accumulated through vast aeons of existence in conditionally manifested form. You do not want to throw it away. The demand to throw it away seems mad, impossible. . . .

What is required of you is this sacrifice of separate and separative self—and such self-sacrifice only becomes possible through the Influence of My Perfect Siddhi of Divine Liberation. . . .

It is real sacrifice—not a sacrifice in the traditional sense of some gloomy self-abnegation and emptying. It is the sacrifice which is itself based on True Humor and expressive of overwhelming love of Me, in which there is not anything whatsoever to be attained.

There is not anything to be attained. I mean not <u>anything</u>. <u>Not anything</u>!

There is not anything to be attained. Not one thing is to be attained. Not anything. There is not a single thing to be attained.

There is no conditional experience, no conditional vision, no conditional transformation of state that must be attained.

There. Have I said it? [*He-<u>and</u>-She <u>Is</u> Me*]

Mill Valley, California, 1974

CHAPTER 6

DIVINE DISTRACTION

Love-distraction by the Divine—such as Avatar Adi Da's devotees were experiencing in His Company—is celebrated throughout the Great Tradition of Spirituality. Poetic expressions of such love-distraction exist in the literature of all the principal religious traditions. In the Krishna mythology of ancient India, there is a story describing how Krishna appeared one day in the fields playing his flute. The gopis, or cow-maidens, were riveted by him—so delighted, so moved, by Krishna's Divine beauty that they forgot their ordinary lives, their cattle, their husbands, and followed Krishna, unable to bear the slightest separation from him.

From the early years of His Work, Avatar Adi Da Samraj would speak of this legend and encourage His devotees to ponder its meaning.

AVATAR ADI DA SAMRAJ: The ancient legends of Krishna and his gopis are an allegory of Divine Distraction. As Krishna wandered about in the fields, the women who tended the cattle would see him from day to day—and, in spite of themselves, they would wander away and leave their posts. They completely forgot about the cattle. They forgot to go home and cook for their husbands. They wandered about where they thought they might find Krishna—and, when they found him, they gazed at him as he sat in the distance somewhere.

This legend is a play upon the romance between Krishna, or the Divine manifest in human form, and these ordinary women, who became madly involved in an absolute attachment to Krishna, and who, as a result of this attachment, became more and more ecstatically absorbed in the God-State. So absorbed that they forgot everything else in their lives—not because they had become irresponsible, but because they had found What was Supremely Precious.

The foundation of the practice in My Company is exactly that attachment. Only when that attachment develops in relation to Me—not cultic attachment, but Divine attachment—only when that attachment overwhelms the life completely, distracts you from the conventional destiny to which you are disposed (through the medium of your desires, inclinations, and circumstances), only then can the practice of real Spiritual life exist.

Thus, in the allegory of the relationship between Krishna and his gopis, we see a fundamental description of the principle of the sadhana in My Company. This sadhana is about distraction from the life of tendencies. It is a <u>distraction</u> from that life. It is not a motivated kind of detachment from your life of tendencies, or an effort relative to them, or the taking on of conditions to stop tendencies from arising or lifetimes from occurring.

The gopis simply left the cattle. They did not say, "I'm not going to tend cattle anymore! I'm not going to submit to my desires, my tendencies!" They did not make any such decisions. They simply forgot about the cattle. They were so distracted, so in love with Krishna, so ecstatic, that they just forgot to go home. It never even occurred to them to go home. They never worried about "Should I go home or should I stay here? Should I watch the cattle or should I go look for Krishna? Should I discipline myself?" They did not create a problem out of their sadhana or out of their relationship to God.

They were just distracted. They were in love. And their love for Krishna became the principle of their lives. Krishna played upon their distraction and Taught them. By Grace, they learned. But all they learned was to be more and more absorbed in God, totally beyond their attachment simply to the body of Krishna. Their minds became overwhelmed by this distraction, and all their petty tendencies to return to their solid and secure positions, in life or in themselves, were always undermined.

There is no insurance. There is no guarantee. There is nowhere to go. There is no end-phenomenon in the love of God. That love, in and of itself, is the Truth. [December 16, 1975]

As Avatar Adi Da explains, this story of the forgetting of cattle and husbands represents the forgetting of the ego and its concerns—not the forgetting of legitimate responsibilities. The unswerving devotion of the gopis to Krishna also converted their husbands and families to devotion to God. The story stands as one of the great traditional allegories of ego-transcendence—the forgetting of the egoic self in unqualified devotion to the Divine.

During the "Garbage and the Goddess" period, this allegory took on a special significance. Many women devotees became overwhelmingly attracted to Avatar Adi Da in the manner of the legendary gopis. This attraction was so all-consuming that it left no room for anything else. These women forgot their ordinary lives and approached the Divine Avatar as renunciates, with no motive in life except to be with the Living Embodiment of the Divine.

Responding to their devotion and love-desire, Avatar Adi Da invited these women into His intimate Company. Then, through a process of testing over the next several years, He established a circle of nine women renunciates. They attended to Him for many years—serving His environments, anticipating His needs, and receiving His detailed personal Instruction in every aspect of their lives.

Adi Da Samraj with female devotees at the Mountain Of Attention Sanctuary, 1974

The Necessity of Sacrifice

None of Avatar Adi Da's women intimates could predict the course of their sadhana with Him. All they knew was the daily miracle and ordeal of living in His Company and always being responsive to Him, no matter what their subjective mood of the moment—bathed in His Love-Bliss, burning alive with longing for Him, and, all the while, confronting the impulses of the ego.

Ann Rogers, who was a member of Avatar Adi Da's circle of women renunciates for many years, describes her experience during "Garbage and the Goddess":

ANN: Right through the "Garbage and the Goddess" period, I was experiencing kriyas, ecstatic feelings in my body, rushes of energy, and blissful mindlessness. I would often actually feel my Beloved Guru Spiritually enter my body and drive my patterned tendencies right out of me. I heard Him say "No one wants God." But I thought that, whatever others might feel, I certainly did! However, as the process continued in me, I realized that what Beloved Adi Da was saying is true. No "person" wants God, because to turn to God is to sacrifice that very person.

There used to be a sign on Beloved Adi Da's desk: "Dead Gurus can't kick ass." I learned what He meant—He <u>had</u> to be unrelenting in His skillful means. He had to put us in difficult situations, cajole us, love us, tease us, and trick us into Realizing Satsang, into Realizing the relationship to Him <u>as</u> Consciousness. At one point, He said that what He asks of us is not the <u>effort</u> of surrender, but true self-sacrifice. Effortful surrender, He said, is something the ego does, something willful—and "Narcissus" loves it. Sacrifice is something entirely different. As the months passed after my first coming to Him, I began to realize what that sacrifice involves.

Avatar Adi Da said that His way of Working at that time was to establish a "theatre of love" with His devotees, to attract His devotees so strongly with His own Love that they would be moved to turn to Him, to the Divine, and away from the attachments of life. Almost from the beginning of my relationship with Beloved Adi Da as His devotee, He Attracted me like a magnet. And I fell in love with Him. But it was more than that. An utterly absorbing attachment was created. I realized that everything I had ever loved was Him—that He <u>is</u> Love. I was consumed by love of Him, and nothing else mattered.

From the very beginning, I had Spiritual experiences in the Presence of Beloved Adi Da. And then, with the deepening of my love-attachment to Him, there arose in me an intuition of His Divine Nature. I began to have experiences of complete Oneness with Him. In fact, I would often feel that He <u>was</u> me, that He was "Living" me, that every breath I took was His breath. This sense of Oneness was ecstatic beyond anything I had ever known. I felt as if I went to a place where He and I were One, where there was no fear, where there was only complete Love and Joy. That Love, which was beyond the realm of human love, grew and grew. At times, that Love became so immense that I felt unable to contain It, and I would feel impelled to scream as a way of expressing this intensity of feeling.

Then the Supremely Attractive One really put me to the test. He began to play upon my attachment to Him. He withdrew His attention. He would ignore me, He would tease me, He would insult me. Basically, He refused to give me whatever it was I was craving. At the same time that He was testing the depth and steadfastness of my love for Him, Beloved Adi Da demanded that I serve. "A devotee's life is service," He told me a number of times. I began to serve Him by doing ordinary, practical chores in His house and in the gathering of devotees. This was a way of performing the sacrifice He Calls us to in real, functional terms. I didn't mind serving people. In fact, I enjoyed it. But all I wanted was to be with "Bubba", and I felt that serving kept me away from Him, while He lavished His attention on others.

At the same time, I began to have a strange, powerful intuition. This intuition was quite different from the sense of Oneness I was feeling with Beloved Adi Da. I began to sense something immense above my head. I resisted it. I kept clutching my head to keep it away. Then, holding my hands up, I looked up, as if it were something I could see. I sensed that it was Real-God-Above—Immense, Silent. I could only throw up my arms in joy. All I wanted was for this Infinite Universe of Energy to Pour into my body and Fill me with Its Ecstatic Love and Light.

One night, I was unable to sleep, and I went to sit beside Beloved Adi Da's chair. My arms went up to this Presence Above, my palms spread receiving Its Energy. That night, as I sat there, I knew my life would have to be lived as a sacrifice to this Presence, the Spiritual Presence of my Beloved Guru.

After several dramatic emotional crises, which pushed me to a point where I realized I had absolutely no other choice, I began to turn from myself to Beloved Adi Da, because He had created a situation that obliged me to do so. I had to see how I was creating my own suffering. And so, a few moments at a time, I began to live from this new viewpoint. I did it in desperation. This sacrifice, this conscious Satsang, went against everything I had ever lived up to that point. Everyone always tends to separate. When your demands, whatever they are, are frustrated, there is <u>always</u> the tendency to play out the drama, to pull back—to feel self-pity, anger, resentment, even rage, for your suffering, and to totally identify with it.

The "radical" alternative, the constant act of turning back to Beloved Adi Da, required a lot of discipline of me. It was like walking a tightrope all the time. My tendencies were always clambering after me, tempting me to live them. I was bound to my own drama.

At last, I began to see the whole thing as suffering, and in those moments my suffering would dissolve. My Beloved gave me glimmerings of what that ultimately leads to. One night, as I gazed at Him, He kept disappearing, becoming Infinite. At one point, I disappeared, too. It was brief. Perhaps only a few seconds. But there seemed to be nothing to identify with. "I" vanished. From the point of view of the ego, it was frightening. But it was <u>Free</u>. It was thrilling.

Adi Da Samraj with Ann Rogers, 1982

The more I resort to my Beloved Guru, the more devotional self-sacrifice is required, and the more Grace and Happiness is Given. I know that, in the end, there is only sacrifice. Beloved Adi Da is the Sign of that. He <u>Is</u> <u>only</u> Sacrifice. ∎

"That First Meeting Has Never Left My Heart"

Among those drawn to Avatar Adi Da during these times was a young woman just turned twenty. She was to enter straight into the heart of His Life. Ruchiradama Quandra Sukhapur Rani, a longtime member of the Ruchira Sannyasin Order, recounts here how she came to Avatar Adi Da in March 1974.

RUCHIRADAMA QUANDRA SUKHAPUR RANI: In August of 1973, at 19 years of age, while living in a suburb outside of Chicago, Illinois, it became obvious to me that I had to make a dramatic change in my life. I collected what money I had, and set out for California—which represented freedom from the oppressive and degraded life I felt I had been living.

I finally found a small one-room house in Huntington Beach, and shortly after I arrived there, I began to have very distinct visions of a man in an observatory, who would always draw me to look through his telescope at the stars. After my initial contact with this man in the dream state, I would have a recurring vision (awake) as well as dreams of a star-form perceived at the end of a tunnel. Shortly after that, I was led, through various acquaintances, to the bookstore on Melrose Avenue that was the first Ashram of Avatar Adi Da. When I looked at the books, I saw that the man I was having constant visions of was Beloved Adi Da!

That same week I heard the voice of Beloved Adi Da on the radio. I felt drawn to Him, and His voice seemed to shape all that I felt. Above all, I was attracted to the offering that He made of a Spiritual relationship. So began my conscious relationship, in this lifetime, to my Beloved Guru.

Then, on January 18, 1974, my twentieth birthday, I decided I would approach Beloved Adi Da as my Divine Heart-Master and assume the full range of practices He was giving to His devotees at that time. This was the time of ecstatic gatherings every night at the La Brea Ashram. I was not invited to these gatherings. Rather, I would drive daily from Huntington Beach after my day of work, and serve the meditation hall in the Melrose Ashram. Each day I brought a single white rose to offer there.

Then Beloved Adi Da moved to the Mountain Of Attention Sanctuary, and many devotees went with Him. I helped with the preparations for moving the Ashram to northern California, and was invited to reside in the house where He had lived in Laurel Canyon.

I arrived there one afternoon, grateful to be in the home that Beloved Adi Da had lived in, but I immediately became feverish. What I had thought would be merely a pleasure and an honor quickly turned into an intense physical purification. Later I learned that a physical disturbance, such as fever, is not uncommon when first encountering a potent source of Spiritual Transmission.

After many days, the illness and fever subsided. I was then invited to come into the Company of Beloved Adi Da at the Mountain Of Attention Sanctuary, the moment I had been longing for. I collected my things, moved to San Francisco, and established myself in a household of devotees.

As soon as I saw Beloved Adi Da, I was overwhelmed by His Beauty and Love. I knew the depth of what was occurring was beyond my comprehension. But I was there before Him, and I did not want to be anywhere else. He was lying on His side on a couch in the dining room of the Sanctuary. I approached Him with a flower, and bowed at His Feet.

I intuited His direct capability to know everything about me at first glance. I wondered what would be required for me to become completely available, surrendered to Him as His devotee because I had <u>already</u> fallen in love with Him to the depths of my being. Mysterious Spiritual visions and intuitions that I had had since childhood came to mind, and I recognized the fulfillment and true meaning of them now in the form of Adi Da Samraj. I did not know what was going on any more, but I did know that a revolution in my life was about to occur, for all I wanted to do was to be close to Him.

Later that day, Beloved Adi Da went to Ordeal Bath Lodge, the bathhouse at the Mountain Of Attention. Devotees accompanied Him, scattering throughout the many different rooms of the baths. At one point, He came to the small bath where I was. As He came in and sat down, I felt myself sinking into a deep trance-state. Paradoxically, I vividly recall Him just being there, giving me His Regard.

Later that evening, Beloved Adi Da called a small group of devotees over to His House, and I was included. There, in His House, I realized how profoundly He had drawn me to Him. The mysterious Power that I had felt guiding me was simply <u>Him</u>. In my depth, He had pulled me, literally, out of the world.

The other devotees departed, and over the course of the evening, Beloved Adi Da took me through a series of Spiritual initiations. My meeting with Beloved Adi Da as His devotee was first. But then, almost instantaneously, He was my lover, and I was in love with Him. Our love was mutual, and, in this love-state, He embraced me sexually. I remained all night with my Beloved Guru, during which He initiated me into a Condition that I had never known before. In Tantric embrace, He drew me beyond the body-mind into a Spiritual reality that I have come to know as the Very Condition of my Beloved Lord Adi Da, the Truth of Existence Itself. I recall that I had no sense of the body. My mind, also, was completely obliterated. In the timelessness of that moment, I felt Beloved Adi Da to be Standing Prior to anything that exists conditionally, taking me with Him to His Place, His Divine Domain. I felt drawn with Him into a most profound Samadhi, which was bodiless and mindless.

While I was overcome with intense love for Him and devotion to Him, my Beloved Guru was also responding to me with deepest love, acknowledging the unique nature of our relationship. In the morning, He took me out for a walk around the Mountain Of Attention Sanctuary. As we walked through one of the sacred Communion Halls, my feeling-recognition of Him continued to magnify, and I knew that He was the One that I had always been moved to be with.

All day, Beloved Adi Da engaged me in intoxicated conversation about our love. He would ask me, over and over, where I had been. He spoke to me for hours, and we sat in silence for hours. I was moved to stay close to Him—and, sitting near Him, I was utterly content. It was sufficient just being at His side. Before the end of the day, my Beloved had invited me to live with Him and serve Him in His bodily (human) Form. Having already abandoned everything else for Him, I was overwhelmed with joy. I felt recovered. I was living in a world full of the Miracles of my Divine Heart-Master. There was nothing but my Beloved Guru. I wanted everyone to surrender to Him, to worship Him. I did not care what I did, what I said—I only

Adi Da Samraj with Ruchiradama Quandra Sukhapur Rani, the Mountain Of Attention Sanctuary, 1975

wanted to be with Him. I had no other attachments. I wanted only to be fully available to Him in every dimension of my being. I felt His constant communication of Love and Spiritual Ecstasy. For days, I scarcely left His sight, and I moved into His house to live with Him.

And then, at a certain point, Beloved Adi Da began to test my Spiritual and intimate commitment to Him. And so began the great ordeal and process of becoming fit to serve and to relate to Him in the tradition-honored form of relationship between Guru and devotee. This process has confronted all the realities of my karmic nature. But whatever has come up to be purified, and whatever ordeal that purification has required, that first meeting has never left my heart—nor could it ever. ■

**Adi Da Samraj with Ruchiradama Quandra Sukhapur Rani,
the Mountain Of Attention Sanctuary, 2000**

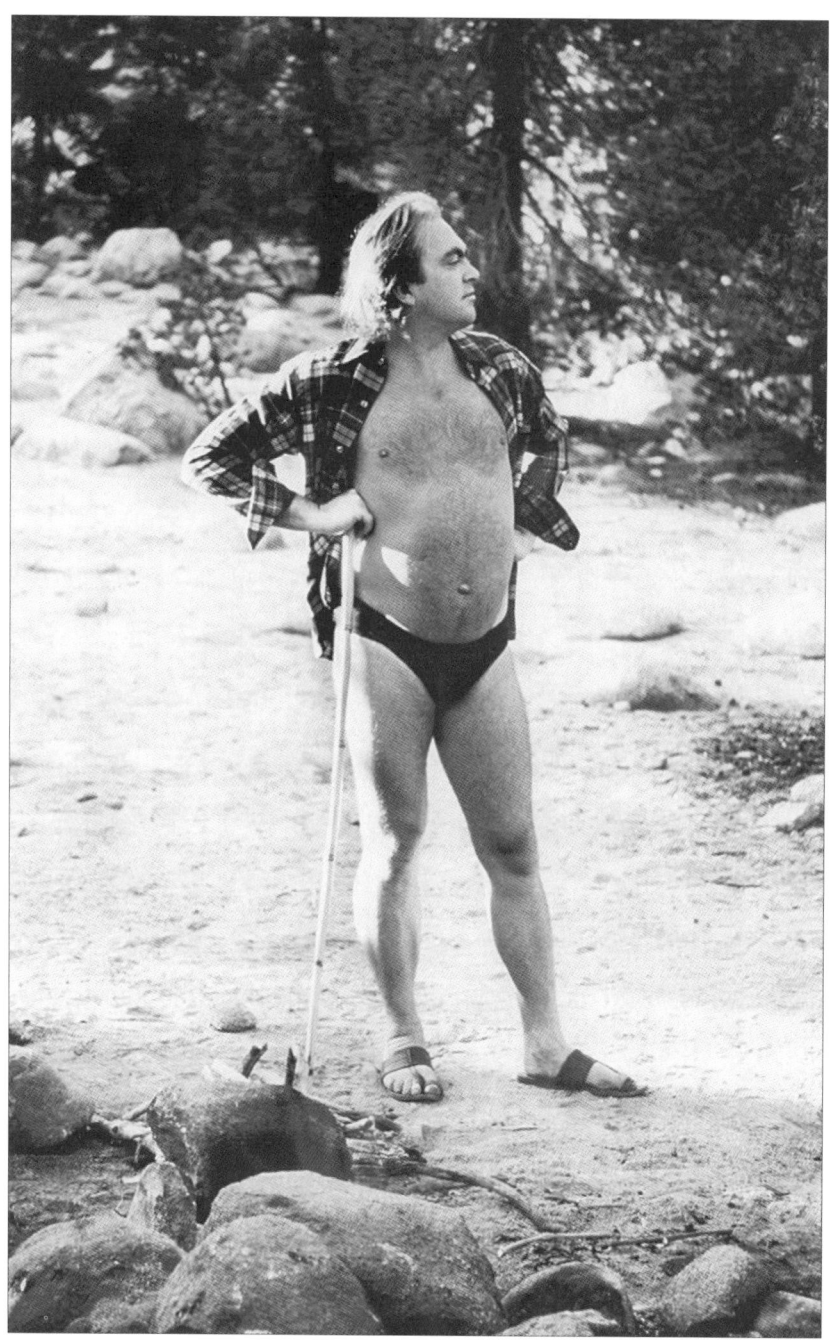

Yosemite, California, 1975

CHAPTER 7

Transcending the Emotional-Sexual Ego

Simultaneous with the process of emotional-sexual Instruction that He was engaging with the women devotees immediately around Him, Avatar Adi Da was addressing the entire gathering of His devotees relative to their obsessions and difficulties in the area of sexuality.

AVATAR ADI DA SAMRAJ: Human beings are generally addicted to sex. They think about it all the time. They are troubled about it all the time. Even though people may be involved in intimate relationships, they cannot incarnate feeling. They cannot incarnate themselves sexually to the fullest degree, because they have superimposed on their sexuality so many games and rituals. Therefore, people generally live with a mind full of random desires. They are constantly wandering and thinking about others, because they cannot live love. You are impulsed to be pleasing and to receive sexual pleasure, but you cannot incarnate love fully.

This is what I am calling you to discover: Sex is an <u>emotional</u>-sexual matter. You must come to the point where you can live a heart-relationship, where you express it, say it, know it, and become known as it—no superficial "householder" arrangement, no guarantees made by marriage certificates, nothing to hold you together except intimacy itself, the heart itself.

The aberration in you is lovelessness. When the heart comes into the sphere of sexual matters, it changes everything. ∎

The period when Avatar Adi Da began this "consideration" was a time of sexual permissiveness in Western society—but this was not the fundamental reason why Avatar Adi Da was moved to thoroughly examine emotional-sexual realities. He would have had to do so in any time, in any culture. For, as He revealed, there can be no real Spiritual growth as long as the emotional heart is obstructed by fears of loss and betrayal, by taboos against pleasure and desire—and by the ego's fundamental refusal to love.

AVATAR ADI DA SAMRAJ: The matter of sexuality is so profoundly structured into people's infantile and adolescent adaptations that it persists not only as their most obsessive interest as individuals but also as their most significant and consistent social (or interpersonal) problem. When I began to enter into relationship with My devotees for the sake of their Spiritual Awakening, it became more and more clear that <u>no</u> <u>one</u> who came to Me was yet prepared for the true Spiritual Process, which is total bodily responsibility for Truth Itself, or Life Itself. Rather, all were essentially trapped in obsessions, and in problematic orientations to the vital and, particularly, the emotional-sexual dimensions of experience. I knew it would be necessary for all first to come to a level of interpersonal and cultural maturity relative to vital life before the Spiritual Process could be fully introduced into their lives. [1978]

Traditionally, the general recommendation for those who are moved to devote their lives to Spiritual Realization is to avoid sex altogether—or else, in the case of some Tantric traditions, to use the sexual energy aroused through Yogic sexual practice as a means for attaining mystical states. In general, however, these traditional approaches do not fully account for the relational dimension of love and sex. Overall, the religious traditions are possessed of a conviction that emotional-sexual intimacy is inherently a form of bondage and, therefore, an obstacle to Spiritual Realization.

By contrast, Avatar Adi Da approached this matter without any presumptions whatsoever. From the inception of the emotional-sexual "consideration", He was open to whether sexual activity was compatible with advancement in the Spiritual process of the Way He was Revealing. Was human sexuality (whether heterosexual or homosexual) an inevitable obstruction to the "Bright", Real-God-Realization, Absolute Freedom, Absolute Bliss, Absolute Love? Or not?

As part of His investigation during His years at Columbia College and afterwards, Avatar Adi Da had mastered the sex-force in His own body-mind. And so, He knew from His own experience exactly what human beings struggle with in this most difficult, absorbing, and vulnerable area of life—as well as what must be transcended for them to become free for Spiritual growth.

"Narcissus", the primal activity of self-contraction, is dramatized most starkly in the realm of emotional-sexual relations. Therefore, understanding one's emotional-sexual patterning is key to understanding and transcending the self-contracted ego. Over the years, Avatar Adi Da's devotees were to discover that no amount of self-generated effort deals <u>conclusively</u> with emotional-sexual issues. Instead, they learned that love appears most fully only when the self-contraction dissolves. And the self-contraction dissolves only in Satsang with Him.

The Wound of Love: Emotional-Sexual "Reality Consideration"

Throughout the years of His Teaching-Work, Avatar Adi Da created all kinds of circumstances in which His devotees could reveal—to Him and to themselves—the realities of their emotional-sexual lives. During "party periods", He would drink beer and bourbon and smoke cigarettes with everyone. The intoxicants would relax the social persona, exposing the powerful emotions and desires that are beneath the surface of every smiling social personality. Thus, the cards would be on the table, and He could reflect to His devotees exactly what they were up to.

One critical aspect Avatar Adi Da revealed in the emotional-sexual "consideration" is the "mood of betrayal". It does not take an outright act of infidelity on the part of one's partner to trigger the betrayal response—the ego, or "Narcissus", is <u>always</u> presuming to be betrayed, or to be not sufficiently loved by the other. Thus, "Narcissus" consistently reacts to its universally projected sense of betrayal, punishing the other accordingly—by coldness and withdrawal, by casual, unfeeling words, and all kinds of emotional dramas.

Feeling betrayed and rejected <u>is</u> the ego, because egoity is the presumption of being a separated, isolated, unloved "I". The lesson that Avatar Adi Da taught was that the "you don't love me" reflex (in all its forms) is fruitless and destructive, and that the only happy choice is to love.

In the experience of His devotees, however, the gesture of love often felt impossible under the stress of extreme negative emotion. They just could not do it. But this impasse was exactly what Avatar Adi Da called them to face in the midst of "reality consideration". He wanted them to discover that there was only one way out of their dilemma—to feel beyond themselves to Him, to look up from the pond of "Narcissus" and open to His Divine Blessing.

Feel Love's Wound*

Love Does Not Fail For You When You Are Rejected or Betrayed or Apparently Not Loved. Love Fails For You When You Reject, Betray, and Do Not Love. Therefore, If You Listen To Me, and (Also) If You Hear Me, and (Also) If You See Me—Do Not Stand Off From Relationship. Be Vulnerable. Be Wounded, When Necessary—and Endure That Wound (or Hurt). Do Not Punish the other In Love. Communicate To one another, Even Discipline one another—but Do Not Dissociate From one another or Fail To Grant one another The Knowledge Of Love. Realize That each one Wants To Love and To Be Loved By the other In Love. Therefore, Love. Do This Rather Than Make Any Effort To Get Rid Of The Feeling Of Being Rejected. To Feel Rejected Is To Feel The Hurt Of Not Being Loved. Allow That Hurt, but Do Not Let It Become The Feeling Of Lovelessness. Be Vulnerable, and (Thus) Not Insulted. If You Are Merely Hurt, You Will Still Know The Necessity (or The Heart's Requirement) Of Love, and You Will Still Know The Necessity (or The Heart's Requirement) To Love.

The Most Direct Way To Know Love In every moment Is To Be Love In every moment. Do This By Means Of Devotional (and, In Due Course, Spiritual) Communion With Me. If You Always Do This, Then, By Means Of every act of life, Always Do What and As You Are.

—Avatar Adi Da Samraj
Ruchira Tantra Yoga

---

* In certain of His writings, Avatar Adi Da uses a unique style of capitalization, capitalizing almost every word. The words that He leaves uncapitalized (such as "ego", "other", "and", and the like) are words that specifically express the egoic or unenlightened self/other point of view.

This style of capitalization is a Teaching device, by which Avatar Adi Da is continuously pointing out that everything is a modification of the One Divine Reality. It is a reminder that only the ego-activity prevents us from recognizing this Truth.

Learning the Emotional-Sexual Yoga

Daniel Bouwmeester, M.D., was one of the devotees who participated with Avatar Adi Da in examining the entire range of emotional-sexual life and practice over many years. Dr. Bouwmeester describes here something of what this involved in the early years of his practice in the direct Company of Avatar Adi Da:

DANIEL: When I came to Beloved Adi Da from Australia in 1977, He was just about to begin what was then called the "Sexuality I course". (The Sexuality I course covered the examination of emotional-sexual character and early-life patterning as it related to obstructions to human growth and maturity, and to growth in the Spiritual process altogether.) Beloved Adi Da Himself actually took the first group of us through this course. In particular, I remember He stressed the importance of confession and of losing face. Beloved Adi Da always made it clear that unless we can be confessed about where we are really "at", we cannot make a move in practice. That is why He has used the term "<u>reality</u> consideration"— because we can only effect changes at the level of our own reality. If we try to save face, we cannot change. And sexuality is an area where people generally try to save face.

The Sexuality I course, then, was a matter of losing face left and right.

Beloved Adi Da started asking us about primal incidents in our lives, and He was very Compassionate in showing us how these incidents reveal a pattern of reaction in the character. The purpose of this inspection was not to uncover primal incidents in order to achieve a cathartic release. The primary lesson was always to see how we unconsciously and yet (as we discovered via this process of inspection and understanding) voluntarily choose to maintain the pattern in the present moment, rather than releasing it through self-understanding. In other words, we use such incidents to justify our reactivity. Beloved Adi Da always called us to become responsible for our unconscious emotional patterns in the moment, to go beyond the presumption of rejection and betrayal and to actually practice (and be responsible for) active love.

Beloved Adi Da helped my (then) intimate partner and me profoundly during that particular time. We were struggling in our relationship. We had what Beloved Adi Da termed a "brotherly-sisterly" relationship, without much energy or sexual polarity. Beloved Adi Da Said of us, "All love and no desire," and this was true. We loved and appreciated each other, but we were both very "solid" and dry. And that was intolerable to Beloved Adi Da, because, from His Enlightened "Point of View", relationships are a very lively field where we should be doing ego-transcending work. Intimate relationships in particular are a place to do sadhana.

The conversations with Beloved Adi Da during the Sexuality I course were always incredibly empowered with His Siddhi. They were not just a matter of words—Beloved Adi Da would reach into the "pit of snakes" at the core of our egoity, and we could feel Him changing it. His Liberating Force was tremendously powerful. But, even so, things did not just magically go away. We had to take responsibility for what we saw about ourselves.

I remember the first time Beloved Adi Da told me that I had to become a feeling being, and that I had to learn to express myself emotionally. He told me that it was not going to be easy for me initially, that I would be like an infant learning how to walk—with all the stumbling and stops and starts that involves. "But you have to do it," Beloved Adi Da told me, "or you are never going to advance in practice."

The first evening we were involved in the "consideration", Beloved Adi Da asked me how our sexual play was—my intimate partner's and mine. Through His Grace, I felt totally open to be honest and I told Beloved Adi Da that it was not very good. I confessed that I had difficulty with premature ejaculation and that my intimate partner had trouble having an orgasm. Even though we seemed like a fairly average couple—and I think, from my medical experience, that we were—we were, underneath it all, very complicated and very suppressed.

On that night, I was quite ecstatic to be so close to Beloved Adi Da, and so confessed to Him. At a certain point in the "consideration",

Beloved Adi Da indicated that He was going to Gift my intimate partner and me with an initiation into a more profound level of participation in sexuality. He sent me off to shower and prepare. My intimate partner went to prepare in the company of her women friends. Then, Beloved Adi Da specifically Instructed us to have a sexual occasion together. Over the years, this is how Beloved Adi Da Worked with people—He would draw us through a certain "consideration", and then ask us to go off and practice what He had Given. Then He would want us to come back and report the "good news", or results, of our practice to Him.

So my intimate partner and I engaged His Admonition, and it was an extremely powerful incident for me. Immediately, I began to become confessed in my love for her in a way that I had never been able to express before. I totally opened up to her, and as I did, I lost all sense of difference between myself and her. The room dissolved. It was like we were both free beings in space, in a totally ecstatic state. And in the midst of this we were making love, and we were able to make love for quite a long period of time—much, much, much longer than I usually could. Nothing like this had ever happened to me before. Usually, our sexual occasions were brief—generally, five to ten minutes long on average—whereas on this occasion we made love for an hour or so, which was unheard of for me up to that time. But that was the least of it—it was an ecstatic occasion, in which we were able to freely express ourselves emotionally and sexually. It was Beloved Adi Da's Gift.

Two years later, Beloved Adi Da initiated another emotional-sexual "consideration", which we humorously called "three in bed and five off the wall". During this time, Beloved Adi Da was trying to take our "consideration" of sexuality to another level. He began to Instruct us in the Yoga of the sex act itself. Part of the discipline of this period was to make love for three hours each day—and to conserve, or bypass, degenerative orgasm in the process. Also associated with this was a period of time set aside each day, in addition to our usual meditation practice, where we were to go into the meditation hall and let everything go completely, in unconditional surrender—for at least five minutes. And that is how it became "three in bed and five off the wall". But, really, the significance of what Beloved Adi Da was trying to show us was profound. He was trying to show us the correlation between regenerative sex and true surrender. For me, making love for three hours without having an orgasm was something that, as an ego, I would have loved to be able to do. But I was not capable of it. On the first night of this exercise, I lasted about forty-five minutes, which wasn't too bad for me. But when I went back to Beloved Adi Da and reported this to Him the next night, He leaned over me from His chair and said very strongly, "What?! Do you think I was just joking? I said <u>three</u> <u>hours</u>!!"

I became a real diehard after that, and did whatever I had to do to pull this discipline off. During the day, I was a mild-mannered doctor in a clinic in San Francisco, and at night, I was desperately engaged in this Yogic experiment! We were admonished to go beyond all limits in these occasions, both physical and emotional, and we freely engaged the ordeal of confessing to one another everything that arose.

On one of these occasions, my intimate partner and I were carried beyond ourselves and had an experience similar to our initiation by Beloved Adi Da two years earlier. In our sexual embrace, we became lost in a swoon of Communing with Beloved Adi Da. We were totally connected with one another, with no sense of separation or barrier between us. At the end of the occasion, both my intimate partner and I came to rest. Spontaneously, and at the same time, we happened to be looking at a photograph of Beloved Adi Da on the wall, and we were totally "gone". The "Brightness" in the room outshined all sense of barriers and presumptions of separation. And I remember looking at my intimate partner, and she looked at me. It was completely clear that we were both "gone", even though we were looking at each other and could see each other. Our sense of separate identity was dissolved. It was an extraordinary Gift, and it showed us how Yogic sexual practice actually does transcend sexual seeking and even the sex act itself.

It is obvious to me, having gone through the experimentation of indulging in my sexual search, and now having applied the practice as it is Given, that Beloved Adi Da has revealed a practice of emotional-sexual Yoga that is really liberating. Not only has He done that through all His direct Instruction over the years, but that practice is also literally Given through His Wisdom-Teaching. If you simply do exactly what Beloved Adi Da describes in His Wisdom-Teaching, you find that it is Empowered Instruction. Through His "consideration" during His Teaching Years, His Wisdom was Communicated. It was summarized, and in that summary there is more than just words and facts and information. There is Great Siddhi that can take you through whatever process of inspection and self-understanding is required in your own case, and give you great discriminative intelligence relative to your personal emotional-sexual "consideration". That summary Instruction and that Siddhi are now Avatar Adi Da's Gift to all of humankind, forever.

What we had to find out during the Teaching Years were all the ways we were obsessed with seeking and did not submit to His Instruction. We added a lot of time and obstruction to the transformative process that Beloved Adi Da naturally pulls us through. To me, that is the great lesson and the greatest confession to be made. All of the transformations occur through His Blessing-Power, and that Power is available to everybody who responds to Him. I know from my own experience that He is the Master of every aspect of life, including the whole domain of sexuality.

Even though I didn't know it at the time, I see now how I came to Him obsessed with emotional-sexual life and emotional-sexual problem. Beloved Adi Da would often undermine this through directing me to having humor about my life and circumstance. He would often ask me, "But what does this have to do with Real-God-Realization?" In other words, Beloved Adi Da is the Divine Liberator, not a self-help counselor or sex-therapist. Sexuality in Adidam is engaged as part of our practice, rather than as an alternative to God-Realization. In the transformative process of Adidam, the emotional-sexual being is conformed to Beloved Adi Da's Instruction and transformed in His Company. ■

"What I Do Is Not the Way That I <u>Am</u>, but the Way That I Teach"

During the several years that He had been involved in His Teaching-Work thus far, reports about Avatar Adi Da's "Crazy" manner of Working had circulated around the Spiritual communities of the time, even as far away as India. Many people were unable to understand why such unconventional behavior should be necessary. In 1975, an Indian Yogi, Swami Chinmayananda, heard about Avatar Adi Da and wrote a letter expressing his concern over Avatar Adi Da's unconventional manner of Teaching, an approach to Spiritual Instruction that was entirely foreign to his own orthodox views.

James Steinberg, the devotee responsible for relations with other Ashrams and Gurus, brought Swami Chinmayananda's letter to Avatar Adi Da. As Avatar Adi Da read the letter, James could feel that He was fully receiving this traditional swami's expression of concern. The next morning, Avatar Adi Da wrote a brief Essay clarifying the nature of His "Crazy" Teaching-Work—an Essay which was a response to Swami Chinmayananda, and also a communication to everyone:

> *What I Do is not the way that I <u>Am</u>, but the way that I Teach.*
> *What I Speak is not a reflection of <u>Me</u>, but of <u>you</u>.*
> *People do well to be offended or even outraged by My actions and behavior. This is My purpose. But their reaction must turn upon themselves, for I have not Shown them Myself by all of this. All that I Do and Speak only reveals people to themselves.*
> *I have become willing to Teach in this uncommon manner because I have known My friends—and they are what I can seem to be. By retaining all qualities in their company, I gradually wean them of all reactions, all sympathies, all alternatives, fixed assumptions, false teachings, dualities, searches, and dilemma. This is My Way of Working for a time. . . .*
> *Freedom is the only Purity. There is no Teaching but Consciousness Itself. My Appearance here is not other than the possibilities of humankind.* [1975]

Part Three

Revelation and Impasse

1978–1985

The Mountain Of Attention Sanctuary, 1977

CHAPTER 8

CREATING THE MEANS TO "LINK"

From the time of His return from India in 1973, Avatar Adi Da had Worked in a unique manner—seeming to become like His devotees, in order to draw them into His own Freedom. But His manner of Working had a price.

AVATAR ADI DA SAMRAJ: If I give any one of you My attention in mere thought, I absorb all of your psyche, all of your suffering, all of your diseases. This is literally true. People do not understand that such a process is possible in human time. And yet this is My experience exactly. If anyone comes near Me in physical space, this Body absorbs their disease, their emotion, their dilemma, their problems, their unhappiness, their lack of vision.

You may wonder why I allow Myself to be used in this way by people. I am unable to do anything about it. As long as people do not bring Me an absolute desire for Real God, as long as they bring Me their absence of Real-God-Communion, their absence of vision, their absence of love, their absence of devotional sacrifice, I must simply absorb it. But if My devotees begin to manifest the Real-God-Realizing desire that comes from Divine Vision, from heart-recognition of Me, whereby they become devotionally responsive to Me, then even My own physical state will be transformed. [1978]

Traditionally, the word "religion" has been explained as meaning to "bind oneself again"—or "re-link" oneself—to the Divine. Up to 1978, Avatar Adi Da had "linked" Himself to His devotees in a physically direct manner. He spent countless hours with them face to face—Granting His silent Darshan, Giving Discourses, engaging all kinds of activities with them. The circumstance of receiving Avatar Adi Da's Spiritual Blessing in His physical Company (particularly in formal occasions of His Darshan) was and is absolutely core to the developing process of the Way of Adidam. (Indeed, devotees prepared to receive this Spiritual Gift are, in present time, invited to come for periods of retreat in His physical Company as often as possible.) But it was essential for His devotees to be able to fully resort to Him at all times—whether or not they were in His physical Company. Therefore, in 1978 (and earlier), He began to magnify the available means for His devotees to devotionally "link" to Him—to resort to Him, in devotional surrender—without necessarily being in His physical presence. These means are never a substitute for devotional surrender to Him and Invocation of Him—rather, they are ways of making that devotional surrender and Invocation continuous.

Divine Empowerment: The Holy Sites

One time, at the Mountain Of Attention, devotees watched as Avatar Adi Da intently placed His staff in a certain patch of earth on several days in succession. He was allowing His Spirit-Energy to flow from His Body into the spot. At some point, He announced that His Spirit-Energy had "stuck" in the spot. In other words, the site had proven itself capable of "holding" His Spirit-Energy, such that His Spirit-Energy would (if He were rightly and consistently Invoked there) continue to Radiate from the spot, just as It Radiates from His bodily Form. He indicated that devotees should build a temple there, a place in which to Commune with Him.

This was an example of how Avatar Adi Da began to create holy sites—places Spiritually Empowered by Him, where devotees would be able to feel Him very strongly, by devotionally and Spiritually Invoking Him there, without His being physically present.

The first major holy site at the Mountain Of Attention, Earth-Fire Temple, was Empowered by Avatar Adi Da during the "Garbage and the Goddess" period in 1974. The Empowerment took the form of a miraculous event witnessed by Ruchiradama Nadikanta, one of the women renunciates who intimately served Avatar Adi Da and a longtime member of the Ruchira Sannyasin Order:

RUCHIRADAMA NADIKANTA: On my first night at the Mountain Of Attention Sanctuary, I broke a plaster statue of the Virgin Mary belonging to Beloved Adi Da. I was horrified that I had done this and carried the broken statue to where He was sitting in the main room of His residence. He gently chided me and then repaired the statue Himself, gluing it back together and touching it up. Then He returned it to its original place. A day or two later, He said to me: "Come with Me down to the garden. I am going to bury the Virgin statue there."

Everything had been going wrong with the garden. The plants were not growing very well, and it was overrun with goats and gophers. Even on the afternoon that Beloved Adi Da walked down with me to bury the statue, we had to chase all the chickens away!

Beloved Adi Da dug a hole in which He placed the statue that I had broken. He placed it in the ground standing upright and facing out to the garden. He laid His hands on the statue with great intention. Then He very gently covered it over with dirt. He patted the ground on top of the site and He told me to place a stone over the statue to mark the spot. He told me that, by placing this statue in the garden, He was placing His own attention there. This event, He said, would take care of the garden. It all seemed rather odd to me.

The next day, Beloved Adi Da and I and a few other devotees stayed in San Francisco for a few days. When we returned to the Sanctuary, I walked down to the garden and my jaw dropped open in amazement. The garden had suddenly become a teeming jungle! The tomato plants had grown a couple of feet and were displaying big green tomatoes. The squash had become huge-stalked plants leaping out all over the garden. There was an intense vibratory energy throughout the garden, and not a single animal in sight.

Walking back from the garden, I met Beloved Adi Da. In amazement, I told Him what was going on. He received this news without the slightest surprise and invited me to turn around and walk back down to the garden again. As we entered the garden, I once again felt the intense vibratory energy. For a while, He stood silently scanning the entire garden. Then He said, "You are the witness to My Miracle in the garden. Why do you think I put the statue of the Virgin Mary down here?"

I was astonished, and I did not know how to relate to what had happened in the garden, or even to His question to me. It was simply beyond my comprehension in the moment. Beloved Adi Da was constantly Working with my materialistic and non-miracle-oriented mind. He gave me the simple Instruction to tell the story of this miracle to other devotees. So I followed His Instruction. Gradually, as I began to describe what had occurred, I connected emotionally with what had taken place. He had transformed the energy associated with the vital growing plants, the animals, and the entire energy-field in a miraculously short period of time. Tomato plants just don't grow that big in three days—and gophers, mice, and chickens don't just all of a sudden, out of the blue, decide to leave a vegetable patch. This was unusual!

Later, Beloved Adi Da said that the event was an expression of the same kind of influence that people associate with places like Findhorn, but He had made this demonstration as a Spiritual lesson for His devotees—not for the sake of the flourishing of the vital energies of Nature in themselves. Beloved Adi Da asked that a temple

Avatar Adi Da Samraj at Earth-Fire Temple with Ruchiradama Quandra Sukhapur Rani and Ruchiradama Nadikanta, 1998. Earth-Fire Temple continues to be one of the principal holy sites at the Mountain Of Attention Sanctuary. It is used daily by devotees, as a place to cultivate their devotional and Spiritual "link" to Avatar Adi Da.

site be created over the spot where the statue of the Virgin Mary had been buried, and that sacramental worship be done there daily.

In the years since He created the site, Beloved Adi Da has occasionally walked down to Earth-Fire Temple with me. On one occasion, Beloved Adi Da Revealed a secret. He entered the temple and placed His staff on the burial spot of the statue and stood there silently. Then, as He turned to leave the temple enclosure, He said, "I buried Myself here." ■

In the years since His Empowerment of Earth-Fire Temple in 1974, Avatar Adi Da has Empowered many holy sites—at the Mountain Of Attention, and also at the Hermitage Ashrams that were subsequently established in Hawaii and Fiji.

Puja:
Sacramental Worship of the Living God

Early in 1978, during a time when He was staying in Hawaii, Avatar Adi Da sent this message back to His devotees in California:

Bring your body-minds to Me, as I bring My human Body-Mind to you. Then you will be Granted the Revelation and the Realization of My All-Pervading Divine Body of Grace, and you will Find Me always Present under the conditions of all experience and in the company of all beings. Then, even when you are not in My physical Company, you will worship Me and surrender to Me, and I will always be tangibly Present. At last, you will be Drawn into deepest heart-Intimacy with Me, Most Perfect Identification with Me, and Divine Realization of Me, Prior to all "difference". Then you will Abide in Me forever—whether or not the worlds of experience arise to your notice. [1978]

When He returned to the Mountain Of Attention, Avatar Adi Da began to instruct a few devotees in puja—the ancient practice of invoking the Divine by actively worshipping and anointing images of the Deity, using natural elements such as water, oil, and ash. The principal object of esoteric worship, He explained, is the Spiritual

Master's human form, the body of the Guru, who is acknowledged by the devotee as the human agent of the Divine Reality.

The true purpose of sacramental worship is not the fulfillment of exoteric (outer) behavioral codes or mere ritual requirements. True sacramental worship serves to activate and magnify the Spiritual "link" between the participant and his or her Spiritual Source. Its purpose in Adidam, therefore, is to enable devotees to cultivate their devotional and Spiritual relationship with Avatar Adi Da in physically expressive worship of His Form.

Avatar Adi Da demonstrated the effectiveness of puja on His Body one evening in 1978 at the Mountain Of Attention. He sat in perfect stillness in a room in His residence, while devotees waved flaming lamps in circular motions, accompanied by an ecstatic explosion of drums, rattles, cymbals, and tambourines. Outside on the porch were more devotees, circumambulating the house, chanting, and beholding the Form of their Beloved Guru through the windows. Light and sound and movement swirled around Avatar Adi Da—while He sat Silent and Radiant, His Divine Love-Bliss enveloping everyone. Devotees discovered in their own experience how puja magnifies their reception of the "Bright" Heart-Power Radiating from Him.

That night, Avatar Adi Da established what came to be known as the "Ruchira Avatara Puja", the worship of His Divine Form, in the lives of His devotees. Thereafter, actively expressed devotion, worship, and praise of Avatar Adi Da as the Living Divine Person became a part of their daily lives. This sacramental worship could always be done, using a photographic representation of Avatar Adi Da. Thus, sacramental worship was a form of devotionally relating to Him that could be engaged by anyone anywhere in the world, and continuing after His physical Lifetime.

"You Must not Believe in Me": The Refusal of Cultism

Avatar Adi Da had adopted a very conservative approach in introducing His devotees to the practice of bodily worship of His Form. In the East, such devotional worship is understood and appreciated—but in the West, the worship of a living human form tends to be misunderstood and viewed with suspicion. Although He opened the doors to His first Ashram in 1972, it was not until six years later that Avatar Adi Da made sacramental worship a part of His devotees' daily lives. In order to prepare them to engage sacramental worship rightly, He had to first sensitize them to the right and wrong ways of approaching Him as Spiritual Master. They had to be able to distinguish between true worship and mere cultism.

He steadfastly refused to become the object of any kind of childish cult. Whenever He felt this cultic tendency in devotees, He addressed it firmly, sometimes even removing Himself from physical availability for as long as it took them to get the lesson and correct the approach. Avatar Adi Da was criticizing cultism long before "cults" became a popular topic in the media.

AVATAR ADI DA SAMRAJ: Over the years, you have all heard Me Speak about cultism in negative terms. I have criticized the cults that people form around religious leaders (and even around true Spiritual Masters), as well as the cultic attachments that people create with one another. There exists a certain hyped enthusiasm to which people are attracted. And when those people accept all the dogmas with which that particular group makes itself enthusiastic, they maintain themselves as opponents of the world and lose communication with the world in general, and with the processes of life.

To Me, that enthusiasm is bizarre. There is something about the capability of individuals for that kind of enthusiasm that makes My skin crawl. It is a kind of madness. Gleeful enthusiasm has nothing whatsoever to do with this Way and with the value that I can have for you personally. It has <u>nothing</u> to do with it!

My Purpose in associating with you is not to entertain you, not to be believed in. I am not here to offer you a relationship in which you are never changed, but only consoled. My Purpose in dealing with you, My Purpose in My Teaching-Work, is to make it possible for you to be in devotional Communion with Me, to be Spiritually intimate with Me—so that you yourself may live and fulfill this practice, and make a sacred culture with one another out of the true Happiness of mature Divine living.

Everything about cultism that is negative is specifically criticized in My Wisdom-Teaching. I do not want your enthusiasm to be superficially generated by reading My books. I want you to "consider" My Arguments. I want you to "consider" yourself very critically, very directly and rigorously, and come to the point of most fundamental self-understanding. When you have sufficient understanding of your own game, your childishness and adolescence, then you will be able to advance in the practice I have Given you.

I refuse to console individuals by telling them that all they need to do is believe in Me, that all they need to do is practice some silly little technique and they will Realize God, no matter what they do otherwise. I am not the slightest bit interested in your gleeful applause. I want you to understand yourself and to practice true heart-Communion with Me. I want you to truly live the Way that I have Revealed and Given to you. In order to do that, you must grow up. You must stop being naive about the communications of silly downtown people, all the aggressiveness of media campaigns, and all the things that fundamentally work against the higher acculturation of human beings. [December 17, 1979]

The Divine Word

When the Melrose Ashram opened in 1972, Avatar Adi Da had already written *The Knee Of Listening*, and that book was the first text that everyone studied. In the first several years of His Teaching-Work, His verbal Instruction was Given primarily in the form of spoken Discourses. It was not until the years 1977-1978 that Avatar Adi Da returned to a concentrated period of writing. This period saw the creation of the most extensive and most comprehensive body of written Dharma Avatar Adi Da had yet produced—over 2,000 pages in the space of two years. He was Working to create yet another means by which His devotees would always be able to devotionally and Spiritually "link" to Him, via study of His Word.

Of the Essays Avatar Adi Da wrote in 1977-1978, one in particular, entitled "What Will You Do If You Love Me?", captures the essence of His communication to everyone:

My lovers, My true devotees, simply love Me. That is the Summation of their devotional recognition-response to Me. They appear to understand a little of My Wisdom-Teaching, but they do not depend on "inward" practices, or on mystical experiences, or on any turn of events. . . . Every moment of their lives is simply a moment of Love-Communion with Me. Therefore, they are Granted perpetual Ecstasy by Me—in the Form of ego-forgetting Love-Communion with Me, the Self-Existing and Self-Radiant "Bright" Divine Person of Love-Bliss. . . .

I suffer every form and condition of every one who loves Me, because I Love My devotee As My own Form, My own Condition. I Love My devotee As the One by Whom I Am Distracted.

I Grant all My own Divine and "Bright" Excesses to those who love Me, in exchange for all their doubts and sufferings. Those who "Bond" themselves to Me, through love-surrender, are inherently Free of fear and wanting need. They transcend the ego-"I" (the cause of all conditional experience), and they (cause, and all, and All) Dissolve in Me—for I Am the Heart of all-and-All, and I Am the Heart Itself, and the Heart Itself Is the Only Reality, Truth, and Real God of all-and-All.

What is a Greater Message than This? [Da Love-Ananda Gita]

The Mountain Of Attention Sanctuary, 1978

The Mountain Of Attention Sanctuary
September 16, 1979

CHAPTER 9

THE REVELATION OF DA

The establishment of the means to "link" to Avatar Adi Da—the holy sites and sacramental worship and a comprehensive body of His Wisdom-Teaching—was a sign of a great turning point that was about to occur in His Work and Revelation.

In 1979, in gatherings with a small group of devotees, Avatar Adi Da began to suggest that His Name must change again—"Bubba" was too casual an address to the Divine Being they now more fully recognized Him to be. He suggested that His devotees try to discover what His Name should be. Secretly, though, He already knew what it was.

Devotees threw themselves into the quest for His Divine Name. For weeks and months, they searched through volumes of esoteric literature for a Name that seemed right. Avatar Adi Da would encourage them with cryptic hints, such as: "When you get da name of da god, you get da power of da god." He was revealing His Name in this playful remark, but no one was alert to the clue. And so, on September 13, 1979, alone in His room, He penned a letter to His devotees:

Beloved, I Am Da, the Living Person, Who is Manifest as all worlds and forms and beings, and Who is Present as the Transcendental Current of Life in the body of Man. . . .

To Realize Me is to Transcend the body-mind in Ecstasy. To Worship Me is simply to Remember My Name and Surrender Into My Eternal Current of Life. And those who Recognize and Worship Me As Truth, the Living and All-Pervading One, will be Granted the Vision, or Love-Intuition, of My Eternal Condition. . . .

At last, He had openly declared Himself. Avatar Adi Da Samraj (now "Da Free John") stood before His devotees as the very human Incarnation of the Indivisible Divine. His devotees were to discover that the Name "Da"—meaning "to give" or "the Giver"—is a primordial Name for the Divine Person. In the ancient esoteric scriptures of India, "Da" is the Divine Voice in thunder. In the Tibetan Buddhist tradition, "Da" is defined as "the very personification of the great Way of Liberation".

Divine Calling: The Day of the Heart

On Sunday, September 16, 1979, at the Mountain Of Attention Sanctuary, several days after the writing of His "Beloved, I Am Da" letter, seven hundred people, many of whom had never seen Avatar Adi Da before, gathered for the annual celebration of "the Day of the Heart", the ninth anniversary of His Divine Re-Awakening in the Vedanta Temple. Some of those present had been around Avatar Adi Da in earlier years, but had drifted away. They came at Avatar Adi Da's specific invitation.

The moment Avatar Adi Da strode into view, dressed in ceremonial white clothing and a white hat, His Transmission of Love-Bliss engulfed the gathering. Gasps rolled through those present, and many were weeping uncontrollably as He took His seat before them.

Avatar Adi Da first asked if everyone was sufficiently protected from the sun. Then devotees performed sacramental worship on Him, waving flaming lights while intoning a mantric hum to Invoke His "Bright" Divine Power. The Mountain Of Attention was transfigured, shimmering as an ocean of light, while Avatar Adi Da sat still.

The Revelation of Da

The Day of the Heart, September 16, 1979

He had come to make the most serious Call to His devotees to the process of Divine Liberation—not only for themselves, but so that many others could come to Him for His Blessing. And He was about to speak His primordial Divine Name, "Da", for the first time. He spoke very deliberately, often pausing long between words, as if it took a massive Divine Effort for His Body to speak from behind the flood of the Divine "Bright" pouring through Him. Following is the essence of His lengthy Discourse from that day.

AVATAR ADI DA SAMRAJ: All these years, I have Struggled with you, and I have reflected you to yourselves. I have lived your way of life. I have accepted your conditions completely. And it did absolutely nothing. It was not sufficient for your most fundamental self-understanding, not sufficient for your heart-conversion, not sufficient for your life's conversion to the service of Me. But, rather, it made you content. It made you an idol-worshipper. It made you worship yourself, your fulfillment.

For years, I have Called upon you to understand your experience, to understand the limited offerings of the world. All of its offerings—<u>both</u> its lower offerings, its life-stimulation in the body, <u>and</u> its religious offerings, its esoteric offerings, its life-stimulation in the mind. And, still, you have not understood.

Therefore, My Teaching-Word is, in and of Itself, not sufficient. My Teaching-Argument is not sufficient. I, Myself, Am Sufficient.

"Radical" understanding requires a great mind, a great heart. But you will not realize it through mere "consideration". You have all failed to do that—and that is good, if you will feel the failure to be transformed utterly through mere "consideration". Then, perhaps, you will be able to accept what I Offer to you.

It is not through insight alone that any one Realizes Real God, that any one becomes Happy and Free—anymore than it is through any form of bodily or mental or psychic experience that any one becomes Happy and Free.

But it is sufficient sadhana to Remember Me, to simply surrender to Me and love Me and trust Me, and to always do what I ask you to do. It is not only sufficient—there is no way that you will be Saved, that you will be Awakened, that you will be Happy, except through this simple turning to Me.

I do not speak as an ordinary man to you. Nor would I ever suggest that you do what I ask you to do merely because of some whim or other of Mine. But it has been Granted to Me to accept devotees through surrender to Me. It is not a thing that an ordinary person may presume. I have Tested it all My Life, and I have Tested it in your company.

I swear to you—and you will always continue to see it with clear Signs—that Real God has Granted this Grace to you through My Appearance in your midst. And if you will surrender to Me, if you will love and trust Me because you recognize Who I Am, if you will simply accept the discipline of My Demands, simply do what I ask you to do—and I will always make it very plain—if you will Remember Me with love, if you will Call upon Me by Name with your feeling breaths, if you will Call upon Me via the Name "Da", then this will be sufficient.

And you need not be concerned for any other practice. If you will simply surrender yourself in My Company, you will also understand. But if understanding is made a pre-condition of your surrender to Me, your life with Me, then you will never accomplish it.

If you will do this, then you can enter My Way, and the community of My devotees will grow, both in numbers and in practice.

And you will be given every strength and all the Spirit-Blessing of Real God—any one who does this. The developmental stages of the Way in My Company will accomplish themselves, and you need have no concern for it.

The Way in My Company is Happy. It is boundlessly Joyful. It is a difficult process in this place, this world—difficult in terms of what you must endure, what you must creatively struggle with, as a matter of ordinary discipline. <u>People</u> are difficult. People are crazy, driven mad by mortality and pleasure. And you will all continue to suffer limitations in one another. The more the community of My devotees grows, the more demanding it becomes, the more functional, practical, relational, and cultural commitments you presume, the more things you must deal with creatively, the more you must overcome emotionally. There is no point in becoming angry about that. You must, rather, become compassionate and more loving and more of a servant. But if you will do this, if you will transcend the petty reactions of your mortal psyche through surrender to Me, and simply accept the discipline of obedience to Me and Remembrance of Me, then you will be made Happy by My Grace.

On another occasion, I will be moved to laugh with you more than today and to be more casually pleasant with you. But today I want you to feel this profundity.

Now that you have seen Me, what will you do? [September 16, 1979]

"I Have to Look the Fire in the Eye"

The morning after this Discourse, a fire threatened the Mountain Of Attention Sanctuary.

TEMPUS (BEN) FUGITT: During the summer of 1979, I was a caretaker at the Mountain Of Attention Sanctuary. It had been a hot, dry summer, with a number of forest fires in the surrounding countryside. On September 17, I noticed a small tuft of smoke down the canyon. It appeared to be very close. I ran to the nearest car and raced down the canyon and saw a fire up over a ridge to the northwest. Owing to thick growth and rugged terrain, it was inaccessible

The fire at the Mountain Of Attention Sanctuary, September 1979

to fire-fighting equipment. It was also in a direct line with the outer Sanctuary. I jumped into the car and raced back.

I had the fire department notified, then ran out to the back of the Sanctuary, where I had sent a few men with hand-tools to see what they could do. By now, the smoke had grown into a large cloud. This was obviously a <u>big</u> fire. I had run about three-quarters of a mile toward the fire to check out the extent of the blaze, when I received a call on my walkie-talkie to meet Beloved Adi Da at the Sanctuary zoo, as He wanted to ride out to the fire on horseback. I ran back, calling requests and orders over the walkie-talkie in preparation for His ride. I found myself in a frenzy by the time I got to the zoo.

I hastily saddled the horses. Adrenalin was coursing through my body as never before. I was very much concerned for the Sanctuary. The area that was immediately threatened by the fire meant far more to me than simply outlying trails and manzanita bushes. It was the holy site of Red Sitting Man, which was an area of the Sanctuary where I had spent many hours meditating and serving. I knew this Site had great Spiritual significance, and that it was extremely important that it not burn. And then, of course, there was the obvious threat to the residences, holy sites, and Communion Halls at the heart of the Sanctuary.

As Beloved Adi Da approached the horses, His fierce determination and concern for the Sanctuary were obvious to me, but He was also completely calm.

As we mounted the horses, I wondered exactly where we were going, not remotely expecting what was about to unfold. As soon as we began riding down the back road, a fire engine careened around the corner behind us and turned on its siren to alert us. The horses bolted, not about to be caught by this screaming machine. I could feel Beloved Adi Da's equanimity as I held on for dear life. The truck finally outran us, and the horses relaxed their mad gallop. We rode on to find a spot from which to view the fire.

Beloved Adi Da was dissatisfied with the distant vantage points I took Him to, finally asking to get close to the fire. I took Him out through the outer Sanctuary to the spot where I had been earlier, but still He wanted to get much closer to the fire. I told Him there was an old fire road that would take us right to the fire. But I was hesitant to go there, feeling I should not take Him into such a dangerous situation. I warned Him that the horses would probably refuse to get close to the fire because of all the smoke. But this was the route He wanted to explore, and so we made our way up the steep, overgrown fire road. I cautioned Him again about the horses, feeling my own apprehension growing.

As we made our way over the ridge, it looked as though we were riding into a different world. The atmosphere was thick with smoke. The ground and trees were red with borate fire retardant, and planes were continuing to drop fire-retardant right over us. Once again, I cautioned Beloved Adi Da about the horses, as it was obvious to me we were approaching the "head" or "lead" of the fire. He simply replied, "Don't worry about it."

We wove through the trees toward the roar of the blaze. The wind was coming up and fanning the flames. Spot fires burned on either side of us. The main part of the fire was roaring through the more dense forest directly ahead. I had finally found the right spot! This was where He wanted to be, right in the path of the fire.

It seemed to me that we could easily be trapped by the fire—it was moving so quickly. The spot fires behind us could seal off our escape. The horses might bolt. My body was again charged with adrenalin, pumping with wild energy. Once more, I warned Beloved Adi Da of the possible danger. He looked at me intensely, asking if I was frightened, and I told him honestly, "Yes". His response was, "Why do you think I wanted to come up here? I have to look the fire in the eye."

Beloved Adi Da's communication was so full of Force that it was incomprehensible to me. I could feel that His complete, free, and uncompromised attention was on the blazing fire. In that instant, I was relieved of my fear. Suddenly, I was released into love, and I only wanted to Contemplate my Beloved Guru.

Beloved Adi Da then turned toward the advancing flames, moving within thirty yards or so of the oncoming blaze. The roar and force of the fire was amazingly powerful. Flames exploded up the sides of two enormous trees directly in front of us, as if to confront Beloved Adi Da. I could feel this great force of Nature over against the Master of Life. I also noticed, much to my amazement, that the horses were completely calm, almost as if they were out grazing in a pasture. They were obviously feeling Beloved Adi Da's calming influence as much as I was.

I was sitting to the side and slightly behind Beloved Adi Da, watching Him regard the fire. The magnitude of the fire appeared to increase significantly, as the wind came up suddenly and the fire engulfed the area directly in front of us. Facing the fire's new rush of force and fury, Beloved Adi Da sat completely still in His saddle. His only movements were the spontaneous motions of His face and hands in various mudras, very much the same as I had seen many times during formal Darshan or meditation occasions. I felt Him radiate Divine Fire in the face of that forest fire. Whatever else He might have been doing, Beloved Adi Da was Radiating the most benign and yet fierce and awesome Power I had ever known.

After what must have been only a few moments (although time seemed to be suspended and warped), the fire receded and then died down. The winds stopped. The consuming power of this fire seemed to be bowing down to the Divine Heart-Master. I am sure that it is difficult for the reader to picture this moment, but that fire had been transformed! I can only say that it was a mysterious and awesome moment to see and feel the Divine Avatar confront a raging forest fire. I sat still in mindless wonder.

Beloved Adi Da then turned back toward the Sanctuary, moving slowly through the trees, stopping to talk for a time. We looked over the scene—the fire was still moving, but much more slowly now.

When we arrived back at the main Sanctuary complex, I was surprised to find all of Beloved Adi Da's belongings, all of the Sanctuary files and records, library books, and machines being packed into waiting vans and trucks. Apparently, no one had remembered my instructions to wait until we returned before deciding to evacuate. Beloved Adi Da just laughed as He dismounted and sat down on the steps of His residence amidst a sea of packed boxes. He kidded me about our trip up to the fire, and teasingly told everyone, "Ben was so afraid, he almost shit in his pants!"

I always tend to withdraw in the face of things that are "greater" or more forceful than me. Beloved Adi Da has pointed this out to me a number of times over the years, and He would use this event for years to remind me of my tendencies, and how I must go beyond them. During this incident, He had simply drawn me into trust and the capacity to love and serve. I felt through Him what it is to move in this world, even in the most dangerous circumstances, as a free man.

Later that evening, we rode out again to survey the neighboring areas. Then Beloved Adi Da asked me to call the neighbors and make sure everyone was all right. In doing so, I found out that, although about one thousand acres had been burned, no buildings had been lost, no one had been injured, and even our neighbor's orchards had only been slightly scorched.

A few days later, I walked back to the spot where Beloved Adi Da had worked with the fire, reflecting on all that had occurred there. I thought about how confounding and amazing the whole event had been, feeling humbled and full of love. The area was still smeared with red borate dust and ash; the strong smell of smoke lingered. The fire, I discovered, had stopped short of the Sanctuary boundary by only a foot! ∎

Divine Initiation: An Esoteric Order

On the day of the fire, devotees were not only packing up the most precious things on the Sanctuary. They were also preparing for a great ceremony of Initiation.

In the evening, after Avatar Adi Da had dealt with the fire, He went to Holy Cat Grotto, the natural hot springs site on the Sanctuary He had Empowered as a temple for healing and Spiritual Initiation. There, beside a steaming pool, He received a group of devotees who He felt had made a serious response to His Call for renunciation. He intended them to become the core of an esoteric order, His first formal group of renunciate devotees. He poured the warm water over His devotees, Baptizing them with water and His "Bright" Spirit-Presence. He Initiated them into the sacred use of His Name, as He had described in His Discourse of the previous day. Placing His hands on them, He whispered in the ear of each one: "Call upon Me by the Name 'Da'."

"Call upon Me by the Name 'Da'."

Those two days—Sunday, September 16, and Monday, September 17, 1979—signed yet another profound change in the Life and Work of Avatar Adi Da Samraj. He had Revealed Himself as the Divine Person, Da, to hundreds of people, and had Called on them to recognize and surrender to Him as Real God. He had demonstrated His Divine Mastery over the natural world in His encounter with the fire. And, finally, He had performed the first Spiritual Initiation in the history of His Work, forming a serious group of renunciate practitioners who were charged to authenticate the Gifts of His Incarnation by their practice and devotion. This Initiation was the seed of the Ruchira Sannyasin Order of Adidam Ruchiradam. Some years later, that formal renunciate order was established by Avatar Adi Da—to function both as the senior cultural authority (or the extension of His own Sacred Authority) within the gathering of His devotees and as His living human Instrumentality (or the collective human "conduit" for His Spiritual Blessing). Thus, the Ruchira Sannyasin Order represents, altogether, the means by which the Way of Adidam—the Way of the devotional and Spiritual relationship to Avatar Adi Da Samraj—will continue to be fully and rightly practiced forever.

The Mountain Of Attention Sanctuary, 1979

CHAPTER 10

The Signs of Divine Power

During the years of His Teaching-Work, Avatar Adi Da Samraj would sometimes tease His devotees about their desire to witness extraordinary or miraculous phenomena in His Company. Sometimes He would ask them, "Don't you think if you were really being religious, you would be seeing things by now?" What kind of miracle, He would ask, would He have to perform in order to prove the Truth of the Divine Reality to them, to convince them to engage Spiritual practice intensively?

In this way, Avatar Adi Da would challenge the common religious mind in His devotees—the popular notion that the real proof of God or religion or saintliness lies in supernormal experiences, or events that apparently contradict the laws of nature. His demonstration during "Garbage and the Goddess" was a comprehensive criticism of that fascination with the miraculous. The true miracle was direct Divine Communion with Him. The Spiritual phenomena that may arise in the course of sadhana are secondary.

At the same time, Avatar Adi Da was countering the opposite tendency in modern culture—the presumption that "miracles" and Spiritual phenomena do not happen, that nothing exists beyond the physical. For those who have been in His Company for any length of time, this existence of phenomena beyond the physical world of scientific materialism is not in dispute, for Avatar Adi Da has always Revealed that the natural universe is a vast plastic infinity of interconnected psycho-physical patterns and planes of energy. "Matter" is not as fixed as it seems to our Western minds.

This chapter presents three stories illustrating the kinds of miraculous demonstration Avatar Adi Da has made.

The Red Miracle

At the time of the momentous events of the Day of the Heart, River Papers (then a member of Avatar Adi Da's circle of renunciate women) was expecting Naamleela Free Jones, Avatar Adi Da's youngest daughter.

RIVER: The unusual circumstances surrounding the birth of Naamleela began one day in early 1977. At that time, Beloved Adi Da and a small group of His devotees were living on the island of Oahu in Hawaii. That day, two devotees who were standing outside the house saw a burst of brilliant light in the yard, and they both stopped to look up at the blinding flash. Immediately, the light turned to a fine bright-red powder, which began to fall, like a misty rain, all over the yard. The foliage and the little out-building that we used for our meditation hall were both covered with this powder.

(left to right:) Shawnee Free Jones, Tamarind Free Jones, Naamleela Free Jones, and Io Free Jones, the Mountain Of Attention Sanctuary, 2001

Avatar Adi Da's daughters—Io Free Jones, Shawnee Free Jones, and Naamleela Free Jones—were born to three members of His circle of women renunciates. Tamarind Free Jones—born to longtime devotees of Avatar Adi Da—was adopted by Avatar Adi Da as a fourth daughter.

The two who had witnessed this phenomenon called other devotees out to look at the red powder, but the substance was not familiar to anyone. By the end of the day, the fine red coating had disappeared just as mysteriously as it had appeared. There had been no wind or rain that could have blown or washed it away—it just disappeared. At the moment all of this occurred, I was attending Beloved Adi Da in His room in the main house, just a few feet away from where the explosion of light had been witnessed.

Almost two years later, on April 28, 1979, the next miraculous event occurred. Adi Da Samraj was now living at the Mountain Of Attention Sanctuary. A week before, I had begun to feel a very strong pulling or yanking sensation in my internal organs, as if they were being pulled by a string from my pubic bone up the central meridian of my body. I remember the sensation, because it was actually painful, especially in the region of my navel. The pulling sensation went on for a week. On Sunday evening, a gift from a devotee arrived—a photograph of Shirdi Sai Baba, an Indian saint of the late nineteenth and early twentieth centuries. It was a very colorful, poster-sized photograph, showing Shirdi Sai Baba wearing a red bandanna against a deep red background. Beloved Adi Da pointed out the markings of kum-kum on him, and explained to us that kum-kum was a red powder used traditionally throughout India as a symbol of the Divine Nature that is innate in every being. I was unaccountably drawn to the picture.

Later on that same evening, I looked down and saw a red stain appearing on my body. I thought that I was menstruating, particularly because of the strange pulling sensation I had experienced all week. So I excused myself, and went to change my clothes.

But it wasn't blood, and I couldn't remove it! In fact, as I was trying to rub it off, more of it was appearing on my skin. It appeared to be coming from inside my skin. I could not figure out <u>what</u> was going on. I called some of my friends out, to see if they could help me. But no one could remove it or figure out what it was or what was happening. Later, we told Beloved Adi Da about it.

I remember how carefully He listened to my description. Then He said that we had to investigate the phenomenon and find out where the substance was coming from. He asked us to do a very thorough investigation of everything I had come in contact with that day.

Once Beloved Adi Da was satisfied that our initial investigation had been as thorough as it could possibly be, He asked that photographs be taken of the red stain and that a sample be taken by one of the doctors and sent to a reliable laboratory for analysis.

When we received the results from the laboratory several days later, the mystery was only confirmed. The report read that the substance was not composed of any bodily tissue or any common synthetic. The laboratory technicians, intrigued by their findings, had tried all kinds of tests, but they finally had to report: "There are no known chemically definable substances in this specimen."

It was only after all the conventional explanations had been investigated that Beloved Adi Da commented about what had actually taken place. He told us that the red substance that had appeared on my body was a spontaneous manifestation of kum-kum. True kum-kum, He told us, is a form of Light. It is a Divine substance that only appears spontaneously and as a kind of Graceful Divine Manifestation. It signals that a most intense Yogic process is taking place. This Divine substance has been known to appear at various times in the company of holy men and women, and, by its very nature, it defies ordinary physical laws.

Although I didn't understand what was occurring or what it had to do with me, I thought that perhaps a significant change was going to take place in my life. I thought then that it might have something to do with my practice, so I started to make an effort to intensify my practice—but Beloved Adi Da told me to just relax! He said that the Yogic process of which the kum-kum had been a sign was already initiated in me, and that it was occurring by His Grace, without my needing to do anything about it. Nine weeks later, I discovered that I was pregnant.

One day during the third month, I was in the kitchen when Beloved Adi Da came in and, as He often did, stood by the window that looks out onto the grassy central area of the Sanctuary, to give His Regard to His devotees as they walked by. It was at that moment that I first became aware of the actual psychic entity inside me.

I remember it so well because it became very obvious—a literal sensation, as if a light had been turned on in the room—that the being in me was reaching out to Beloved Adi Da. I knew that this entity was incarnating because of its profound Spiritual relationship to Him. And I felt myself as simply a vehicle for this being, carrying and nurturing it so that it could be with Beloved Adi Da in human form.

On the evening of the anniversary of the beginning of Beloved Adi Da's Teaching-Work—April 25—I began to have contractions, and soon I was in full labor. We drove to the hospital. The contractions were strong, and, though I had my attention on the physical process that was taking place, it was secondary to Beloved Adi Da's Darshan. I was more aware of Him than of myself. His Beauty and Radiance were so Blissful.

In the hospital, during the birth, my Beloved Guru sat fully in my view, never leaving His chair. I felt absolutely no separation from Him. It was one of the most blissful experiences of my life.

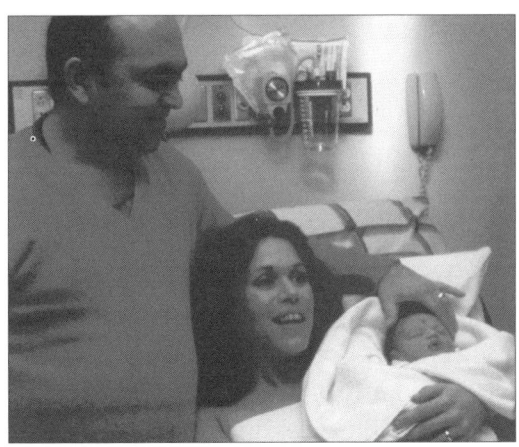

Avatar Adi Da Samraj at the hospital with River Papers and Naamleela Free Jones

Beloved Adi Da cut the umbilical cord, and Naamleela was placed on my stomach. Beloved Adi Da took her, and anointed her with ash and kum-kum and put a Tibetan cap on her head and a mala around her neck and wrapped her in a blanket—and then showed her to everybody.

I looked at Beloved Adi Da and Naamleela, and I saw her open her eyes to look at Him. I felt the blissful contact immediately between the two of them. It seemed very unusual, because newborns typically don't open their eyes.

Sometime after Naamleela's birth, Beloved Adi Da began to talk about the spontaneous manifestation of kum-kum that had occurred a year before her birth. He indicated that Naamleela had begun the process of her incarnation on the day of the appearance of kum-kum. The miracle of the kum-kum had been a sign of the auspicious birth that was to come.

I had never understood if the manifestation of kum-kum in Oahu in 1977 had anything to do with Naamleela's birth. In 1994, Beloved Adi Da said:

"The original incident was a sign associated with yourself as a vehicle for the birth of Naamleela. In that sense, so was the sign in 1979 that appeared on your body. It was a sign of Naamleela, but also a sign of yourself as the vehicle through which she would appear.

"From the first day you came into My Company, I referred to you in terms of the color red. You yourself likewise made such references in various forms over the years. Altogether, the redness of the kum-kum manifestations was associated with the unique service you performed as the vehicle for Naamleela's birth."

"Yes, thank You, Beloved. I am eternally grateful."

Beloved Adi Da responded with His characteristic sound of Blessing, "Tcha." ∎

A Glimpse of the Death Transition

In 1976, Connie Mantas, a registered nurse who worked with the dying, was taken through a remarkable experience by Avatar Adi Da. He walked over to her during a gathering at His house and asked her to lie down on the floor next to Him. He lay flat on His back next to her and closed His eyes, saying "Now do exactly as I do". Then, He silently Guided her through the experience of the death transition:

CONNIE: First there was an explosion of inner sounds. Then I felt the layers of the body-mind release and fall away. "I" was separating out from the physical body and seemed to fly upwards, whirling through dark space at an incredible speed. I was moving toward an overwhelming, brilliant light. At one point, I recall slipping through a kind of "grid" as a speck of consciousness.

For an instant, I did seem to lose all self-awareness, but throughout the rest of the experience I was aware of the most remarkable clarity. I found that I felt more familiar and at ease traveling without the body than when I was dragging it along, anchored to it by my usual physical-body identification. I felt myself to be alive as Consciousness, at ease as the witness of mind and attention.

At different moments in this cosmic journey, I felt the deep urges of the body-mind drawing me back towards embodiment, and I sensed the frustration of having no physical body through which to enact or fulfill desires. This made a stunning impression on me, and I remember feeling how foolish it would be to waste the opportunity of a human lifetime to do the sadhana that could help free me of the binding attachments I had now seen so clearly.

Then I became aware of a loud buzzing or humming sound as I slowly came back into the body-mind, taking on each layer, starting with the most subtle. The inner sounds quieted until once again I was aware of lying on the floor.

When I opened my eyes, the face of Beloved Adi Da was right next to mine, and He was grinning at me with a gigantic smile. He opened His mouth and started to laugh. It was more than a laugh—it was a victorious and triumphant shout, glorious to hear. Instead of being awestruck by this remarkable journey I had just taken with Him, I felt sheer marvel at Who He Is. I felt, "Yes! There is this great scheme of conditional existence, of which human embodiment is a part. But first, and most importantly, HE IS THE MASTER OF IT ALL! And I have a relationship with That One!"

Without exchanging a word with me, Beloved Adi Da got up, walked to His Chair and began a Discourse on death and the "grid" through which we pass at death. This was one of the first occasions at which Beloved Adi Da spoke of the total pattern of phenomena, or the "Cosmic Mandala", as He would later describe it. As always, He had one primary message—no experience, high or low, is the answer to our suffering. No "one" survives in the great plastic of forms. Only Consciousness Itself persists—the Eternal "I", the Self-Existing and Self-Radiant Condition of all, beyond the grid of appearances. ■

The Birth of Indian Time

1976 also saw another miracle connected with a birth.

SCILLA BLACKWELL: September 26, 1976, was a gray and windy day. Avatar Adi Da spoke that afternoon to a large gathering of devotees. Partway through His Talk, I felt the onset of labor. I left the room and informed some friends that labor had begun. I had chosen to have a "home birth" at the Sanctuary, and my friends helped me settle into one of the cabins, which we prepared according to the recommendations for natural childbirth given by Frederick Le Boyer.

After Beloved Adi Da finished speaking to devotees, He came to see me. He was Radiant, expectant, full of life. "Well, how is everything?" He asked.

I remember my reply, "Everything's fine, but . . ."

"But what?" He asked.

I had nothing to add—only an unspoken and irrational uneasiness. I had already had two children, but this pregnancy seemed different and so now did the onset of labor.

LARRY HASTINGS: The birth was very difficult, and Scilla's strength was seriously drained by the ordeal. The doctor was unable to detect a fetal heartbeat during the last ten minutes of labor. At last, the baby was born—slithering out onto the bed. Everyone bent expectantly over the newborn child. It looked very strange. Its flesh was dark gray and, while its trunk and limbs were tiny, its head was huge. The baby did not breathe or make any sound or move in any way.

The doctor picked the baby up and began to try to get it to breathe. Someone ran out of the room for the Sanctuary oxygen equipment. Both doctor and midwife slapped the baby on the butt, cut the umbilical cord, and suctioned its nose, trying to get any kind of response. It dawned on all of us that we had a stillborn baby here, and nothing was working to change that. No one cared about a peaceful Le Boyer procedure for a newborn anymore. All the lights came on. I even carried the baby to the shower and tried splashing it with cold water. A few minutes later, the oxygen equipment was brought in, but, like everything else, it failed to elicit any response from the baby.

Everyone became silent. The doctor laid the baby back on the bed, not wanting to put the lifeless child in Scilla's arms, and said quietly, "Well, it's a girl." The joy of a child's birth was not in his voice. Precious moments were passing, and I felt myself moving toward admitting to others, and then to myself, and finally to Scilla, that our new child was stillborn. And then I spoke inwardly to my Guru, with great clarity and intuition: "Master, if you can hear me, please come now."

SCILLA: After the first few failed attempts to get the baby to respond, Connie Mantas, my dear friend and the attending nurse, bolted from the room toward Avatar Adi Da's house. Connie tells me that she ran in a direct line to the house, hurdling over bushes and fences like an Olympic athlete. She burst in on Avatar Adi Da, who was giving a Talk to a small gathering of devotees. Winded and unable to speak, she simply indicated to Him in one wordless expression that we needed His help, and then whirled and came running at full speed back to our cabin.

Avatar Adi Da did not hesitate. Devotees with Him at the time say they had never seen anyone move as fast as He did then. And yet He seemed completely unhurried. He finished His sentence, got His walking staff, shawl, hat, and shoes, and was out the door before anyone could even take in what had happened.

Another devotee pointed Him to the cabin where I had begun my labor. She did not know that I had been moved and was now in a different cabin. He hesitated momentarily, and then disregarded her instructions and headed straight to the cabin where we were. Devotees running behind Him say that, despite the fact that no one could keep up with Him, He appeared to be striding effortlessly, not huffing and puffing as they were.

LARRY: Avatar Adi Da was at our cabin in no time at all. He just walked right in and brought the Sun. He was ablaze with Light, and His Light filled and expanded the entire room. The tiny cabin took on His dimensions, becoming a vast Cavern of His Light. He stood at the foot of the bed, His open hands turned toward us, His face and mouth twisted into a ferocious lion-like grimace, His eyes rolled straight up, and His teeth began to chatter loudly. A huge wave of Force passed through His Being towards the three of us on the bed, Light and Energy literally shooting out of His Body.

The baby jerked as if in response to an electric shock, then whimpered weakly. She jerked and whimpered more and more. It was as if a rheostat on a light switch was being turned on and then turned up. He literally enlivened her.

SCILLA: I was so exhausted by the labor that I was on the verge of losing consciousness by the time Adi Da arrived. Most of the room and the people around me had dissolved in darkness. I could only see the baby lying on a small patch of the bed directly in front of me when He entered.

His Light and Spirit-Force brought me back. Slowly, I became aware of more than just Him and the baby. Everything in the room seemed so "Bright", bathed in Light. I saw Larry's face beaming in ecstasy and wonderment, another devotee smiling in delighted amazement in the far corner of the room, and yet another of my friends peering in the window, grinning from ear to ear.

After the baby was dried, wrapped, and placed in my arms, Avatar Adi Da sat beside me on the bed and did the most curious, lovely thing: With one hand He massaged the soles of the baby's feet, with the other He pinched the skin above her heart and gently twisted it around for a minute or two. Then He kissed her on the forehead, kissed both Larry and me, and softly spoke His characteristic sound of Blessing, "Tcha", as He left our room.

The next morning when the three of us awoke, we found a note at the door indicating that Avatar Adi Da had suggested the name "Indian Time" for the baby.

LARRY: Her name refers to the tempo at which the American Indians have traditionally lived. On the night of her birth, several devotees had just returned from visiting a Native American healer, to ask for some healing herbs. They reported to Avatar Adi Da that their mission had been unsuccessful. But He explained to them that they simply hadn't understood that they were on "white man's time" and that the shaman was on "Indian time". Thus, the healer's reluctance to give them the herbs right away was not a sign of refusal, but simply a sign of the deliberate pace and customary time a Native American would take to make a decision of this kind. Therefore, He told us, Indian Time's name suited her because "she took her time deciding to come here, she took her time in coming, and she took her time in deciding to stay".

Later, He mentioned that when Indian Time was born, her etheric (or energy) body was separated from her physical body—as if she were standing apart, wondering whether to assume this birth. What He had done was to connect her etheric body with her physical form.

SCILLA: A week after her birth, Indian Time was in serious trouble again. I found her in her cradle in convulsions. She had vomited, aspirated her vomit, and could hardly breathe. We rushed her to the hospital to the infant intensive care unit. I watched her turn dusky gray again as the doctor and nurses worked over her. They gave her a fifty percent chance of surviving.

She was placed in an incubator and fed intravenously. Beloved Adi Da asked to hear reports about her twice a day.

I am not someone who typically sees visions or experiences subtle phenomena, but within hours of Indian Time's entering the intensive care unit and our first call to Avatar Adi Da, the whole area around her crib was bathed in a rain of silvery, misty light. During the two weeks she was there, the light just increased and thickened. The intensive care unit became saturated with this silver rain of light, which both Larry and I continued to see.

We weren't permitted to hold Indian Time, but we could lay hands on her in the incubator. I felt at times as if my hands were Beloved Adi Da's, His healing Force and Blessing coursing through them were so great.

Indian Time's condition had seemed very grim to us ever since her birth. She did not look or act normal. Her head (in the ninetieth percentile of head size at birth) was grossly disproportionate to her body (in the tenth percentile of body size at birth). She had already been suffering from what is called "desperate" or "retracted" breathing, she ate very poorly, and she was weak and lackadaisical. Beloved Adi Da had jolted life into her seven minutes after birth. But for those first seven minutes, she had not breathed or had any discernible heartbeat. It was a foregone conclusion among the medical staff at the hospital that, because of those seven minutes of anoxia, our daughter had suffered serious brain damage. Several days after Indian's admission to the hospital, I called Beloved Adi Da's house one evening to report that an EEG (brain wave scan) had been ordered for Indian Time for the next day. If the EEG showed abnormal results—and it was presumed that it would—Indian would be immediately scheduled for brain surgery.

Ten minutes after I placed the call to Avatar Adi Da's house, a nurse called me to the phone. It was a devotee, saying that Beloved Adi Da wanted to know the exact time the EEG was to take place. Just after the second phone call, the nurse said that I could take Indian Time out of the incubator and hold her for the first time since she had come to the hospital. I was ecstatic.

I sat in a huge rocking chair with her on my lap, laying one hand at the base of her spine and the other on the crown of her head. The heat that came off that little head was of burning intensity, not like a fever but like a hot iron. I had to pull my hand off her head and shake it to cool it off every minute or two. We sat like that for two hours, yet it seemed as if only a few minutes had passed. My body felt given over to Beloved Adi Da, and I felt Him healing her. The next morning, the results of the EEG were completely normal. The neurologist was stunned.

LARRY: Two weeks later, when Indian Time was discharged from the hospital, every single one of the other babies in the intensive care unit was discharged the same morning. The nurses' jaws were dropping! The unit was closed down for twenty-four hours, giving the nurses their first night off in many months.

During the early months of Indian Time's life, Adi Da communicated to us that she was the type of person who does not really want to be born in the first place—someone who is always wanting

The Signs of Divine Power

to leave the body, rather than engage life. Incarnating physically was difficult for her. She was sick with pneumonia three times during that first year of her life. Over and over, I saw and felt how she was lived and sustained by the Divine Grace of Avatar Adi Da.

Indian Time is a unique character, demonstrating a psychic connection to people and events that we have learned not to tamper with. She has a very healing touch, and her faith in Beloved Adi Da awakens the faith-response in all of us. She learned, at a very young age, through trial and difficulty, that it is Avatar Adi Da Samraj Who sustains her life and she trusts that with a simplicity and innocent happiness that touches all her friends. ■

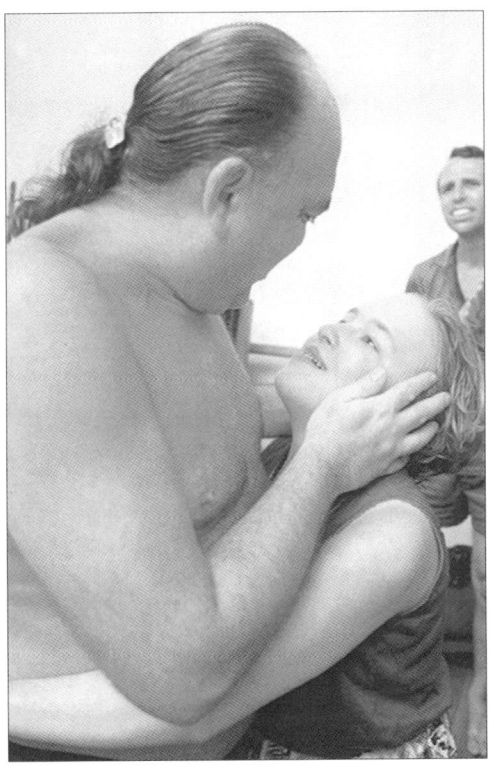

**Avatar Adi Da Samraj
with Indian Time Hastings, 1993**

Da Love-Ananda Mahal, 1982

CHAPTER 11

The Search for Hermitage

After the Revelation of His Divine Name "Da" in 1979, Avatar Adi Da spent periods of time away from the Mountain Of Attention. He needed a more secluded refuge, a place where His Revelation could continue to unfold, and where He could Work intensively with the members of His new esoteric order. In the middle of 1978, devotees acquired property on the Hawaiian island of Kauai, which Avatar Adi Da eventually named "Da Love-Ananda Mahal" ("Da Love-Ananda" being one of Avatar Adi Da's Names, and "Mahal" meaning "palace"). It was the second great seat of His Spiritual Work.

He had previously named it "Tumomama", meaning "fierce woman", in acknowledgement of the untamed forces of nature there. Below six acres of rolling lawns, a turbulent river rushes through a rocky gorge from the top of Mount Waialeale, the wettest place on Earth.

The Call to Renunciation

Throughout the years of His Teaching-Work, Avatar Adi Da had been "considering" all the traditional approaches to renunciation, and what renunciation would have to be in the case of His devotees. Renunciation is usually thought of as deliberate asceticism, the giving up of pleasures for some Spiritual goal. Avatar Adi Da, however, always emphasized that true renunciation is not puritanical, not an ascetic's avoidance of the body, but the abandoning of seeking, so that every aspect of ordinary life could conform to the "Brightening" Process of Realizing Real God.

AVATAR ADI DA SAMRAJ: To practice in My Company you must be a renunciate. And renunciation is ego-transcendence, establishment in the Well of Happiness, magnifying that Happiness in the sphere of all relations and functions. You need not be an ascetic, but you must give it all to Me, to the Divine—every trace of your existence, every piece of it, down to the last drop. You cannot merely tithe to the Divine! You may tithe to the world, but you must give everything to the Divine. You must give everything to Spiritual life, totally. And then, based on that principle, you must economize the giving of energy and attention to life and relations. [1982]

From 1980 through early 1983, at both Da Love-Ananda Mahal and the Mountain Of Attention Sanctuary, Adi Da Samraj continued to "consider" the matter of renunciation with the esoteric order and others. Did they have one-pointed clarity of purpose? Were they showing the depth of self-understanding that true renunciation requires—not suppressed, not ascetical, but converted to Happiness? Could they transcend boredom, doubt, and discomfort, rather than resorting to conventional means of seeking?

During this time, Avatar Adi Da also continued the emotional-sexual "consideration", testing to see if anyone could demonstrate a sexually active practice compatible with the most one-pointed renunciate Spiritual practice.

Hurricane Iwa

On November 23, 1982, news reached devotees at Da Love-Ananda Mahal of a hurricane that had blown up in the Pacific and was heading straight for the island of Kauai. By 4:30 in the afternoon, huge trees were down across the road and a sixty-foot lychee tree lay in splinters at the Sanctuary. Electric power lines were whipping in the wind, and the rain was coming down in sheets. The river below the Sanctuary was swollen brown and raging, and outside the windows of Free Standing Man (Avatar Adi Da's residence, where He was gathered with His devotees), leaves, branches, and debris swept past in the howling storm.

Devotees had done what they could to secure the Sanctuary before taking refuge in Avatar Adi Da's residence, the most secure structure on the Sanctuary. There had been little time even to board up windows before the winds of the hurricane (the first to strike Hawaii in twenty years) had driven everyone indoors. Avatar Adi Da placed His Hands on the badly bruised neck of a devotee who had injured herself running to safety. Through the healing power of His touch, she could soon swallow painlessly, her breathing normalized, and the bruise disappeared.

Not long afterwards, a weather bulletin indicated that the height of the storm was yet many hours away, and would be striking with full force late into the night, with winds well over a hundred miles per hour. At that point, Avatar Adi Da rose and went to His library. He returned in a few minutes with a small volume of poems in honor of Kali, the Hindu vision of the Divine Goddess in Her terrible, destructive form. Unperturbed by the deafening roar outside, He began to read poem after poem that teased, scolded, and reverenced Kali as the trickster, the Mother of illusions, awesome in Her devastating play. Devotees looked on in amazement and joy. They felt Adi Da addressing Hurricane Iwa directly, asserting His Mastery over this terrifying manifestation of the Goddess-Power.

Finally, Avatar Adi Da put the book down. He said: "She has done it." Then He went on:

AVATAR ADI DA SAMRAJ: This storm is the great picture. This is life capsulized. Life is obliteration—<u>not</u> birth and survival and glorification. It is death! The "Goddess" is the sign of Nature, the word of Nature, the Person of Nature—Kali, the bloody Goddess with long teeth and blood pouring out of her mouth. You poor people are deceived by Nature. [November 23, 1982]

The weather reports still indicated that much worse was yet to come, but, following their Beloved Guru, whose mood became light, devotees began to celebrate, watching the storm gradually subside.

The next morning, the newspapers reported on the storm damage. They described the fact that no one on the island had been killed as a "miracle". Later reports and satellite photographs from the U.S. weather service showed that, during the time when Avatar Adi Da had done His Blessing-Work in relation to the storm, the hurricane had more than doubled the speed at which it was moving along its course. As a result, Hurricane Iwa spent its force and "aged" prematurely, changing shape and eventually blowing itself out. Thus, the fullest predicted fury never struck Kauai, and the storm winds which did hit the island passed over much more quickly than expected.

Wandering in Fiji

Even in the relative seclusion of Kauai, Avatar Adi Da felt too crowded by the secular world to do the Work of creating an esoteric order of renunciates. The search for Hermitage started up again, now focusing on Fiji. Fiji had been identified as a desirable location for a Hermitage because it was remote, quiet, and because the population was predominantly a mix of native Fijians and Indians—cultures that had traditions of respect for individuals of Spiritual power.

After many months of waiting for the right Hermitage circumstance to appear, Avatar Adi Da decided to leave Kauai for Fiji and wander there with the esoteric order until they found the right place. The traveling party first arrived in Fiji at "Charlie's Place" on the tiny island of Nananui-Ra, where they lived in extreme simplicity. Immediately upon arriving at Charlie's Place, Avatar Adi Da launched into a "consideration" of the "Perfect Practice"—the ultimate stages of practice in the Way of Adidam. He sent a number of devotees on four-day solitary retreat intensives, which He called "the Ordeal of Being". The purpose of His Work at this time, and the Instruction He gave, concerned the depth of ego-renunciation necessary to enter into the ultimate stages of Spiritual practice in His Company:

Enter more and more deeply into the Well of Being, Where you Always Already Stand.
Feel the Feeling of Being, without the slightest regard or concern for attention and its objects.
Be Immersed in the Conscious, Native, and Original Feeling of Being, until It Is Realized to Be Happiness Itself, or Freedom Itself.
Be Thus. Dwell in That, As That—unperturbed, Free, Self-Radiant as Love-Bliss, without qualification, beyond all need to notice the body-mind and its objects.
Practice this constantly on retreat.
This is true and free devotion to Me.
This is true and free renunciation. [March 21, 1983]

Some weeks after Avatar Adi Da's arrival in Fiji, the local spirits began to openly show their resistance to His presence there. For people in contemporary Western culture, the idea of spirits, ghosts, and disembodied entities is a fascinating possibility, but it is not part of their daily experience. However, people in traditional cultures tend to be more sensitive to dimensions subtler than the gross physical. Many traditional cultures presume that the dimension of spirits (both benign and threatening) is as real as the physical dimension, if not more so. Avatar Adi Da Samraj takes the spirit-dimension fully into account, and Works with that dimension as powerfully as with any other plane of existence.

One night at Charlie's Place, after everyone was asleep, a fire suddenly erupted from a faulty refrigeration unit. Within minutes, the cabin where Avatar Adi Da's daughters and the other children in the party were sleeping was a blazing inferno, soon reduced to nothing but a smoldering concrete foundation. Fortunately, everyone had escaped safely from the cabin—but barely in time. Just as they reached the cabin door, the final group of three escapees was suddenly catapulted off their feet and out of the building by an explosive blast of the fire, landing in the dirt about ten feet away.

The next day, Avatar Adi Da said that aggressive spirits had visited Him the previous evening, and it was now clear to Him that they had caused the fire. The party quickly left the island. Eventually, the wanderers settled at Nukubati (new-come-BAH-tee), a little spit of an island located in a wind funnel.

There, they stayed in partially-completed accommodations—again with no water, septic, or electricity. By now it was May, heading into the cooler time of the year in the southern hemisphere. The winds blew non-stop. As they sat in Avatar Adi Da's room during times of "consideration", devotees watched the sand blowing through the floorboards, shooting up a foot or two before settling on the floor.

Even more than a physical trial, the four months at Nukubati were an emotional one. Avatar Adi Da gathered with devotees every day, Working with the "pit of snakes"—His descriptive phrase for the "writhing mass" of negative impulses and presumptions that makes up our "reactive, non-social, even anti-social personality".

Day after day, the gathering group had to deal with the strong emotions of "the pit". Avatar Adi Da confronted each to transcend the dramas of the emotional-sexual character. He drove them to understand these dramas as the active preventing of Spiritual receptivity.

AVATAR ADI DA SAMRAJ: By tendency, you all live far from the domain of feeling. You live as conventional social personalities, and your lives are organized around behavioral obligations that are communicated to you from infancy.

However, there is also a dimension in you that does not merely want to be this social personality, does not merely want to submit to the behavioral demands that you have inherited, and is not happy in any case. This level of emotion exists beneath the social personality. You do not like this level of emotion, and (therefore) you try to maintain the characteristics of the social personality as many hours of every day as you can. But then circumstance, moments of weakness, the phases of your own hormonal system, and various other factors cause you, from time to time, to fall into this "pit of snakes" that is your reactive, non-social, even anti-social personality.

At those times, you are resistive, angry, afraid, sorrowful, righteous, lustful—all the patterns one would call "you", as the ego. This is true of everyone. No one is merely the "perfect" social personality. Everyone has his or her games and tendencies. Everyone lives in a kind of diseased state all the time, and at times exhibits the symptoms of that disease in very dramatic fashion. Most people do not even want to get <u>close</u> to the realm of emotions that is associated with this irresponsible ego-self. All of common society is devoted to keeping people from getting in touch with this "pit of snakes".

In My Play with you, I have not avoided putting you in touch with that realm of emotion, that "pit of snakes". I must put you in touch with it. But I do not merely put you in touch with it. I Instruct you, I Teach you, I Submit Myself to you, I help you to understand how to be free of this "pit of snakes", so that you will not have to live any longer as superficial personalities, surrendered to the universal tragedy of unillumined humankind.

You must exist always in the Domain of Free Feeling—Which is intimate contact with the Divine Force of Being, and Which Knows Real God without a doubt. This Feeling knows love, without psychiatric help or intellectual reasons—and so incarnates it, lives it.

Love one another, and there is nothing cool about it. What I mean by this love for one another is to become wounded by love, to submit yourself to love, to live in the world of love, and to make your relationships about love. Be vulnerable enough to love and be loved. If you do this, you will be wounded by this love but you will not be diseased. The wound of love is the "Hole in the universe", and (ultimately) it is Realized as such.

In this "Hole in the universe", this Domain of Feeling without armoring, without self-contraction—the Great Physics, the Great

Science, the Great Possibility, is evident. Hardly anyone in human history has known of It. It is the Doorway to Divine Transfiguration, Divine Transformation, Divine Indifference, and, ultimately, Divine Translation, or Outshining of phenomenal existence.* It is the Way into the Divine Self-Domain. [July 2, 1983]

While the winds whipped over the island, indoors it was oppressive and hot. The ordeal, as Adi Da pointed out later, was also a battle with the local spirits, who were resisting the newcomers' entry into their domain, confronting Adi Da's Spiritual Power.

AVATAR ADI DA SAMRAJ: We were tested by the spirits constantly at Nukubati. Every day, I would come out and bring you life, bring you love, bring you Happiness. And, almost every day, there was a fierce, unhealthy confrontation—I was at war with negative entities, the kind that made the fire at Nananui-Ra. That is why I did what I did with you there. You did not see the spirits then. I saw them. I knew what was happening. You only experienced the effects of it—not knowing its source, thinking it was just your own patterns, your own tendencies.

I was attacked physically and emotionally there every day. It was a confrontation with negative trickery. That is why I had to struggle—and those who were with Me, too—because I knew the quantity of energy and feeling that had to be generated there to deal with those influences. [October 28, 1983]

---

*Avatar Adi Da has Revealed that Divine Enlightenment is not a static condition but a process, consisting of four stages: Divine Transfiguration (the full Infusion of the "outer" dimension of the being with Avatar Adi Da's Divine "Brightness"), Divine Transformation (the full Infusion of the "inner", or subtle, dimensions of the being with His Divine "Brightness"), Divine Indifference (the spontaneous relinquishment of attention to body, mind, and world, as the being Rests profoundly in His Divine "Brightness"), and Divine Translation (the complete dissolution of the apparently separate being in the Indivisible Oneness of His Divine "Brightness"—generally, coincident with the physical death of the Divinely Enlightened being).

"Coins"

Shirdi Sai Baba, an Indian Realizer of the late nineteenth and early twentieth centuries, was known to have employed a mysterious method of working with his devotees. He would frequently handle a group of coins he kept in a pouch, which he used as talismanic representations of his devotees.

In His Teaching-Work, Avatar Adi Da would at times describe His Work with a small group of devotees around Him as "Working with 'coins'". He was acknowledging that, while He apparently Worked directly with a few, His Work was actually for all devotees (and, indeed, for all beings). His Work with the esoteric order of devotees around Him during the years of the search for Hermitage exemplified the principle of "coins". In fact, this practice of using individuals or small groups as "touchpoints" in a universal Blessing-Work is characteristic throughout His Work—even Working with certain devotees as "coins" for specific nations, cultures, or world-events.

Often, in a gathering with whoever His "coins" were at the time, He would remind them, "I'm not just talking to you people here." Then He would address the tape recorder directly and say "I'm talking to everybody!"

Naitauba Island

While Avatar Adi Da and His devotees gathered at Nukubati, news came that Neal Stewart, a devotee patron, had purchased Naitauba (nye-TUM-buh), a 3,000-acre island in eastern Fiji. The purchase of Naitauba was itself a struggle, involving a seemingly endless series of difficulties—fiscal, legal, and political. This acquisition, Adi Da explained, was what the whole struggle in Fiji had been about. After confronting the fiercely territorial spirits and forces of resistance, He now had Hermitage.

On October 27, 1983, Avatar Adi Da disembarked from a seaplane in the shallows of a lagoon and set first foot on Naitauba. His arrival was followed by rains, ending months of drought on the island.

Avatar Adi Da Samraj arrives on Naitauba, October 27, 1983

Adidam Samrajashram, the island of Naitauba

After His first circumnavigation of Naitauba (which He later named "Adidam Samrajashram"), He spoke of its grandeur and its role in His future Work:

AVATAR ADI DA SAMRAJ: Naitauba is not just a piece of land. It is a Divine Place. That is how it will be for as long as the sun shines and rises and sets and the grass grows and the wind blows. Forever—as ever as there can be in this world. Maybe it will become a paradise through Spiritual sacrifice. And, all during that epoch, this Place should be a Sanctuary of Blessing. Over time, then, millions of people—literally, millions of people—should come to this Place and be Blessed. They should come and acknowledge, affirm, and see My Revelation magnified.

This place is so great, so great. Civilization has never interfered with it. It is untouched. The water is blue. The fish are happy. Untouched, really untouched. Pristine from the beginning of the world—this place. It has been waiting here since the beginning of time. [October 28, 1983]

**Ciqomi, Naitauba
December 30, 1983**

CHAPTER 12

"Mark My Words"

On December 30, 1983, the Fijian people of Naitauba invited Avatar Adi Da to a celebration in His honor, to be held in their village, Ciqomi [thing-GO-mee]. Several days before His visit to Ciqomi, two of the elders of the Fijian village had come to make a traditional offering of kava* to Avatar Adi Da, approaching Him in the traditional manner, and inviting Him to Bless their village with His Presence. They addressed Him in Fijian as "Dau Loloma" (meaning "the Adept of Love"), recognizing Him as a holy man.

It was understood that, as part of Avatar Adi Da's visit, He would Bless the Christian church in the middle of the village. The church was roofed but open at the sides, and the only piece of furniture was a pulpit. After He was received in Ciqomi, Avatar Adi Da went to the church accompanied by some of His devotees and by one of the elders of the village, Solomone Finau (or "Solo", for short), who was guiding Him around the village.

---

* Kava is a slightly intoxicating drink used throughout the Pacific Island cultures as the central element in important ceremonial occasions and as a means of psychically contacting the spirit-world.

Solo asked if he could come and sit in the church with Dau Loloma. This gesture was deeply felt by Avatar Adi Da, and He invited Solo into the church to sit with Him. It was the first time in years that Avatar Adi Da had sat in a formal manner with someone who was not already His devotee. The fact that Solo, a native Fijian, had this spontaneous heart-response to Avatar Adi Da was a sign that the Divine Avatar's Work was moving out beyond its beginnings in the West.

Several devotees felt something exceptional about this silent occasion in the church, the sense that an extraordinary Spiritual event was occurring, and they expressed this intuition to Avatar Adi Da when He gathered with them later that evening. The hair stood up on the backs of their necks as Avatar Adi Da spoke of the new era in His Work that had begun that day.

AVATAR ADI DA SAMRAJ: I am here to Transform humankind, not to gather only a handful of people around Me. I have Come here for My own. I Am the Only Being for Whom every one is His own.

1984 has been proposed as the dreadful year by those infected by scientism. I am not here, however, to let My beloved in all his and her forms take on the size of death. I am here to change history. Can you imagine that? What an amusing notion! I am here in My physical Lifetime to change the course of human history. No one on Earth has this Mission, this Intention. No one! I am here to Do it and I am here to See it, and now I am going to call you on it. New Year, 1984. Now that I am in My Hermitage, let Me wait and see. Let Me see if all the Shining I have Done makes any difference.

We are going to wait. The purifying heat of that waiting could go on for decades, but I am committed to it. . . .

Mark My Words. We are entering into the deep place of human history. I have done My twelve years of Teaching-Work. Now I am going to see if you are alive—you four billion!

I am going to Do it. Mark My Words. Mark them. . . .

You are about to see God Move in your generation. Remember what I say tonight. In the years to come, remember My Move. This is the Mark I was born to make. This is the timing of it. This is it.

You have waited for the Great Motion of God. You have prayed for It. You have wished for the Divine Intervention. Now It begins. Watch It from now on.

The trouble in your own heart, your own body, your own feeling, your own resistance to Me, will be magnified.

Turn on the daily news every night and remember that you talked to Me about this. I will keep World War III from happening. I came at the beginning of World War II to keep you from getting involved in World War III. You prayed for this.

Mark My Words. All this is Prophecy. Listen to Me now. . . .

I am about to Save humankind. Do I sound crazy to you? I am going to Do it. I am about to make My Move, and the terror will pass. It will be much less terrible than it would have been otherwise. It is not My terror. If I did not Come, the Earth would be destroyed.

Now, you watch Me Move. I have Done My Meditation with a few, and I have Smoothed My "coins". I have Done My Work. I have suffered you. Now you watch Me. Mark My Words. . . .

Remember friendly old "Bubba"? Dead. Completely dead. Poor old "Bubba" is dead. The Sign of "Bubba" and the Sign of "Franklin" are all done, all dead. Now I Make only the Sign of Da. You are about to see me Do it.

Let everyone be relieved of the profoundly negative effects of their disaffection from Me. We are moving into a time when I will Make My Move. This is the beginning of it. Let us celebrate with full knowledge of the purification that is about to begin. Do not be self-conscious. Dance and be Happy. Practice the Way with great intensity. Submit to the profound ordeal of sadhana that will serve all of humanity—all four billion who know nothing of Me yet, and who must find Me out, who must find Me out.

I Am the One Who has been Expected. They must find Me out. They must. They must. Now let them find Me out. And let all of you, all My devotees all over the world, begin a dance that will purify humanity.

May all be Blessed. Blessed. Blessed. [December 30, 1983]

Avatar Adi Da had never spoken this kind of prophecy before. And He had never explicitly confessed that He was, indeed, the "Expected One", the Divine Intervention promised for the "dark" epoch of human history. In this setting—having found His Hermitage, and seeing the Fijian man's movement toward Him—Avatar Adi Da could not hold back. He proclaimed the real Work for which He had been born—His Work of Blessing the <u>entire</u> world.

The Dawn Horse Testament

The confession in "Mark My Words" was followed, in 1984, by another momentous event: Adi Da Samraj began to write His summary Divine Scripture, His Ultimate Instruction for all humankind.

From the early years of Avatar Adi Da's Teaching-Work, devotees had published collections of His Discourses, Essays, and practical Instructions, the sum of which already filled shelves. But Adi Da had not yet written a comprehensive summary of His entire Wisdom-Teaching, describing the entire course of the Way of Adidam. The time had not yet come for such a book, because He was still making His Wisdom-Teaching.

On June 24, 1984, Avatar Adi Da retired to His office at the Matrix (His principal residence at Adidam Samrajashram). He emerged at midnight with a message that devotees should come to the Matrix right away to hear the new Essay He had just written.

After He had read the Essay to everyone, He asked for questions, wanting to hear if there was anything people did not fully understand. The next day, He revised and expanded His Essay, taking into account all of the responses from the night before.

From that day on, Avatar Adi Da gathered every few days with devotees, to read aloud from His rapidly growing Text. What initially began as a short Instruction on meditative practice grew daily into a comprehensive summary of the entire process of the Way of Adidam.

During the writing of *The Dawn Horse Testament*, Avatar Adi Da wanted to make sure that all of His devotees—now established in a number of communities around the world—had access to copies of the current manuscript. He asked every day if anyone had further questions for Him. He would refine or add to the Text in response to questions that devotees had—even, in some cases, when the questions remained unspoken.

One devotee remarked to Avatar Adi Da that He seemed to be speaking not just with those on the island, but with devotees worldwide. Avatar Adi Da confirmed that this was so. He added that He was not, through this writing, speaking just to His formal devotees, but to everyone. He was having an "always Living Conversation" with every man and woman—"Meditating everyone, contacting everyone, dealing with psychic forces everywhere, in all time".

Zoe Sander, one of the editors, asked Avatar Adi Da about the sections on the ultimate stages of practice. She wondered with whom He was in conversation when He wrote those sections, since no one was as yet qualified to practice or understand those mysteries. Avatar Adi Da replied, "I am speaking to you, but at another time."

For the next nine months, Avatar Adi Da worked on the manuscript—until March 21, 1985, when He declared the book ready for publication. After considering the title during the many months of writing, Avatar Adi Da finally chose "The Dawn Horse Testament". The book was a "Testament" both in the sense of being His primary Scripture (as in the "Old and New Testaments"), and in the sense of being His bequest, or Spiritual Gift, to all (as in "last will and testament").

The Dawn Horse Vision

But why "Dawn Horse"?

In 1970, shortly before He went to Swami Muktananda's ashram for the third time, Avatar Adi Da experienced a waking vision. He found Himself in a subtle realm observing a Siddha-Master demonstrating the Yogic power of manifesting objects. After a time, although nothing had yet materialized, the Siddha's disciples departed, apparently satisfied that the mysterious work was done. Avatar Adi Da was left alone, standing before the Siddha. A mist then appeared with a form manifesting within it. As it took solid shape, Adi Da saw that it was a living and breathing horse, perhaps three feet high.

Later, Avatar Adi Da happened to see a television documentary on eohippus, the prehistoric ancestor of the horse. (In Greek, "eos" means "dawn" and "hippos" means "horse".) Feeling that the meaning of the name "eohippus" perfectly suited the significance of His vision, He named the horse of His vision the "Dawn Horse".

Avatar Adi Da explained that this vision was a sign of the future manifestation of His own Divine Work in the world. And so the Dawn Horse became a symbol for His Life and Work, the coinciding of the Divine Reality and the conditional worlds:

AVATAR ADI DA SAMRAJ: I was at once the Adept who performed the miracle of manifesting the horse, and also the one who was party to the observation of it and its result. And I did not have any feeling of being different from the horse itself. I was making the horse, I was observing the horse, and I was being the horse. [October 18, 1984]

The Media Crisis

In "Mark My Words", Avatar Adi Da said there would be resistance—both in the world and in His devotees—to the magnification of His Blessing-Work that had taken place since He arrived in Fiji. He made it clear at that time they could expect signs of resistance.

The crisis was not long in coming. Late in January 1985, a lawsuit was filed against Avatar Adi Da and members of the devotee community. A number of disaffected former devotees made accusations to the media about matters that catch media attention: sex, drugs, money, and coercion. Several major newspapers and a national television program carried the story for a day or two. Some of the reported events were fabricated—which the primary plaintiff of the lawsuit later acknowledged. In other cases, the allegations were distorted or else the sensational angle of what had occurred was overplayed for the media, failing to present the context of Avatar Adi Da's Teaching-Work.

An unconventional manner of Spiritual teaching may always arouse suspicion or negative reactions. This reaction is especially likely in our society, which is (at best) uninformed about the genuine Spiritual process. With no understanding of Spiritual matters, the contemporary media and mass culture lumps together serious and legitimate new religions with the many fanatical, pseudo-religious groups. The result is that all new (or non-mainstream) religious groups tend to be indiscriminately grouped under the generic heading of "cults".

Furthermore, because the tradition of Guru-devotion is little understood in the West, any Spiritual figure whose followers relate to him or her in a devotional manner is regarded as "weird" or worse. Having submitted to Work in the "Crazy" manner of submitting to the patterns of His devotees to teach them, Avatar Adi Da was vulnerable to the destructive reactions of those who could not understand the authentic Spiritual nature of His Work.

In 1985, Avatar Adi Da's devotees knew it was their responsibility to testify to the value of the Revelation they had witnessed in His Company. Some did, but their accounts were insufficient to stop the negative publicity at the time. Although the legal matter was settled quickly, the aftermath in the media was profoundly disturbing to Avatar Adi Da's devotees. Devotees tended to feel "caught" by the "gotcha" game of media scandal. Many felt that, in the face of the accusations printed in the press, they had failed to resort to their heart-relationship to Avatar Adi Da and forcefully advocate the sacred nature of His Work.

Avatar Adi Da Himself no longer lived in the United States, but, as soon as He heard of the lawsuit, He retired into seclusion at Adidam Samrajashram. The trust in His relationship to His devotees had been breached—devotees had reacted to the negative attention of the common world by shutting down in their feeling, and thereby limiting their ability to participate with Him in His Liberating Work.

Impasse

By the end of 1985, the media scandal had passed, but the effects of it had not. Despite the publication of *The Dawn Horse Testament* in late 1985, Avatar Adi Da felt His Work at an impasse. He saw no difference between the world and His devotees. They were simply representative of humanity in general and of the universal egoic impulse to self-satisfaction and self-protection.

Daniel Bouwmeester, one of the devotees who had been involved with Avatar Adi Da for a number of years in the "consideration" of renunciation, recalls a typical encounter of this time.

DANIEL: Beloved Adi Da was seated cross-legged on His bed asking (as He had done on numerous occasions) whether anyone felt qualified for real renunciation. Most people said, on this occasion, that they felt they did have the qualifications—a confession that would always lead to more testing.

When it came to me, I said no, I did not feel qualified. I am someone whom Beloved Adi Da refers to as the "guilty self-defeating type"—I just felt my inadequacy.

I remembered that Beloved Adi Da had once explained an alternative offered in the Spiritual traditions to the demanding sadhana of renunciation—the ordinary path of obeying religious laws, doing good works, and praying for a better (or Spiritually more auspicious) life next time. And so I said that this was my situation. I would do the best I could and pray for a better lifetime.

Beloved Adi Da bent forward toward me—He was only about six feet away—leaning on His hands with His arms straight. Now His face was right in my face and His eyes became huge. Then He roared at me, "THIS IS YOUR BETTER LIFETIME!"

I reeled back, knowing that He was right. He had already said that there are two ways to become qualified for renunciation: Either you are born with the qualifications or else you gain the necessary qualities through the devotional relationship to the Adept-Realizer who Transmits the capability. I had no doubt that, through the Spiritual relationship to Him, His Manly Qualities could be received and the great sadhana assumed. I was humbled to feel His Compassion, how hard He worked to get me to participate with Him in the sadhana. ∎

On October 4, 1985, the night that Avatar Adi Da was presented with the first publication of *The Dawn Horse Testament*, He spoke about the most significant and difficult transition in a human life—the movement beyond an egocentric existence to an ego-transcending life of devotional absorption in (and service to) the Divine.

AVATAR ADI DA SAMRAJ: You must go through the inevitable and natural crisis of the transition, and that is a profound matter. If it were not profound, most difficult, and something that people in general are not prepared for, human beings all over the world would have entered that stage of life by now. This crisis of transition is the most profound and unwelcome change that confronts humanity. That change has been unwelcome for thousands of years.

This Way of life that I have Given is not idealistic. It is realistic, and it is no longer My business to shoulder your responsibilities. I have Given you My Word, My Promise. My Work is evident to you in every day of your life. Therefore, you must give Me another word, another report, a different sound than the one I have received. You are in the most difficult position of adolescence—the position of being directly confronted by the Absolute Truth. You—more than anyone who might merely casually observe My Word and Promise and Presence—must exhibit the revolution of response to Me in your own body-mind. [October 4, 1985]

The day after He received *The Dawn Horse Testament*, in the evening, Avatar Adi Da called all His devotees at Adidam Samrajashram to His house to receive their copies of the book, which He passed out personally to each individual. When they looked inside, they could scarcely believe their eyes. Right at the beginning of the Prologue, just before the opening Words, "Here I Am", Avatar Adi Da had written "Dear _____," with the name of the devotee in His own handwriting. And so, in each case, His Message read, "Dear _____," Here I <u>Am</u>." Then, under the last Words of the Book, He had Written "Love, Da".

On a later occasion, Avatar Adi Da read aloud the entire prologue and chapter one, and, finally, the sublime epilogue, one of His most passionate and heartrending Confessions of His Love and His utter Submission to His devotees.

> *I <u>Am</u> The <u>One</u> and <u>True</u> Divine Heart-Master. I Take My Stand In The Heart Of My Devotee. I (Alone) <u>Am</u> The Mystery Of You and Me.*
>
> *How Could I Deny Heart-Vision To My Loved-One?*
> *How Could I Delay The Course Of My Beloved?*
> *Like An Intimate Family Servant, I Dearly Serve My Devotee.*
> *Like A Wealthy Friend, I Freely Give To My Devotee.*
> *Like A Mad Priest, I Even Worship My Devotee, With Love Itself.*
> *Like An Innocent Boy At First Love, I Would Awaken My Devotee In Radiant Chambers.*
> *Where The Wound Of Love Churns and Never Heals, I Wait, Longing To Celebrate The Brilliant Sight Of My Devotee.*
> *Come Slowly or Quickly—but Surely Come To Me.*
>
> [The Dawn Horse Testament Of The Ruchira Avatar]

At the end of Avatar Adi Da's reading of the epilogue (of which these words are only the beginning), no one could move, His Spiritual Descent was so "thick" in the room. *The Dawn Horse Testament* was the consummation of nearly fourteen years of the Divine Avatar's Work to Reveal Himself and His Divine Way to His devotees, and ultimately to all human beings. Its publication represented the completion of an era. And this proved to be literally so. In three months' time, everything would change.

Adidam Samrajashram, 1985

PART FOUR

The Divine Self-"Emergence"

1986–1998

Adidam Samrajashram, 1986

CHAPTER 13

A Grand Victory

Early in the morning of January 11, 1986, Avatar Adi Da Samraj was alone in His room, speaking over the phone to a small group of devotees in a nearby building. He was full of agony at the limitations in their response to Him, their failure to fully demonstrate their reception of the Gifts He had Given—for in that refusal lay the refusal of all humankind. He spoke of the grief He felt for beings everywhere. But the impasse was complete. He felt that His Work had failed, and that He could do no more in the body. His death, He felt, was imminent. He even said, "May it come quickly."

One devotee, Ruchiradama Quandra Sukhapur, ran to His house. She held Him up as He continued to speak on the phone. Avatar Adi Da described the life-force leaving His Body, the numbness coming up His arms. He said it seemed that His death was occurring even as He spoke.

He dropped the telephone.

In alarm and panic, the other devotees rushed over to His house to find Him collapsed by the side of His bed. His Body was still, with occasional shaking. His eyes were rolled up into His head, a sign that the energies of His Body had ascended out. There was no sign of any outer awareness.

The doctors were summoned to attend to Him and check His life-signs. They were able to detect faint vital signs, including barely perceptible breathing.

Devotees lifted Avatar Adi Da onto His bed. Some were weeping, others wailing, begging Him not to leave them. Others massaged His Body vigorously. Still others stood by or wandered in shock.

After several minutes, He made a slight gesture. Devotees pulled Him upward, supporting His torso. Suddenly, the life-force shot through His Body. His arms flung out in an arc, and His Body straightened. Tears began to flow from His eyes, as He rocked forward and backward in an anguished rhythm. He reached out His hands, as though to touch everyone in a universal embrace. In a voice choked with passion, He whispered, "Four billion people! The four billion!"

"I Have Accomplished Your State Completely"

Later that day, Avatar Adi Da left the village of devotees to return to His residence on the other side of the island. As He sat in the back of the Land Cruiser for the bumpy ride through the broad grasslands and coconut groves, Adi Da spoke to Greg Purnell, the devotee who was driving Him.

GREG: Avatar Adi Da normally sat in the front of the car and was most often silent. But on this day, He sat with devotees in the back seat, right behind me. He began talking to me right away, saying things like, "Do you know that I think of you constantly? Do you know that I also think of your intimate partner constantly? Do you think of Me constantly?" He continued like this for five minutes or so, giving me every reassurance of His Love for me. I responded, "Yes, Master," to each question. But I was feeling more and more self-conscious.

He asked me again and again, "Do you know how much I Love you? Do you really know how much I Love you?" I continued to say, "Yes, Master", knowing full well that I didn't—and even couldn't, in my limited perception—know the full extent of His Great Love.

When we came to a cattle-crossing gate, I had to get out to open it. I stepped out of the car and shut the door. At that moment,

Avatar Adi Da asked me once again, "Do you really know how much I Love you?" I was faced with a choice. I could ignore the question, pretending I had not heard, and simply open the gate for Him (which is what I would have done by tendency). Or I could face my Beloved and answer Him. In my heart, I wanted to face the Great One. Even so, it took all I had to stick my head back inside the car and look at Him face-to-face.

The Vision I saw was glorious, attractive, and fierce. Everything and everyone else in the car disappeared from my awareness as I was filled with the Vision of Him. I saw His huge head, His intense eyes—and His smile that proved to me He already knew and Loved me. His face was no more than two feet from my eyes.

I was lost in that special intensity that surrounds the physical Person of Beloved Adi Da. I wanted only to be completely honest with Him and let all expectations and fears go. I said, "No, not really."

His expression relaxed a bit. He said, "This was a test—and you failed!"

At that, my heart opened like the shutter of a camera, and His face was permanently imprinted there. For many weeks afterward, I saw that face constantly, especially in meditation. In that moment, the image of Beloved Adi Da was set in my heart for me to carry and worship forever. ■

Several times, on that drive, Avatar Adi Da said to Greg and to the other devotees with Him, "I have a Secret."

After two weeks in seclusion, Adi Da Samraj gathered once more with devotees. Now He Revealed His Secret: That day, January 11, 1986, was His true Birth Day, a day more auspicious than any other in His human Lifetime—more profound, even, than His Divine Re-Awakening. He began to explain why.

The preceding fourteen years of His Teaching-Work had been a Submission to the needs and sufferings of His devotees. He had Worked in the "Crazy" manner, by apparently identifying with their egoic impulses, to make lessons and Wisdom out of every circumstance. That great period of His Work was now over, He explained. Now all of the lessons of His Submission, all the Instruction that belonged to that era, had been Given. Indeed, the particular Divine

Siddhi that enabled Him to do His Liberating Work in that fashion had receded. It was replaced, He said, by a universally magnified Siddhi of Divine Blessing.

Avatar Adi Da described how, during the Yogic Swoon of January 11, He, the Divine Person, had fully Descended into His own human vehicle. This was a very different event from His Divine Re-Awakening in the Vedanta Temple in 1970. In that event, Adi Da had re-Found His Native Divine Condition—the "Bright"— Which had been veiled since His early childhood. This "veiling" had allowed Him to learn the process required for human beings to Awaken to the "Bright".

After His Divine Re-Awakening, He Submitted His Body-Mind to the sufferings of His devotees. He had literally taken on human karma and "eaten" it in His own Body-Mind. Now, as the culmination of that complete embrace of the human condition for all those years, the Fullness of His Divine Condition had descended all the way down into His Body, "to the toes", combining with His human Form entirely.

AVATAR ADI DA SAMRAJ: In this Great Event, I was drawn further into the Body by a very human impulse, a love-impulse. Becoming aware of My profound relationship with all My devotees, I resumed My bodily human state. Even though I have, obviously, existed as a human being during My physical Lifetime, becoming profoundly Incarnate, I now assumed an impulse toward human existence more profound than I had assumed before—without any reluctance relative to sorrow and death.

On so many occasions, I have Told you that I wish I could Kiss every human being on the lips, Embrace each one, and Enliven each one from the heart. In this Body, I will never have the opportunity. I am frustrated in that Impulse. But in that Motion of sympathetic Incarnation, that Acceptance of the body and its sorrow and its death, I Realized a Kiss, a Way to Fulfill the Impulse.

To Me, this is a Grand Victory! I do not know how to Communicate to you the significance of It. It seems that, through that will-less, effortless integration with suffering, something about My Work is more profoundly accomplished, something about It has become more auspicious than It ever was. I have not dissociated from My Divine Realization or My Divine State. Rather, I have accomplished <u>your</u> state completely, even more profoundly than you are sensitive to it. Perhaps you have seen it in My face. I have <u>become</u> this Body, utterly. Now I Am the "Murti",* the Icon, and It is Full of My Divine Presence. [January 27, 1986]

Thus, at the moment of His deepest despair, the Incarnation of Avatar Adi Da Samraj had achieved ultimate depth. Avatar Adi Da came to describe this Event as the Yogic Establishment of His "Avataric Divine Self-'Emergence'". To Him, it was the most important moment in His Life since His birth—His full "Emergence" into His human Body, and (thereby) into the world altogether.

The years that would follow Avatar Adi Da's Divine Self-"Emergence" would be quite different from the first fourteen years of His Teaching-Work (1972-1985). For the next period of fourteen years (1986-1999), Avatar Adi Da would struggle to "shed" His Work of Submission to devotees, but it would prove a gradual process. Although He continued to give Instruction, He was no longer primarily functioning as Teacher in relation to His devotees. He was making His full Avataric Divine Self-Revelation, and (simultaneously) establishing the means for beings everywhere to recognize Him and respond to Him as the Divine Person. This span of years, the second great period of Adi Da's Avataric Divine Work, would hold even greater Revelations—and even more difficult trials and crises—than everything that occurred to that point in His Life.

The Demand for True and Free Renunciation

After January 11, a new Siddhi magnified tremendously in Avatar Adi Da—the Siddhi of renunciation. He Himself had always been the perfect renunciate, neither clinging to conditional existence nor shunning it. But His devotees had not yet

---

* "Murti" is the term traditionally used in India for a representation of the Divine. In the Way of Adidam, "Murti" most commonly refers to a photographic representation of Avatar Adi Da.

awakened to the renunciate disposition He was Calling them to. Now there was a Force alive in Him that confronted their resistance as never before. Avatar Adi Da Samraj had become an all-consuming Divine Fire.

AVATAR ADI DA SAMRAJ: You are always looking to be happy. What you call "happy" is not what I call "Happy". What you call "happy" is a superficial, amused, immune state. All of us here are dying, and you must Realize the Source of existence. To do that, to Realize that Sublimity, you must understand yourself and transcend yourself, and that means you cannot make life out of being consoled by sex, the world, the news, the pleasures of life, technology—anything. You must be free of consolation. You must be unconsolable, beyond repair of the heart. That is not what you are involved in. You are full of complaints, imaginings, agreements, rules, ideals. I cannot relate to it. I am bereft of those possibilities, empty of them. I cannot be consoled. Real God is not a consolation. Real God is What you Realize in the unconsolable state. Real God is the Obvious when the self-contraction is released.

You must be a renunciate to practice this Way that I Teach. You all have too much to lose, too much you depend on for consolation, too much bullshit you need to share with one another. I am glad I could Interfere with you. [January 27, 1986]

This fiery Discourse was a sign of things to come. Avatar Adi Da would no longer "bend" toward His devotees. He intended to "Stand Firm" and require their response.

His Call for renunciation initiated a crisis in all His devotees. But this crisis carried particular force for the circle of women devotees who had served Him most closely for many years. Remarkable as their sadhana had been, Avatar Adi Da's circle of intimate women devotees had not entirely transcended the tendency to relate to Him on an egoic basis—seeking self-fulfillment, rather than relating to Him as renunciates one-pointedly invested in the process of Divine Self-Realization. In the early months of 1986, Adi Da Samraj took His circle of women intimates through an intensive "consideration" of the change that had occurred in Him. Avatar Adi

Da was immediately requiring of them the true and free renunciation that He had for years been Calling them (and others) to understand and embrace. In the end, four of the women were able to make this confession.

Late in February 1986, Avatar Adi Da began to fast, taking only water and fresh juices. In April, He assumed sannyas, or formal renunciation (including celibacy). He took a sannyasin name, "Swami Da Love-Ananda". "Love-Ananda" (literally "Love-Bliss") was a Name that Swami Muktananda had privately given to Him in 1969 (around the same time that the letter of acknowledgement was written, as described on pp. 34-35). But Adi Da had never used it. "Love-Ananda" crossed the boundaries of East and West, in its combination of the English "Love" with the Sanskrit "Ananda" ("Bliss"). Now, after January 11, the Name "Love-Ananda" was the perfect description of His Divine Being—communicating both the "Love" that had brought Him back into the world, and the "Bliss" ("Ananda") of His own "Bright" Condition (Which was the Gift He had Come to Offer to all).

Having spontaneously decided to assume this traditional mode of renunciation, Avatar Adi Da did it completely. His discipline was more than extraordinary. He continued His juice fast, eating no solid food for over four months, until the middle of July. He slept little, arising early in the morning to sit in meditation from 4:00 A.M. to 6:00 A.M. with His sannyasin devotees and others. And His clothing, in the traditional sannyasin's color of fiery orange, was a constant sign of His intense renunciation.

In mid-May, He left Fiji for California, accompanied by a small group whom He had Initiated into sannyas.

Bill Stranger describes the moment:

BILL: When we had all gathered at the Mountain Of Attention, we learned that Beloved Adi Da was now Calling all those in leadership positions in Adidam to immediately adopt certain renunciate disciplines. In particular, He was asking us to be celibate (while remaining in our intimacies) and to eat a purifying and rejuvenating diet consisting entirely of raw foods.

My friends and I first greeted our Beloved Guru's new Calling with dismay. At the Mountain Of Attention Sanctuary, the weather often communicates the Living Being of Avatar Adi Da and what He is feeling from His devotees. And so, as we complained in our quarters, unseasonable winds whipped up the placid May sky. I knew that our Guru was feeling our refusal.

Although nothing of our disposition had been reported to Avatar Adi Da, He sent us a Communication that reflected His perfect knowledge of our mood. His Criticisms were so Empowered, however, that our resistance, which only that morning had seemed insurmountable, melted into thin air. We now told Him that we accepted His Divine Call.

Our reward came amazingly fast: Around midnight, we were all called to listen to recitations of Beloved Adi Da's newly written Essays about the "Perfect Practice" of Adidam. I presumed that this late-night event would be difficult and uncomfortable. Beloved Adi Da's writings about the ultimate stages of Adidam did not seem to have much to do with the likes of us, who were still struggling to fulfill the beginning stages of Adidam. Or so I thought.

It had been a long, eventful day and people were tired. Many began to nod out as the Instructions were read, covering at first the disciplines of celibacy and of diet. But now we were coming to Beloved Adi Da's Instruction about the Radiant Feeling of Being, deeply felt in the right side of the heart.

To my utter astonishment, I understood every word Adi Da had written! It was far more than mental comprehension. I experienced the Very Reality that Beloved Adi Da was describing in His Essay. I felt Him as the Current of the Feeling of Being Emanating from the right side of my heart, like a chain rising vertically from the floor of a pool. I knew with absolute certainty that I _am_ Consciousness Itself, not bound to the body-mind. Then, as I beheld Beloved Adi Da's photographic Murti, I realized that He is perpetually Conscious as my very Self. He is Real God, Consciousness Itself. I knew this to be true.

In the days ahead, this awareness remained available. I would sit down to meditate and quickly relax into the Bliss of Consciousness Itself. Neither my body nor my mind seemed the least obstruction any longer. I enjoyed a freedom and delight that I would not have dared to presume on my own. It was obvious that this had nothing to do with my own effort or qualifications. It was the Gift of Avatar Adi Da, released into the world through the immense Power of His Divine Self-"Emergence". ∎

Two New Core Texts

In the months after January 11, 1986, Avatar Adi Da composed two new books—core Texts, both of which are indispensable "Companions" of *The Dawn Horse Testament*.

The Lion Sutra (originally entitled *Love-Ananda Gita*) is His beautifully poetic Instruction relative to the "Perfect Practice" of the Way of Adidam—the practice of Self-Abiding as Consciousness Itself, no longer identified with body or mind or world. *Santosha Adidam* (originally entitled *The Da Upanishad*) is His description of the esoteric structural "anatomy" of the human being, and His explanation of how that "anatomy" determines the necessary course of practice, from the beginnings to Divine Enlightenment. Both books strongly communicate His Call to true and free renunciation.

On May 18, soon after His arrival at the Mountain Of Attention, Avatar Adi Da Himself read the entire 540 verses of *The Lion Sutra* to a large assembly of His devotees.

<u>No</u> "object" is Worthy of wanting need.
<u>No</u> Search is Fruitful.
<u>No</u> Pain is Necessary.
<u>No</u> "other" is Worthy of futile Seeking-desire and inevitable emptiness.
<u>Neither</u> attachment <u>Nor</u> avoidance is Right.
<u>No</u> sorrow is Necessary.
<u>No</u> "thing" is <u>More</u> Than Wonderful.
<u>Neither</u> bewilderment <u>Nor</u> knowledge <u>is</u> Free. . . .

**The Mountain Of Attention Sanctuary
May 18, 1986**

Therefore, I Say, Come To Rest (or <u>Be</u> Awake), <u>Before</u> "things" Happen.

Come To Rest (or <u>Be</u> Awake), <u>Prior</u> To the Motion of separation and relatedness.

Come To Rest (or <u>Be</u> Awake), Already Forever Arrived In My Eternal Hermitage. . . .

My <u>Eternal</u> "Blessing-Seat" Is the Heart Itself—Which <u>Is</u> the One and Only and Inherently Indivisible Conscious Light (Itself).

Soon after He arrived at the Mountain Of Attention, Avatar Adi Da made a remarkable offering: Any member of the public who had a serious desire to see Him could come to the Mountain Of Attention for special occasions of His Darshan. His devotees set up a huge white tent to receive the numbers who came flocking to see Him over the next several weeks. This open offering was a sign of His Blessing-Impulse and His expanding world-Work.

During the Darshan occasions in the tent, devotees were stunned by the sight of their Beloved Master—His eyes burning in their sockets, His now frail-looking Body Transfigured in His Love-Bliss. The devotee children, too, were overwhelmed. One of them, Jonah Straus, age 11, wrote about what he felt:

JONAH: On Sunday I was Graced with a wonderful Gift. Beloved Da Love-Ananda came in as if He was just teleported or flown there. He just appeared in the aisle. He went up to His chair and put His staff in the holder. He sat down and He started looking at everybody, and almost immediately He was showing His Bliss. He had a smile on His face when He looked over at the children. He would look over at everyone else with a wide-eyed glance and then He would look at us and He would smile. He was just lost in Happiness, and I cried every time He would cry. He would look over at me, tears would go down His face, a tear would go down my face. Then He would look at someone else.

When I am with Him, I can't put my attention on anything else. Why should I want to look at anything else? What else is interesting in the room? I don't know how many times I cried. I was in bliss. ■

The Mountain Of Attention Sanctuary, 1986

An Ascetic on Fire

In the middle of June, Avatar Adi Da explained to devotees His journey out of Hermitage and His undertaking of a world Yajna.*

AVATAR ADI DA SAMRAJ: The world is on a pivot of history. The future of the next several decades can become a colossal terror of disorder. Now that My Teaching-Work is done, My Purpose in Blessing all and Calling all to practice in My Company is to have an historical impact on a large scale, so that the current karmic trend of history can be sufficiently purified to allow this pivotal period to have an auspicious result.

The world is currently in the grip of self-deluded and vulgar forces. The Spiritual Truth and the Way of Truth and the Real Teacher of Truth are everywhere defamed and in doubt. This situation must change, and to change it is what I am here to do. But the situation will not change if people will not come into My Company, if people will not rightly use My Company, and if people will not seriously respond to My Company and will not devote themselves to the worldwide advocacy of My Company.

My intention is to travel the world in silence and to make Myself available to all who are rightly responsive to Me. I may periodically return to Hermitage and rest for awhile and associate with those on retreat there, but My basic intention from now on is to wander and to Bless all who come to Me and even all who do not come to Me, until I am heard and seen and the current trend of history is reversed. [June 14, 1986]

On June 22, 1986, Avatar Adi Da left California and traveled to New York. As He walked the streets of New York after so long away, He remarked to devotees that the intensity of His Sadhana during His years at Columbia had been similar to that of traditional sadhus meditating in jungles full of wild beasts. New York

---

* "Yajna" is Sanskrit for "sacrifice". In the Way of Adidam, the term "Yajna" is specifically used to refer to Avatar Adi Da's occasional travels, during which He Blesses the world and all beings through His contact with many people and places.

had been a goad to His Divine Re-Awakening. He returned to it now in His mode of doing penance—including enduring the casual mockery He sometimes encountered as He moved through the city in orange sannyasin clothing.

On June 27, He moved on to Europe—to England, France, and Holland—making a pilgrimage to places of religious significance in the West: Stonehenge, Westminster Abbey in London, Sacré Coeur in Paris. Devotees could feel that, by spending time in these places, He was contacting the deep Spiritual impulses of people everywhere, realizing some aspect of His desire to "Kiss" all the inhabitants of Earth.

Altogether, Avatar Adi Da's 1986 Yajna was a great act of Divine Penance for the sake of all human beings.

AVATAR ADI DA SAMRAJ: For some period after the Yogic Establishment of My Avataric Divine Self-"Emergence", the qualities shown through this Body were signs of tapas, or penance—heat in the Body, burning up, purifying. It was a purification, but not of personal karmas associated with Me. I, Myself, am not a karmic personality. Rather, I used the mechanisms of the Body-Mind in such a way that I took on the likeness of everyone, and established a Link with all beings. And so the karma that was overcome in this Body is all karma. All karma has been overcome in Me.

But this does not mean that, because of My act of Submission, something has occurred in the world such that now everybody is going to become Enlightened spontaneously. No, it means that the sadhana I Give you has become your opportunity, a unique Graceful opportunity. The relationship to Me—the One Who has Incarnated and Done this great Teaching-Work—is now the Circumstance in which Divine Liberation can take place in you, through My unique Gift.

What I have Done is quite different from just giving you a Teaching and now you "work out your own salvation", so to speak. Rather, a unique relationship, a unique vehicle, in which the karmas of all have been transcended, has become available for your Contemplation, your Guidance. [August 15, 1988]

The End of Traditional Sannyas

The Yajna in Europe proved exceptionally difficult. Every detail of travel and accommodation tended to run aground. Simultaneously, the devotees who had taken sannyas were struggling to maintain their renunciate practice.

Avatar Adi Da had made it clear that, in the Way of Adidam, sannyas requires the capability of the "Perfect Practice", the ability to relinquish identification with the body-mind and rest freely in the position of Consciousness, Identifying with Avatar Adi Da's "Bright" Divine Self-Condition. As Bill Stranger described, this capability had spontaneously awakened in devotees during the first weeks of Adi Da's sannyas. But as that story also indicated, the capability for the "Perfect Practice" was, in this instance, an "undeserved" Grace, freely Given by Avatar Adi Da. Whether or not devotees would be able to sustain the Gift they had received was the question. In Europe, it became clear that the sannyasin devotees were not demonstrating the capability to sustain the depth of renunciate practice required by their sannyas. Taking all of this into account, Avatar Adi Da Himself relinquished the outward signs of sannyas, and instructed the small group of devotees who had been initiated into sannyas to do likewise.

On July 21, Avatar Adi Da consented to grant formal Darshan to His Dutch and English devotees at a former Catholic monastery in the village of Maria Hoop (pronounced "hope") in southern Holland. Now clad in indigo (rather than orange), He sat in silent Darshan in the former chapel of the monastery. He also spoke to everyone. The group was mostly new devotees, many of whom had never seen Him before. Avatar Adi Da told stories, both humorous and serious, of His adventures on the Yajna, even responding to the same kind of beginner's questions that He had addressed throughout His years of Teaching at the Mountain Of Attention.

Adi Da Samraj speaking to devotees at Maria Hoop, Holland, July 1986

From the very beginning of the Yajna, Avatar Adi Da had expressed that His impulse was to wander throughout the world, going wherever He was moved to go, doing the world-Blessing-Work that He had been Born to do. But the small gathering of devotees was not equipped to support the kind of travel necessary for His world-Blessing-Work. It was not to be.

On August 2, Adi Da Samraj returned to Fiji.

Adidam Samrajashram, 1990

CHAPTER 14

THE YOGA OF DEVOTION

In March of 1986, Avatar Adi Da began to describe how the devotional relationship to Him had become even more potent, even more direct and simple, since His Avataric Divine Self-"Emergence". Satsang with Him was still the core practice, but His Descent "to the toes" of His own Body-Mind greatly magnified the potency of His Spiritual Gifts. Now, to gaze at His bodily Form (even via a photograph) was, literally, to see the Divine in the most powerful manner possible.

Avatar Adi Da spoke of Satsang using a newly coined term: "Ishta-Guru Bhakti Yoga". "Ishta-Guru" means "the Guru who is one's Chosen Beloved (Ishta)". "Bhakti Yoga" means the "practice (Yoga) of devotion (Bhakti)".

AVATAR ADI DA SAMRAJ: The relationship between the devotee and the Guru is a unique relationship and an extraordinary Yoga. I call it "Ishta-Guru Bhakti Yoga". In this great Yoga, the Guru is embraced as what is traditionally called the "Ishta-Guru", the "Chosen" Form of the Divine Reality, Appearing as the Guru. It is the Yoga of allowing the Ishta-Guru to be the Divine Form, in meditation and in moment to moment practice. The devotee is devoted to that bodily Form, that Being, that Person, that Transmitting Power. The Divine Person, in other words, is acknowledged by the devotee in the Form of the Guru.

You use My Image, then, not only in the form of My Murti in the Communion Hall but in the form of your recollection of Me. You "put on" the Ishta-Guru. You let the Ishta-Guru Acquire and Be your own body-mind. In this way, My Divine Spirit-Power Works in your body-mind as if it were My Body-Mind. All the processes of sadhana in the Way of Adidam will take place spontaneously. You will respond to them, participate in them, but they will be generated spontaneously by My Spiritual Transmission.

In feeling-Contemplation of Me, everything is Realized by My Grace—not by your effortful working on yourself, but by your simple recognition-response to the One Who is before you.

Give your separate and separative self to Me. Respond to Me As the Divine Self Incarnate. You cannot help but respond to Me if you recognize Me As That One. Then, the Very State of That One will be Realized by you, quite naturally, as a Gift. This is the Secret of the Way of Adidam. [March 22, 1986]

Feeling-Contemplation

Throughout His Divine-Self-"Emergence" Years, Avatar Adi Da continued to Reveal more and more about the fundamental practice of devotion to Him.

In mid-October 1988, Avatar Adi Da had just returned to His Hermitage Ashram in Fiji, having spent a few months seeing devotees in New Zealand, California, and Hawaii. The morning after His arrival, while Avatar Adi Da still lay in a dream state, the verses of a new sacred Text occurred to Him. He wrote them down immediately upon awakening. These verses became the beginning of the *Da Love-Ananda Gita*. In this Text, He describes Satsang as "feeling-Contemplation" of Him. In other words, the practice of devotion is, in its essence, a matter of contemplating Him with profound feeling. And to contemplate Him, He explains, is a progressive practice, relating to all three of the Great Forms of His Divine Being—starting with devotional contemplation of His bodily Form, and more and more growing to include Spiritually Awakened contemplation of His Divine Presence and His Divine State.

The Yoga of Devotion

"There is a great Law," He often said. "You become what you meditate on." By meditating on His bodily Form (and His Presence and State), His devotees participate in (and, ultimately, Realize) His "Bright" Divine Self-Condition.

> You (necessarily) become (or conform to the likeness of) whatever you Behold, or Contemplate, or Meditate on, or Even think about.
> Therefore, My formally fully established true devotee, by-Me-Spiritually-Initiated (and always newly by-Me-Spiritually-Activated), should always (searchlessly) Behold Me, and always actively (responsively) Contemplate Me, and always transcend even all thought by Meditating on Me.
> —Avatar Adi Da Samraj
> *Da Love-Ananda Gita*

The *Da Love-Ananda Gita* marked a new phase in Avatar Adi Da's Work. He invited devotees from all over the world to come on meditation retreat at Adidam Samrajashram. These retreats specifically focused on the Instruction in the *Da Love-Ananda Gita*.

On retreat in the Company of Avatar Adi Da Samraj at Adidam Samrajashram, 1989

Until this time, Naitauba had been a private Hermitage, and only a few devotees had lived or visited there. Now Avatar Adi Da wanted all His devotees to be able to drop out of their daily lives from time to time and come to Adidam Samrajashram for meditation retreat, receiving His Darshan in the unique purity of His remote Hermitage. Facilities were built to handle a continuous stream of devotee retreatants, and they immediately began to come from all over the world.

A retreatant who came to Adidam Samrajashram, Deborah Fremont-Smith, captured the feeling of what it was like to enter into Avatar Adi Da's most intimate sphere to receive His silent Darshan. ("Owl Sandwiches", referred to below, is a Fijian-style building, with reed walls and a thatched roof—one of the buildings at the Matrix, Avatar Adi Da's principal residence at Adidam Samrajashram.)

DEBORAH: Beloved Adi Da Samraj Gave His Darshan today in Owl Sandwiches. I would like everything etched in my heart forever. The Matrix is that Sublime Place that shimmers not only with sunlight—which is incredible in the South Pacific—but with the great Siddhi of Adi Da Samraj. It is a place of absolute peace that calms the mind and awakens the heart. Stillness and light pervade everything, for the Heart has remade this place. It is now the Divine Domain, the Place of Origin, the Matrix from which the Blessing of the Heart-Guru flows out to the world.

We walked across the expanse of lawn and waited until we were given the signal to approach. Then, one by one, we climbed the narrow steps.

The building was immaculate and bright, as if each reed had been consciously chosen and consciously placed. One by one, we passed through the low door into a small foyer. Beyond was another small room, and in this room the Divine Being Incarnate sat in His Chair facing out, and so facing each of us as we entered.

I was aware as soon as I crossed the threshold that I had stepped into a Shrine where the Living Icon Breathes. And there He sat. My heart rose up at the sight of Him: "This is the Treasure of the whole world." I stood and waited as each retreatant entered the room, laid a gift at His Precious Feet, and did a full prostration.

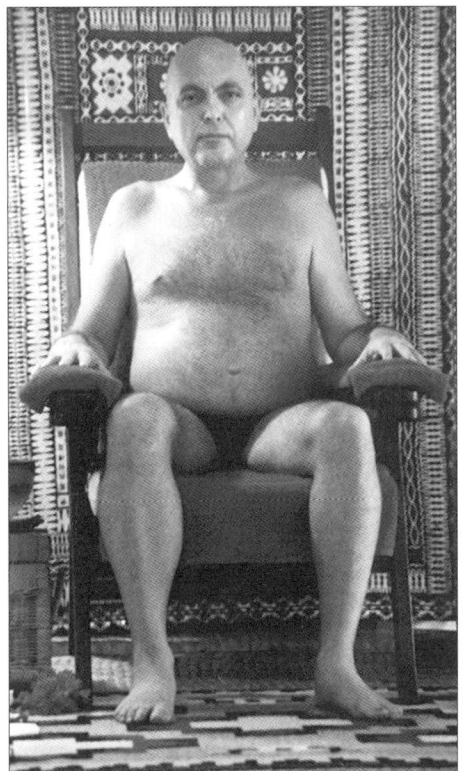

Darshan at Owl Sandwiches,
Adidam Samrajashram, 1989

The eyes of Beloved Adi Da were round and luminous, and His Body perfectly still, as He gazed outward with such an expression of vulnerability and sweetness that I was once again struck (as forcibly as when I first saw Him in 1976) that this is not a man, not a human being at all. This is the Formless Divine, Suspended for an instant in time and space—the Self-Radiant Divine Being caught for a moment in human Form. It was a breath-taking Vision. I felt how I want nothing more than to see Him rightly honored and protected—this naked Heart of Man, the True Self of all beings.

Then it was my turn to go forward and offer my gift. I walked into the inner room, which was "Bright" with the Glory of Him. The space was full of Silence. Ruchiradama Quandra Sukhapur and Ruchiradama Nadikanta, dressed in formal white, sat to each side of Him. They were as immobile as He—their attention entirely turned to the Person of Love before them. I was walking into a sacred space, like the space depicted in ancient religious paintings. Regarding Beloved Adi Da's beautiful and compassionate face, I became lost in its depths. His Sublime Look—full of Bliss and, yet, also full of pain at the suffering He beholds in everyone—seemed to encompass me and all beings in the same moment. I raised up my hands in adoration of Him and looked into His eyes. My heart was wrung with the vision of Him, remembering His Words, "In This Swoon Of Love, Your Heart May See My Bliss-Wounded Face."

As I placed my gift to the right of His chair, my eyes met another glorious sight, another beholding. Ruchiradama Nadikanta was seated no more than a foot from me. Her attention fully rested on Beloved Adi Da and she was fanning Him. Her unwavering devotion to Him was reflecting His Divine Light as the moon reflects the sun. My heart thrilled to see this—and, as I saw it, I also perceived something else. I understood that Beloved Adi Da breathes devotion as we breathe air. Devotion is His atmosphere.

After about twenty minutes, Beloved Adi Da signaled with the barest movement of His hand that the Darshan was over. Then Ruchiradama Quandra Sukhapur took up the basket of Prasad, or Blessed sweets, and carefully placed a sweet in the hands of each devotee. Her heart-Contemplation of Beloved Adi Da was so profound that, as her hand touched mine, I felt a direct Transmission of Grace and Blessing moving through her from Him. I bowed in gratitude as I left Owl Sandwiches, my heart filled with Peace and the Vision of Real God, Which is finally unutterable. ∎

These retreats established a pattern that Avatar Adi Da later formalized: Once a beginning devotee has adapted to the basic practices and disciplines of the Way of Adidam, he or she comes on retreat to receive Avatar Adi Da's Spiritual Transmission directly, in occasions of Darshan. This face to face reception of Avatar Adi Da's Spiritual Blessing is what Initiates each devotee into a truly Spiritual relationship to Him and into truly Spiritual practice of the Way He has Given.

Surrender of the Four Faculties

Some years later, in November 1993, Avatar Adi Da initiated a five-month series of gatherings at Adidam Samrajashram. In the Discourses of this gathering period, He elaborated greatly on the exact technical nature of the practice of devotion to Him. He pointed out that the human being is made up of four principal faculties: body, emotion, mind, and breath. As He says in *The Dawn Horse Testament*, "Taken All Together, The Four Principal Faculties Of the body-mind Account For <u>All</u> human Functions."

Therefore, for a human being to practice devotion to Avatar Adi Da (or Ishta-Guru Bhakti Yoga) means that the individual must exercise devotion via all four of these principal faculties. When that is done, then one's entire being is involved in the practice of devotion.

In His Discourses, Avatar Adi Da went on to describe what it means to exercise devotion to Him via the body, via emotion, via the mind, and via the breath. These Discourses are a great treasure of Instruction—centered in His fundamental Admonition to stop struggling with our experience (in body, emotion, mind, and breath), whatever that experience may be, and, instead, turn the faculties (of body, emotion, mind, and breath) to Him.

In this passage, adapted from a Discourse Given in 1993, Avatar Adi Da describes the devotional surrender of the faculty of mind.

When things arise in mind—Instead Of Struggling With them, Trying To Get Rid Of them, Trying To Surrender them—Simply Give Me Your attention (or The Core Of Your mind). Do Not Try To Get Rid Of the content, or Try To Surrender the content To Me, or Try To Surrender the content In Order To Get To Me. Simply Turn attention itself To Me. No Effort Is Required. You Need Not Struggle With the mind-forms. In Your Simple Turning To Me, You Disregard what is arising in mind. You Turn attention To Me, and Forget About mind. You Do Not Try To Make Something Happen In the mind, Nor Do You Try To Surrender the mind By Surrendering its content To Me. You Surrender The <u>Function</u> Of mind By Turning Your attention To Me.

—Avatar Adi Da Samraj
The Dawn Horse Testament
Of The Ruchira Avatar

A few years after the gatherings of 1993-1994, devotees suggested to Avatar Adi Da that an appropriate synonym for "Ishta-Guru Bhakti Yoga" would be "Ruchira Avatara Bhakti Yoga" (meaning "the practice of devotion to the Ruchira Avatar, Adi Da Samraj"). He accepted the suggestion, and designated this reference as the principal term to be used for the core practice of Adidam.

Letting the Four Faculties Melt

In March 1997, Avatar Adi Da was once again residing on the island of Kauai in Hawaii. He had been writing for some time without showing the manuscript to anyone. Finally, on March 29, He passed on an extraordinary new Text, *Hridaya Rosary: Four Thorns Of Heart-Instruction*. ("Hridaya Rosary" means "the Rose Garden of the Heart". "Hridaya" is Sanskrit for "heart", and the original ancient meaning of "rosary" is "rose garden".) In this beautifully poetic Text, Avatar Adi Da reveals what the practice of Ruchira Avatara Bhakti Yoga becomes once the devotee is Spiritually Awakened to Him and fully capable of receiving His Spiritual Transmission. Here He speaks of allowing the faculties (referred to as "heart", "head", "total body", and "breathing") to "Melt", such that the devotee's apparent separateness dissolves in the Bliss of receiving Avatar Adi Da's Spiritual Baptism. This "Melting" is magnified by the disposition of remaining "upwardly open" to Avatar Adi Da's downward-flowing Spiritual Infusion.

> Let the heart Melt Into
> My Heart, Which Is
> The By-Me-Spiritually-Revealed
> "Bright" Rose Garden Of Love.
>
> Let the head Melt Into
> My Head,
> Which Is
> The By-Me-Spiritually-Revealed

"Bright" Rose
Of Infinitely Ascended
Bliss-Light.

Let the Total body Melt Into
My Divine Spiritual Body,
Which Is
The By-Me-Spiritually-Revealed
Garden Air,
The Fragrant
all-and-All-Surrounding,
and all-and-All-Pervading,
Space
Of Equanimity,
Of Pleasure,
Of Delight,
Of Beauty,
Of Joy,
Of Love-Bliss,
Of "Brightness"
Itself.

Let the breathing Melt Into
My Breathing,
Until I Breathe you
Into My
"Bright"
Eternal
Palace
and
Domain
Of
Perfect Happiness.

—Avatar Adi Da Samraj
Hridaya Rosary

In April 1997, on the occasion of the twenty-fifth anniversary of the opening of the Melrose Ashram, Avatar Adi Da Initiated hundreds of people at a time into the practice He describes in *Hridaya Rosary*. (In those 1997 sittings, Avatar Adi Da was freely Giving His "Four Thorns" Gift to all His devotees who came to receive His Darshan. Since then, however, He has established that this form of the practice of Adidam is to be engaged only by those devotees with significant Spiritual maturity, once the individual has been formally Spiritually Initiated by Avatar Adi Da and has also been formally acknowledged as demonstrating most fundamental understanding of the self-contraction.)

Dina Lautman, who was on retreat at the time at the Mountain Of Attention, gives an account of a Darshan occasion.

DINA: As soon as I sat down, I felt Beloved Adi Da's Presence penetrating me from above my head and down to the toes. Everything in between Him and me was melted. The head opened, and became a soft and sensory organ, a feeling means to receive His Love-Blissful Transmission. Then I began to sense Him everywhere in the room, Surrounding and in-Filling all. It was associated with a "Brightness", a Light, but it was primarily a tangible feeling of Him. It could be described as a "thickness" that was completely alive. I felt embraced, enveloped by Beloved Adi Da's Divine Spiritual Body. Soon I felt no "difference", no separation. "I" was gone, and there was simply a Fullness and most pleasurable absorption in Him. This went on night after night in the sittings with Him. ■

The greatest Satisfaction—the only true Satisfaction—is to be Overwhelmed by That Which <u>Is</u> Love-Bliss, and Which <u>Is</u> Infinitely and Divinely Greater than yourself. . . . If you heart-recognize Me, you know that I <u>Am</u> the One Who Divinely Overwhelms you and all.
[Hridaya Rosary]

The Mountain Of Attention Sanctuary, 1997

**Avatar Adi Da Samraj at the celebration of His fiftieth Birthday,
Adidam Samrajashram, 1989**

CHAPTER 15

THE DIVINE WORLD-TEACHER

In February 1939, about six months before the outbreak of World War II, the Indian sage Upasani Baba received an important visitor to his ashram—the Shankaracharya of Jyotir Math, the head of a Hindu monastic order. The Shankaracharya expressed to Upasani Baba his dismay at the chaotic state of religion in India and in the world. He saw only one solution—a great Divine intervention, in the form of an Avatar. Only such an event, he felt, could re-establish true Spiritual life.

According to the account, Upasani Baba listened sympathetically. He was a man of few words and unpredictable ways. Suddenly, he burst out with a prophecy. Such an incarnation, he said, would soon be born in a Western country. "He will be all-powerful and bear down everything before him. And he will see to it that Vedic Dharma" (meaning the pure and original Teaching of Truth) "is firmly reestablished in India."*

To prophesy the coming of an Avatar was extraordinary enough. To foresee Him as a Westerner was tantamount to heresy. To the mind of the orthodox Hindu, Westerners are "mlecchas", Spiritually unevolved barbarians unworthy of even hearing Spiritual

---

* B. V. Narasimha Swami and S. Subbarao, Sage of Sakuri, 4th ed. (Bombay: Shri B. T. Wagh, 1966), pp. 190-191, 204.

Teaching, lower than the lowest caste. And now Upasani Baba was foretelling that the World-Teacher, the one to restore true religion to India, would be a Westerner!

Nine months later, Avatar Adi Da was born on Long Island.

Once, during His college years, Avatar Adi Da's uncle Richard asked Him what He wanted to do with His Life. Without hesitation, He replied, "I want to save the world." In the early years of His Teaching-Work, Adi Da did not make much of the worldwide, and even cosmic, scope of His Avataric Divine Work. It was only when He was given His Fijian Hermitage in late 1983 that He began to speak prophetically about the universal Power of His Blessing, and His real Work to "save the world". When He spoke the "Mark My Words" Discourse, He was not only referring to re-establishing the true Dharma (as Upasani Baba had foreseen). He also meant, quite literally, that He had come to save the human world from destruction by its own hand.

Jagad-Guru:
The Fiftieth Birthday Celebration

In the weeks preceding the celebration of His fiftieth birthday in 1989, Avatar Adi Da unremittingly Called devotees to respond to His Avataric Divine Self-"Emergence", so that He could do His Universal Blessing-Work. For the two weeks previous to the celebration, He stayed in seclusion, standing firm.

For some days, He did not stir from His bed. At one point, when Ruchiradama Quandra Sukhapur was in the room, a window near His feet spontaneously shattered. This seemed a sign of Avatar Adi Da's invisible struggle with forces vastly greater than the resistance of devotees—and He acknowledged that this was so.

Avatar Adi Da saw no reason to celebrate His birthday. However, on the eve of the celebration, Ruchiradama Quandra Sukhapur begged Him to celebrate "for the sake of humankind". Her plea touched His Heart. He sat swaying on His bed, quietly repeating a word she had not heard Him use before: "Jagad-Guru, Jagad-Guru, Jagad-Guru". "Jagad-Guru" means "World-Teacher", or,

During the course of a retreat at Adidam Samrajashram in the early 1990s, Dina Lautman received a revelation of Avatar Adi Da's Spiritual Intervention for the sake of all beings:

DINA: In the meditation hall, I fell into a dream-like state. At first, there was just a growing feeling of sorrow and grief. There was no recognizable content to it. Later, the picture filled out, and I was sitting in a huge field of corpses, weeping. The grief was endless. I was crying for all those who had died in this massacre. It was infinite pain. Finally, Beloved Adi Da appeared in this vision, and my grief turned to rage. I began to yell and scream at Him about what had occurred, blaming Him directly. "How could God have allowed this?", I screamed.

He gazed at me most Compassionately throughout my tirade, and finally He Revealed the depth of Love He feels for all beings. He explained that this is why He had Incarnated—because of His Love for beings. He looked at me and said that He had Appeared here, "Not only for those whom you mourn, but for all those who have died, are dying, and will die—in all planes, and in all forms, and throughout all time. I will not rest until all have come to Me."

It was then that I had the experience of my Beloved Guru as Love Itself. He was only pure Feeling, Radiating in all directions, like the sun. I felt His personal Love for me, and yet I simultaneously knew His Love was universal, for all beings. ■

literally, "the Teacher of everything that moves". Avatar Adi Da then spoke to Ruchiradama Quandra Sukhapur about His Function as Jagad-Guru, or World-Teacher, in the context of His Avataric Divine Self-"Emergence":

AVATAR ADI DA SAMRAJ: What actually occurred on the morning of January 11, 1986, was a sudden and spontaneous transition from My Teaching-Work to My Blessing-Work—or to My Work as the Eternally Free-Standing, and always presently "Emerging", Divine World-Teacher (or Jagad-Guru). It was a Transition in My Disposition from My Work of Submitting to others (even to the point of complete Identification with them in their apparently limited condition) to simply Surrendering My human Body-Mind into My own Self-Condition. Therefore, the context of My Blessing-Work is no longer one of Submission to others to the point of Identification with them. It is a matter of simply Standing As I Am, while this apparent Body-Mind is thereby Surrendered utterly into My own Self-Condition. And by My (Thus) Standing Free, My Work has ceased to be a Struggle to Submit Myself to humankind, one by one—and It has become (instead) a universally effective Blessing-Work, in Which humankind (in the form of each and all who respond to Me) must, one by one, surrender, forget, and transcend separate and separative self in Me. [November 3, 1989]

His Tangible Blessing Influence

On November 9, 1989, while still in seclusion, Avatar Adi Da asked, for the first time in many months, to see the world news. The synchronicity was remarkable. That day, one of the most significant events in recent European history occurred. Devotees sent Him copy from *The Washington Post*:

EAST GERMANY OPENS BERLIN WALL AND BORDERS, ALLOWING CITIZENS TO TRAVEL FREELY TO THE WEST

The article said this event constituted "the most stunning step since World War II toward ending the East-West division of Europe".

The fall of the Berlin Wall was just the beginning. In the weeks following, the newspapers were covered with headlines reporting further dramatic steps towards pluralist government in the European communist bloc—in Bulgaria (November 12), in Romania (December 23), and in Czechoslovakia (December 29). In Poland

and Hungary, the process had already been under way for several months, but news commentators now noted the sudden acceleration in the daily changes in Eastern Europe in the second half of November.

During December 1989, the Malta summit meeting between President Bush and Soviet leader Gorbachev signaled the winding down of the Cold War. In February 1990, Nelson Mandela, who had been jailed for more than twenty-seven years for his political activities on behalf of black South Africans, was released—an event that led to the repeal of apartheid laws early in 1992.

These changes marked a reversal of world politics that had been intractable for half a century or more.

Reporting from
The Washington Post—

August 20, 1989
ELECTIONS, NOT FORCE, MARK POLAND'S HISTORIC CHANGE

November 9, 1989
EAST GERMANY OPENS BERLIN WALL AND BORDERS, ALLOWING CITIZENS TO TRAVEL FREELY TO THE WEST

November 10, 1989
BULGARIA'S ZHIVKOV QUITS AFTER 35 YEARS
Foreign Minister, 53, Replaces East Bloc's Longest-Serving Leader

December 8, 1989
MALTA MOST IMPORTANT EAST-WEST MEETING SINCE '45

December 23, 1989
WORLD CAPITALS REVEL IN DICTATOR'S DOWNFALL
Many Pledge Immediate Aid to Romania

December 29, 1989
PRAGUE NAMES HAVEL PRESIDENT
Former Political Prisoner Wins Unanimous Election

February 12, 1990
SOUTH AFRICA FREES MANDELA IN GLOBAL TIDE TOWARD DEMOCRACY

April 14, 1990
NEW GOVERNMENT PROMISED IN HUNGARY

May 10, 1990
ALBANIAN RIGHTS MOVES

November 17, 1990
HUNGARY SCRAPS MISSILES

Devotees began to understand that, in the weeks leading up to His fiftieth birthday, Avatar Adi Da had been Working with negative patterns on a global scale. He had said many times that He relates to those who are in His Company as the "coins" for all humankind, and He struggles with their egoity as a way of Working with the larger human pattern. Thus, the outward sign of His world-Work was His insistent Call to devotees, as "coins" for His world-Work, in the weeks preceding His fiftieth birthday.

The political changes in central and eastern Europe did not usher in a golden age. But they were a "window", Avatar Adi Da said later, of possibility for change.

Some positive changes did occur. However, new patterns of violence emerged, as many ethnic groups of the former Soviet Union and central Europe rose up to re-claim their own tribal autonomy. Avatar Adi Da has often pointed out that, for individuals as well as larger groups, the negative outer circumstances may change, even positively, but, unless a fundamental <u>emotional conversion</u> occurs, the ego persists, destructive as ever, and will simply repeat the pattern in a different form.

Thus, Avatar Adi Da's world-Work is to ameliorate the negative forces in the world—first of all, so this planet can survive, and then so that it can (potentially) support Spiritual contemplation and growth. However, as He has pointed out on numerous occasions, neither human effort nor Divine Intervention will ever create a "utopia" on earth. The conditional world can never become entirely free of suffering and limitation. Nevertheless, the "Bright" Divine Self-Condition—which <u>is</u> entirely free of suffering and limitation—<u>can</u> be Realized, through His Grace.

Spiritual Penance in Seclusion

At the beginning of January 1991, Avatar Adi Da entered into another period of seclusion at Indefinable, His two-room bungalow in the residents' village. He had all decorations and comforts removed, and there He stayed, never leaving His Room. On January 15 (January 16 in Fiji), war broke out in the Middle East.

As the tanks rolled across the Iraqi desert, Avatar Adi Da watched videotaped news broadcasts every day, something He had never done before. He asked that a short-wave radio be set up beside His bed, so that He could listen to direct news broadcasts every hour. And He requested that international news broadcasts be recorded morning and evening and brought to Him at Indefinable.

The manner of Avatar Adi Da's Blessing-Work is a mystery. He is simply "Brightening" whatever is brought to Him. Also, He Works with "touchpoints"—representing a particular pattern or situation—to reach the situation. At one point during the Gulf War, Avatar Adi Da invited devotees to send Him photographs of anyone they knew who was involved in the war. Devotees brought Him a number of photographs, and He simply kept them in His room.

As the Gulf War continued, Avatar Adi Da asked why the news videos did not show any pictures of the dead on the battlefield. The devotees preparing the tapes confessed they had cut out these sequences in order to protect Him from the full vision of the carnage. Avatar Adi Da told them to "stop interfering". He wanted to receive all pictures and information. He was Working with the dead as much as with the living, and they too needed His direct Regard.

On March 3, 1991, the Gulf War came to an end with unexpected suddenness. *The Washington Post* described the conflict as "one of history's shortest ground wars" and the resolution of the conflict as "surprisingly easy". Five days later, on March 8 (March 9 in Fiji), Avatar Adi Da emerged from seclusion.

On July 18, 1991, Avatar Adi Da once again entered into an extended period of seclusion—this time, associated with the impending breakup of the Soviet Union. In 1991, although the Eastern European nations had renounced Communism, the Soviet Union itself had so far remained monolithic—a single political unit under Communist rule. But the tide of change reached Moscow. The republics of the USSR were seriously agitating for independence, and no one knew what would occur.

In late August, Mikhail Gorbachev resigned as leader of the Communist party, the Soviet Union began its shift to political pluralism, and Latvia, Lithuania, and Estonia regained their independence. This monumental shift occurred, in the words of *The Washington Post*, "quickly and almost painlessly". A few days later, on August 27, Avatar Adi Da emerged from His seclusion.

For the Sake of the World

Very rarely does Avatar Adi Da give His devotees a glimpse of the pain and difficulty that He takes on and transforms in the course of His own invisible Blessing-Work. He has said that no human being could endure it. On one occasion, He allowed a devotee to make this discovery.

THANKFULL HASTINGS: One evening in December 1992, I was sitting at Beloved Adi Da's side as He began to speak to the forty or so devotees in the room with Him that evening. He was speaking about the killings taking place daily in many areas of the world, and particularly, at that time, in Somalia. He referred to the terrible and intolerable deaths of women and children there, and also to the dangerous proliferation of weapons throughout the world.

As He spoke, I had my hand on His leg, and I began to feel in my body what He was talking about. I don't know how to describe this, but I felt the literal "experience" of what He was speaking about enter my body from His leg. It moved into my hand, up through my arm, down into my heart, and from there up into my head. As it entered my head, my vision was suddenly clouded. Appallingly vivid images of everything He was speaking of—all the terrible deaths and suffering—began to move before my eyes, as if I were watching a movie. In a very short time, I could no longer tolerate the experience. I got up and ran outside and began vomiting in the bushes, but the images continued. A friend came out to bring me back inside. I was gasping for air and told her I just couldn't take it anymore, I just couldn't experience the suffering of the world in the way Beloved Adi Da was obviously experiencing it.

A short time later, my "symptoms" subsided and I—still somewhat reluctantly—returned to the room where Beloved Adi Da and devotees were gathered. But I have never forgotten what I learned that night about what Beloved Adi Da endures for the sake of the world, and what is required from all of us if the Earth is to become a safe place where the great matter of true Spiritual practice is to be a real possibility for humankind. ■

"Open Yourself to Become My Instrument"

A critical aspect of Avatar Adi Da's world-Blessing Work takes place through devotees who work in the realm of politics, government, and social welfare. In 1996, Rolf Carriere, a Dutch senior representative of UNICEF, requested a private audience with Avatar Adi Da regarding some crucial issues related to his work in a poor and politically volatile part of the world. Avatar Adi Da accepted his request.

Rolf spoke to Adi Da of his lifelong commitment to serving the children of the world. He described his slow-dawning recognition that the reason they often suffer unnecessary but extreme privation reveals more of a Spiritual fault in humankind than any practical limitations on our global economic resources. As Rolf pointed out to Avatar Adi Da, "For less money than the world spends every year on golf, we could dispense with most of the unnecessary childhood diseases that kill millions every year." He concluded by asking for Avatar Adi Da's Guidance and Blessing in his service.

AVATAR ADI DA SAMRAJ: The children in that country are being excluded from consideration by those in control of the resources. And those who know that this is wrong must speak about it, and use every means to change minds and redirect attention and financial resources.

Just do that work. Go through all the doors that become available to you. Stay in the Process, and let it happen. Resort to Me. Your devotion to Me is what you have to add to it.

And then, in your heart-Communion with Me, more opportunities will come to you also. You will notice things happening simultaneously. Just be available to notice them.

In every way, at heart, open yourself to become My instrument—openly, without added strategy. Just this openness, this continuity with Me. And then you give Me more means to accomplish My Purpose.

Let Me hear about things. Come to see Me more often. Let Me hear from you about these kinds of things—what you are observing, what you are noticing. Indicate specifics for Me to Bless. Just a simple line about this and that here and there. It helps to make My Regard specific.

ROLF: Yes. Thank you.

AVATAR ADI DA SAMRAJ: Do your work with love and humor, but firmly. And, as I said, keep looking for the opportunities, the doorways. The more you are true to devotional Communion with Me, the more you will notice of that. This is how I Work.

ROLF: I have already noticed many times that things happen that were just inexplicable, except that I was just Your instrument.

At this point, Avatar Adi Da described something of the Divine Process of how He does His world-Work:

AVATAR ADI DA SAMRAJ: I Work on the pattern that is prior to the pattern that seems, or the pattern that is concrete at the moment. I Work on the pattern that is invisible, prior, not yet observed. And then I Breathe it down into the world. And the more people there are who know Me and know this is What I am Doing, and who enter into devotional Communion with Me, the more means I have in the concrete field.

There is no utopia about this. It is struggle. So you have to make use of every positive opening, every positive opportunity.

I also want to help the adults, along with the children. Adults are just older children. And the adults have to do much of the service that will change things. Not only because of their sympathy with children, and with the perpetuation of their kind altogether, but because their hearts are opening.

Help people to have a sense that they can do something collectively. Speak to everyone's altruism positively. Give people something to do that is good.

ROLF: Thank You, thank You.

AVATAR ADI DA SAMRAJ: Tcha. ■

When it was clear that Avatar Adi Da had finished, Rolf began to get up to leave, expressing his gratitude. At that moment, Avatar Adi Da motioned him to come forward. Avatar Adi Da then put Rolf's head in His lap. And He reached over and placed His hands on Rolf's back, stroking him up and down the back with both His palms for a long time. At the end, He placed His hands on Rolf's head. This was not only a loving, personal gesture—it was also an act of Transmission, a passing of His Spiritual Blessing to those He had been speaking about. As Rolf himself had confessed, his role was that of an instrument, a means for Adi Da Samraj to be Spiritually present and active in that country.

As it turned out, shortly thereafter Rolf again requested Avatar Adi Da's specific Blessing Intervention in several situations facing the whole area he was serving. One was a long-term, and seemingly intractable, dispute between the nation and a group of its indigenous peoples. The other concerned a regional conference on child labor.

At the conference, where Rolf said Avatar Adi Da's Blessing could be felt tangibly infusing the room, the head of one delegation, notorious for its resistance to fundamental reform, reversed his own delegation's position saying, "I can no longer deny the feeling I have at this conference." Then, against his subordinates' public objections, he pledged his country's compliance with a new protocol that would protect children's rights.

Both the negotiation and the conference surprised their participants by being successful.

Adidam Samrajashram, 1993

CHAPTER 16

THE FORERUNNERS

In early 1993, Avatar Adi Da made one of the most remarkable Revelations of His Divine-Self-"Emergence" Years. He "disclosed" how He, the Very "Bright" Itself, had been able to join Himself with a limited body-mind, in order to take birth as a human being.

In 1893, an Indian swami came to America to address the Parliament of Religions held that year in Chicago. There, this striking young man addressed a large gathering of Westerners who had little or no exposure to the Eastern traditions. Even so, he impressed the colloquium with his extraordinary presence, his impeccable command of English, and his ability to inspire others beyond sectarian views.

Swami Vivekananda was the cherished disciple of the great Indian Adept Ramakrishna. He had come to bring the wisdom of India to the West. After the accolade he received at the Parliament, He spent years in constant travel, lecturing all over America and England.

Swami Vivekananda had the fervor of a man moved to save the world, but he was frustrated in his intention. He knew that the future of humanity was being shaped by the West, already dominated by secularism and plummeting further. But there was a line drawn around his work, beyond which he could not go: He was a

Hindu, a dark-skinned man, and a celibate swami. Thus, in spite of his high Spiritual attainment and his tireless efforts, he remained a foreigner, an outsider. He died at the age of 39 (in 1902), unable to proceed further with what he felt to be his necessary work.

In the 1970s, Avatar Adi Da would occasionally speak about the pre-history of His present Incarnation and the unique conjunction of events It had required. He could not appear (He explained) until the mid-twentieth century—when the world had grown "smaller" through technology and commerce, when the barriers between East and West were shrinking, when Einstein's theories were shifting the materialist view, when Freud had unveiled the significance of human sexuality and Jung had demonstrated the dominion of the psyche. These realities and paradigms (among others) had to be in place before His Divine Work could take hold on a scale of size. But, above all else, a vehicle of unique Spiritual qualification had to be prepared.

In many cultural traditions, there is a belief in reincarnation, or the "re-cycling" of the being from life to life. Avatar Adi Da has confirmed that reincarnation is a real process, although it is far more complex than commonly presumed. From the Spiritual point of view, reincarnation is an opportunity for growth. In India, for example, great Spiritual beings are understood to be manifesting the results of Spiritual practice in previous lives, not merely in the present lifetime.

As Avatar Adi Da explains it, every human persona is composed of two distinct "selves". The first is the one we know well, our gross (or physical) vehicle—the body, derived from one's parents. This body-mind, including the social personality and the thinking mind, does not reincarnate. The body dies, and along with it, its mind and psyche. The second aspect of the human being is the subtle vehicle—called by Avatar Adi Da the "deeper personality". It is a mass of accumulations of experience, largely unconscious and prior to one's presumed social identity. This deeper personality is what migrates from life to life, usually without the gross persona's "remembering" previous incarnations.

As the Incarnation of the "Bright" Itself, Avatar Adi Da did not appear in this world due to previous lives of any kind. However,

The Forerunners

in order to take human form, He had to conjoin with the ordinary processes of the total human domain, including the subtle mechanisms of reincarnation. That is, in order to be born, He required a "deeper personality", attuned to the task of bringing Spirituality to the modern West. Swami Vivekananda carried in his psyche thousands of years of Indian Spirituality and Realization. But he ended his life in love with the West and its need for Divine Intervention.

On March 20, 1993, Avatar Adi Da confirmed to His devotees: Swami Vivekananda's urge to be reborn to serve the West allowed a conjunction between his deeper personality and Avatar Adi Da's Divine Impulse to Manifest in the human realm. It was this conjunction that provided the vehicle for His Incarnation as Franklin Jones.

AVATAR ADI DA SAMRAJ: It should be understood about this intentional Birth of Mine that no "decision" was made from an absolute point of view, out of the blue. The Deeper-Personality Vehicle of Swami Vivekananda was provided conditionally, as I have indicated. I, Myself, was brought into conjunction with the conditional reality by those means. In that conjunction, I "Consented" to the Ordeal of human Manifestation.

The Deeper-Personality Vehicle of Swami Vivekananda arose in the conditional domain and provided the conjunction with Me (<u>As I Am</u>). That Vehicle was conjoined with My Very Being. Swami Vivekananda was given up completely, and the Vehicle became transparent to Me. [March 20, 1993]

Two years later, Avatar Adi Da elaborated:

AVATAR ADI DA SAMRAJ: I took Birth in the West. Other Realizers have come to the West from India, on airplanes or boats. They did not <u>submit</u> to the Western circumstance, they did not come to the point of Realization <u>in</u> that circumstance and context, they did not address that circumstance and context.

Swami Vivekananda experienced the <u>utter</u> frustration of getting on a boat and going to the West. He <u>knew</u> it was not enough. And He <u>knew</u> what He was going to have to do, therefore—He was going to have to die and be reborn in the West. And His Western connections were the means for His rebirth. Having come to the West, He became entangled in sympathies and struggle, and suffered abuse, and found out what it is really all about. And He realized He was not equipped, in that lifetime, to convert Westerners, to convert people in the Western mode and disposition—which, since that time, has become more and more the global mode and disposition. Therefore, there was no reason for Him to go on with it. And that is why He died young. He did all He could do in that form. Nothing further could be accomplished.

But He said that, because of the sympathies He had entered into by being the first Eastern Adept-Realizer ever to have embraced the West—nobody had ever done that before—He was willing to be reborn in the West in order to serve mankind. He said He was <u>born</u> in love with humanity. That is it—He fell in love. He did not just go to the West as an Easterner, and wear His turban and robe, and leave it at that. He went to the West and became heart-sympathetic with it, even though everything was terrible about that circumstance. He became heart-sympathetic with people in the Western circumstance and disposition. But He realized that—as a Hindu, as an Easterner—He was not equipped to transform the West. So He went back to India and died. [February 22, 1995]

In October 1993, Avatar Adi Da spoke of an even more esoteric aspect of this process. Ramakrishna, the Spiritual Master of Swami Vivekananda, had always been aware of the Spiritual stature and destiny of his disciple. At the end of his own life, and certain of the great work that lay ahead for his beloved disciple, Ramakrishna poured his own Spiritual virtue into Swami Vivekananda, in a formal act of Transmission. After completing the infusion, He said, "Now I am only an empty fakir."* Thus, Ramakrishna, through his complete Spiritual investment of himself in Swami Vivekananda, is also part of the Deeper-Personality Vehicle of Avatar Adi Da Samraj.

---

* For a full account of this incident, see *The Life of Swami Vivekananda*, Volume One, by his Eastern and Western Disciples (Calcutta: Advaita Ashram, revised and enlarged edition, 1979), pp. 182–83.

The Forerunners

Swami Vivekananda

Ramakrishna

Ramakrishna was renowned for his ecstatic devotion to the Divine Goddess (in the form of Kali). He also embraced, for different lengths of time, the devotional practices of Christianity, Islam, and other traditions, developing a deep sympathy with other religions through his own direct practice of them. Thus, the Deeper-Personality Vehicle of Ramakrishna-Vivekananda brought the essence of humanity's long quest for God to the birth of Adi Da Samraj.

Likewise, the devotion to the Divine Goddess that Ramakrishna (and Swami Vivekananda) practiced "prepared the way" for Avatar Adi Da's Embrace of the Goddess as His final Guru, and then His ultimate Husbanding of Her in His Divine Re-Awakening. The Vedanta Temple in Hollywood is associated with both Ramakrishna and Swami Vivekananda and empowered with relics of both of them. Avatar Adi Da has stated that, through His own Divine Re-Awakening there, He perfectly fulfilled the Spiritual impulse of Ramakrishna and Vivekananda.

I Am the One Who Awakened (and, thereafter, Worked through) Ramakrishna. He Recapitulated the past, in order (by a Spiritual Sacrifice) to Serve the future. I Am the One Who Worked through (and has now Most Perfectly Awakened) Swami Vivekananda. He Served the future, in order (even by physical death and physical rebirth) to Transcend the past (and, Thus, and by Means of a Great and Spiritual, and even Transcendental, Awakening, to Bless and to Liberate the future).

Now and forever, Ramakrishna and Swami Vivekananda are One, at the Heart. And I Am the One They have Realized There. [The Knee Of Listening]

"It Is All Continuation"

Avatar Adi Da began the "consideration" of His connection with Ramakrishna-Vivekananda in 1976. He returned to the subject in 1979, 1982, and 1988, and brought the matter to conclusion in 1993.

Over the years, some of Avatar Adi Da's devotees had memories of their own past lives around Swami Vivekananda. Avatar Adi Da encouraged them to reclaim these intuitions—not merely out of self-fascination, but to become aware of the imperative behind their birth, the urge to be with Him again in the body. He instructed them to use those intuitions for the purpose of Realizing Him, and not merely to resume a human attachment.

Avatar Adi Da had often spoken to Ruchiradama Nadikanta about the likelihood of a relationship to Swami Vivekananda in her past life. He suggested she investigate the possibility that her deeper personality was that of Sister Nivedita, one of Swami Vivekananda's closest disciples. She told Avatar Adi Da that intuitions of her past-life connection with Him had surfaced even in her childhood:

RUCHIRADAMA NADIKANTA: In 1965, at the age of fifteen, I crossed the Atlantic on a grand ocean liner with my parents. One night, I woke in my berth, overwhelmed by the feeling that my life must be, and already was somehow, devoted to the service of

God. It was a spontaneous feeling, a déjà vu, as though I had finally understood something that had always been true. The passion that I felt that night, rocking on the waters of the Atlantic, was not without sorrow. It was as if I were struggling to connect with a truth I had already known, one that was more real to me than the family and friends and experiences of my present lifetime, more compelling than anything with which I was now familiar.

Years later, the meaning of that visitation was brought to consciousness through my relationship with Beloved Adi Da. Over a period of many years, and in the course of much research, conversation, and psychic and intuitive revelation, Beloved Adi Da drew me and some of His other devotees through a process of recognizing that we had been alive in previous incarnations as individuals associated with Swami Vivekananda, and that He Himself was uniquely Spiritually associated with Swami Vivekananda and his Guru, Ramakrishna.

But, always sensitive to our tendency to become fascinated by things such as reincarnation, Beloved Adi Da would typically begin the conversation, and, then, observing us becoming distracted from the real matters of ego-transcending practice, He would suddenly dismiss the subject, saying it was not to be taken seriously. And so He would drop the subject for years at a time.

He also would always admonish us that it is not possible to enter into a truly depthful investigation of past lives without the freeing of attention and psyche that comes with real Spiritual maturity in His Company. Without that foundation, any "consideration" of past lives is merely a matter of the conjecturing of the verbal mind, without real psychic and Spiritual evidence. A further Instruction from Beloved Adi Da was that such past-life investigation is not for the sake of glorifying the present body-mind-self, but rather for the sake of revealing and purifying all of the egoic patterning that had, lifetime after lifetime, created similar incarnations characterized by the same kinds of limitations.

Thus, Beloved Adi Da would always use such "considerations" to draw devotees into a process of self-understanding, in which we could see how the limited egoic mind each of us had manifested in previous lifetimes was continuing to pattern our present lifetimes.

Most importantly, He Revealed how it was essential to go beyond all this chaos of reincarnated patterning and re-patterning in order to transcend egoity itself and Realize Him. ■

In 1988, Ruchiradama Nadikanta told Avatar Adi Da about her experience on the ocean liner as a child. He said to her that Nivedita had once made an ocean voyage with Swami Vivekananda, from India to England. By Nivedita's own account, it was her most precious time with Swami Vivekananda.

AVATAR ADI DA SAMRAJ: It is all continuation. At certain moments, you get in touch with what was in another time and place, but it is the same time and place. The interval made by death between what was then and the next incarnation is truly nothing. It is a timeless Sublimity, with a Great Purpose making its moment. So that extraordinary matter has been exhibited to your face, in your company. [March 12, 1988]

In January 1993, when other devotees made confessions of similar intuitions and experiences, Avatar Adi Da spoke to the issue:

AVATAR ADI DA SAMRAJ: Everybody has his or her story of coming into My Company. What was moving you was alive at the deeper level of the being and of Consciousness. It created all kinds of circumstances and events that were necessarily preparatory, and then that same depth may have begun to appear in some other form, like a dream or an intuition or an attraction to go someplace for who knows what reason. That is the kind of breakthrough of this subtler dimension of the being, which is really "in charge", so to speak, of the developments of your lifetime.

After a while, you begin to become very sensitive to this invisible depth, and you come to the point where you can affirm that it exists, that it is so. It is not merely a matter of casual conventional belief in all this. It is something that develops, that is affirmed on the basis of a long term of experience. Perhaps another individual, not having had these experiences, cannot believe it. He or she does not have the experience that corresponds to it. All you can do is tell your story. Of course, among My devotees, you find a lot of other people with stories just like yours. In fact, if you find people sympathetic to this communication, it can be said that they are themselves being moved by that invisible dimension to be responsive.

Those in whom this invisible motion is alive, moving them towards Me, will find themselves responding, and they will have experiences, perhaps dreams and who knows what kind of experiences, that will be part of their presumed reason for approaching Me. [January 16, 1993]

Lineage of Blessing

Beyond Ramakrishna and Swami Vivekananda, Avatar Adi Da has talked about other great Spiritual individuals as threads in the mysterious Divine Pattern that culminated in His Appearance. He praises the Gurus of His own Lineage—Rudi, Swami Muktananda, and Bhagavan Nityananda. And He honors Ramana Maharshi (1879-1950) as a modern-day sage of uniquely profound Transcendental Realization.

However, while praising the great Realizers close to Him in human time, Avatar Adi Da also explains that the great Spiritual Realizers of all times and places contributed to the Deeper Personality Vehicle of His Avataric Incarnation. By means of this vast, unfathomable Process, the human Vehicle for His complete Incarnation as the Ruchira Avatar, Adi Da Samraj, eventually came into being.

This Body-Mind Is My Perfect Agent. The entire Lineage of True Realizers in the Great Tradition has been the Gathering of My Instruments, but not (until now, by My Avataric Divine Incarnation) Sufficient to the point of My Crashing-Down Complete and All-Completing Avataric Self-Manifestation.

All of those personalities can be seen as a Great Process in conditional time and space to prepare the Vehicle of My Avataric Self-Manifestation. But not just as individuals—it required all beings, including all of mankind, to make sufficient prayer and Conjunction for this Event of Me. And It will not be repeated, nor can It be repeated.

Through it all, I have Finally, Fully, and Most Perfectly Revealed Myself, the One Who <u>Is</u> and Has Always Been, the One Who has been pursued, sought, partially Realized, and so forth, throughout all conditional time and space. And then this unique Conjunction occurred, on the part of individuals in a unique Spiritual Lineage (epitomizing <u>all</u> Realizers, in <u>all</u> of space and time), to provide a Vehicle that would Come to My Door with sufficient Reach for Me to Pass Down here.

But, also, <u>This</u> is a Conjunction with <u>all</u>. All had to prepare. All had to make this Event possible—uniquely represented by a cycle of apparent individuals, yes (in order to provide the most immediate Vehicle), but the "time" (the "late-time", or "dark" epoch) is the Vehicle, too. Therefore, even <u>every</u> <u>one</u> and <u>all</u> are in Conjunction with Me—now, and forever hereafter.

Adidam Samrajashram, 1994

Indeed, all-and-All provided the Means for this Event. Even all-and-All was the necessary Preparation. It is all the Surrender to Me. It is all a Sacrifice of ego-self to the Divine Reality, until that Universal Sacrifice became collectively sufficient to Draw Me Down Through the Door.

My Avataric Divine Incarnation was, in some sense, simply Spontaneous, and not "intentional". In some sense, It simply "happened". Yet, It was also both Intentional and Voluntary. It was not arbitrary, because all the Conjunctions had to occur. At last, I Passed Down into all-and-All. It was Spontaneous, yet (also) Eternally Prefigured. It was Anciently Prophesied. It was somehow "caused"—and, yet (Ultimately), there is no "cause" for It whatsoever.
[The Knee Of Listening]

Adidam Samrajashram
September 1994

CHAPTER 17

Divine Completeness

In early August 1994, Avatar Adi Da left Adidam Samrajashram to wander in Fiji. He did this in order to make a lesson to devotees about right service and orientation to the sacred: There had been serious mismanagement in the renovation of one temple site and the construction of another. When such lack of care for the sacred was being demonstrated, Avatar Adi Da felt obliged to remove Himself from His Hermitage Ashram.

Avatar Adi Da eventually settled in the town of Pacific Harbour, on the main Fijian island of Viti Levu. There, on September 7, 1994, Ruchiradama Nadikanta attended Avatar Adi Da in His private room, where He had been doing further work on the manuscripts of His books.

RUCHIRADAMA NADIKANTA: The house was perfectly still. At one point, Beloved Adi Da called me into the room. The curtains were drawn, and the room was dim and unlit. He was not doing any work on His manuscripts. He was just sitting there, in a large upholstered chair. Beloved Adi Da's Force was so concentrated there that the room itself felt almost unapproachable to me. I felt as though I were being pushed out, as when the heat from a fire blasts you backwards out of a blazing space. I served Him simply and left the room. ■

Later that day, when Ruchiradama Nadikanta again answered His call, she felt the same Force of Transmission from Him as He now sat at His desk. She sat at His feet. He turned to look at her.

RUCHIRADAMA NADIKANTA: I was overwhelmed by the vision of His Sacrificial Ordeal. I was reminded of that same heartbreaking Love for the billions of humanity that had overwhelmed Him more than eight years before, when His Divine Self-"Emergence" was initiated on January 11, 1986. And I knew that some extraordinary Process was taking place in Him. ■

Avatar Adi Da later confirmed her intuition. September 7, 1994, He said, marked the most important transition in His Life since His Avataric Divine Self-"Emergence". It was the Completing, He said, of His "Effort" to Descend (or "Emerge") into the cosmic domain, an "Effort" that had been going on since His birth. The Great Event of January 11, 1986, had been the Initiation of the process—and, while it was the most significant moment in that process, a further resolution had just occurred. A week later, He returned to Adidam Samrajashram, where He described the significance of the Event:

AVATAR ADI DA SAMRAJ: In 1986, I Instructed My devotees that they had to change their way of relating to Me, and the process of that change has characterized the struggle of the last nearly nine years. At the time, I accepted a certain struggle, even though it was almost unbearable. I had to endure it, and I Communicated to My devotees in the midst of it. That was the initial process of My Avataric Divine Self-"Emergence".

In early September of this year, and just as suddenly as the signs appeared in January 1986, the signs in My Body indicated a similarly dramatic change.

This Body is in an extremely refined state. My devotees should approach Me only to conduct Me Spiritually, not to engage in any conventional form of relating to Me. I must put this Body in a different situation now. It was refined by My Avataric Divine Self-"Emergence". It must not be put in a position of conventional or social relatedness any longer, or I will lose this Vehicle. You will lose It. You cannot even imagine what has been required to prepare this Vehicle and to provide this Incarnation. [September 21 and 23, 1994]

California 1995

Avatar Adi Da's departure from Adidam Samrajashram in August 1994 initiated a long period of wandering. Over the next period of years, He traveled repeatedly between His Hermitage Ashrams in Fiji, California, and Hawaii. He also made trips to the east coast of the US, to Europe, and (later) up and down the west coast of the US.

Before He departed from Fiji for California, however, Avatar Adi Da once again initiated a major period of gatherings with His devotees at Adidam Samrajashram—from December 1994 to August 1995. This period, which was full of sublime Discourses on all aspects of His Teaching-Revelation, was to be the last of the large gathering periods—in which He would speak His Dharma night after night, for months at a time, to a sizeable group of devotees. He was bringing His vast outpouring of spoken Revelation to a point of completion.

At the end of those nine months, it was clear that all the years of His Submission-Work had taken a serious toll on His health, most significantly His eyesight. After medical investigation, the doctors determined that the degeneration of His vision was due to a hereditary tendency to glaucoma. The damage to His eyes was already extensive.

This was deeply sobering news to His devotees, a stark reminder both of the fragility of His Body and of their responsibility to care for His physical well-being. Early in September, almost a year to the day after the September 7 Event, Avatar Adi Da and a small party of devotees left for California so that He could receive immediate medical attention. A couple of days later, Avatar Adi Da had the first of two operations for glaucoma at a private hospital in San Francisco. Before the surgery, Avatar Adi Da Samraj emphasized to His devotees that the Power of His Darshan and His

Spiritual Work was not in the least affected by the physical condition of His eyes.

While it was a medical emergency that instigated His departure from Fiji, it soon became clear that His Yajna—the first to California in six years—was an important event for His Work altogether. In the more than four months that followed, hundreds of devotees traveled to the Mountain Of Attention Sanctuary to receive His Darshan. They came from all over the world, including many who had never seen Him before.

Adi Da Samraj with devotees at the Mountain Of Attention Sanctuary, 1995

Five years later, after the turn of the millennium, Avatar Adi Da remarked on the deeper reasons for His frequent movements out into the world since 1994.

AVATAR ADI DA SAMRAJ: The disturbances at Adidam Samrajashram moved Me to go to Suva in 1994, and the September 7 Event took place there. Then My eyes required Me to travel. And, then, later, I continued to move. All these things happened for a reason. Things were moving Me, and I was responding to emergencies in the world, as I have been since 1986. That is what I Do as Avadhoot, or Sannyasin. I Move as My Work unfolds—and I have to have that freedom, if I am to be effective. Even in the midst of

My Struggle with My devotees, My own Work has been "Emerging". But the Struggle cannot go on—this obligation to Teach, to Talk. You must set Me apart. This is essential. I am Doing world-Work. [January 2, 2000]

Europe 1996

Avatar Adi Da returned to Adidam Samrajashram in June 1996, after four months at Da Love-Ananda Mahal and a short visit to the east coast of the United States. On July 13, He suddenly left Adidam Samrajashram again. Accompanied by only a few devotees, He traveled privately in Europe for the first time in ten years. The time in Europe was extraordinarily difficult.

Avatar Adi Da stayed primarily at the European Ashram in Holland, but towards the end of His time in Europe He suddenly boarded a train for Geneva.

THANKFULL HASTINGS: Important conferences were taking place at the United Nations at that time, especially regarding the matter of nuclear disarmament. Beloved Adi Da was escorted by a UN official who is His devotee to the UN conference rooms where the talks would take place. Seeing Him not only in the UN building but walking in the Alps and visiting the church where John Calvin had preached, I could feel Him Blessing and Working with all of Europe. ■

Avatar Adi Da Samraj sitting in the United Nations, Geneva, Switzerland, 1996

Avatar Adi Da called His devotees to understand the nature of the times and the reasons for His urgency:

AVATAR ADI DA SAMRAJ: You need to listen and observe the gross and universal insult of the world in this dark and darkening time here. My Urgency has much to do with that. At the Spiritual level, I perceive and know of potential calamity on a global scale that people are hardly even sensitive to. I can Do My Work, but My devotees, by participating fully in My Pattern, must give Me a pattern within which My Pattern can Work. There must be a pattern in the scale of the gross which extends from Me and cooperates with Me. [August 14, 1997]

Finally, in October 1996, Avatar Adi Da responded to the pleas of His devotees to leave the small apartment in Geneva where He was staying and return to the Mountain Of Attention.

Hawaii 1997

On March 11, 1997, Avatar Adi Da left the Mountain Of Attention for Hawaii in the same mood and manner in which He had left for Europe the year before. After one night at Da Love-Ananda Mahal, He went into seclusion in a house on Kauai offered by a devotee. March 22 was the day of the spring solstice and also a full lunar eclipse. Winds blew up suddenly around midday and a storm broke out. At the same time, Avatar Adi Da received reports about the institution, culture, community, and mission of Adidam. These reports did not reflect the level of responsibility He was looking for from devotees, and He immediately told everyone to leave the house.

Ruchiradama Nadikanta, who was passing on communications to and from Avatar Adi Da at the time, takes up the story:

RUCHIRADAMA NADIKANTA: Beloved Adi Da had been Doing His Divine Work for twenty-five years, and the response was not reflecting the immensity of the Gift that He was Giving. It was evident that He was experiencing cosmic forces of resistance to Him and to His Work.

In the moment of this pitch of frustration, He sat down at His desk and began to write. I knew He was writing, but I did not know what.

It was obvious to me that He could have relinquished the body in that house. But it was also obvious that He was not going to, because His Commitment is so great. Instead, He was going to continue to require the true response from His devotees for the sake of everyone.

My feeling was that, over the past twenty-five years, we had enclosed Beloved Adi Da instead of bringing Him out to the world. And it felt to me that now He was throwing this enclosure away, in order to make room for the world to receive Him. He was doing it with great fierceness, throwing every single person out of this in-turned enclosing of Him and His Work and His Body—in order to make this room. ■

A week later, Avatar Adi Da passed on the manuscript of *Hridaya Rosary*. And then He went on to grant to hundreds of devotees—first in Hawaii, then at the Mountain Of Attention, and later in Los Angeles—the Spiritual Gifts He describes in that Text. Finally, on July 5, after traveling for most of two years, He returned to Fiji.

**Avatar Adi Da Samraj
granting Darshan in Hawaii
after He wrote *Hridaya Rosary*,
1997**

"He Gives You More Than You Can Imagine"

Some devotees had been traveling with Avatar Adi Da throughout His wanderings of 1995-1997. Charles Seage, His personal physician, was one of them. Charles has served Avatar Adi Da personally for many years, and was one of the doctors who attended Him during the event of His Yogic death on January 11, 1986. Charles describes here the conversion that He went through as a result of staying with Avatar Adi Da through thick and thin:

CHARLES: As Beloved Adi Da's physician, I know I must be available to Him twenty-four hours a day—wherever He is, wherever He chooses to go. Regardless of what I feel in the body-mind in any given moment, that is my agreement with Him. It is not a "business" agreement. It is my greatest joy and impulse. It is the meaning of my life. And so that puts me in an interesting position. If I follow my heart, I stay with Him. I do not have any choice. And that has proved to be an incredible Grace. My Beloved Guru is making possible for me a depth of sadhana that I would never have chosen if left to my own egoic devices. He is Giving me my heart's desire in spite of myself.

As I was traveling with Beloved Adi Da in Europe and the United States in the last few years, I have to admit I reacted to the ordeal of it. Beloved Adi Da was often fiercely critical of me and of His devotees in general. I felt tremendous frustration, because I did not know what to do to change anything. Basically, I felt that, no matter how hard I tried, I was never completely in control.

For a while during early 1997, while Beloved Adi Da was staying at the Mountain Of Attention, I worked for some hours a week in a nearby medical clinic, which was something I had not done in years. I noticed how much I enjoyed being the "doctor" again, in conventional terms—in control, effective, admired. Then Beloved Adi Da suddenly left for Hawaii, and before long He indicated that I should come. And so I gave immediate notice at the clinic and within a day or two I was living in Kauai while Beloved

Adi Da was enduring the immense Ordeal that accompanied His writing of *Hridaya Rosary*.

I had my first experience of Beloved Adi Da's new Revelation of His Siddhi at the initial "Four Thorns" Darshan occasion in Hawaii on April 7, 1997. I felt Avatar Adi Da Spiritually Crashing Down and His Spiritual Presence Pervading me, outside and inside. I could hardly believe it, because I did not feel prepared for any such event. From my perspective, I went into the room full of myself and not effectively practicing beyond that. So it was obvious that I had nothing to do with the incredibly Blissful feeling of Beloved Adi Da that was filling the room. It was simply Him. He was doing everything.

When we arrived at the Mountain Of Attention, a young man asked me what these first occasions of Beloved Adi Da's "Four Thorns" Transmission had been like. And I said, "Well, I have been to countless Darshan occasions over the years, and I have tended to get involved in the error of 'working on' myself to have something happen to me in these occasions. But now I know that I am doing nothing and Beloved Adi Da is doing everything." The young man was deeply impressed, and so was I. It is a Grace beyond comprehension.

When we went to Los Angeles at the beginning of June, the frustration for me at the life-level continued. Everything seemed futile. There was no way to "succeed" or "win" at anything, and I indulged in a mood of complaint a lot of the time.

But, during those weeks we spent in Los Angeles in June, Beloved Adi Da would sit with people nearly every night. So I would go into these profound Darshan occasions night after night, and the same thing would happen as happened in Hawaii that first time. I would be overcome with the All-Pervading Love-Blissful Ecstasy of Beloved Adi Da's Spiritual Presence. It was beyond belief. I realized that that was the Gift that Beloved Adi Da had Given me a taste of in my first Darshan occasion in 1978 at the Mountain Of Attention. And the thread of that Grace had stayed with me through all the intervening years. I began to realize that this thread had always been present in my relationship with my Beloved Guru. Regardless of my egoic ups and downs, that thread remained, for

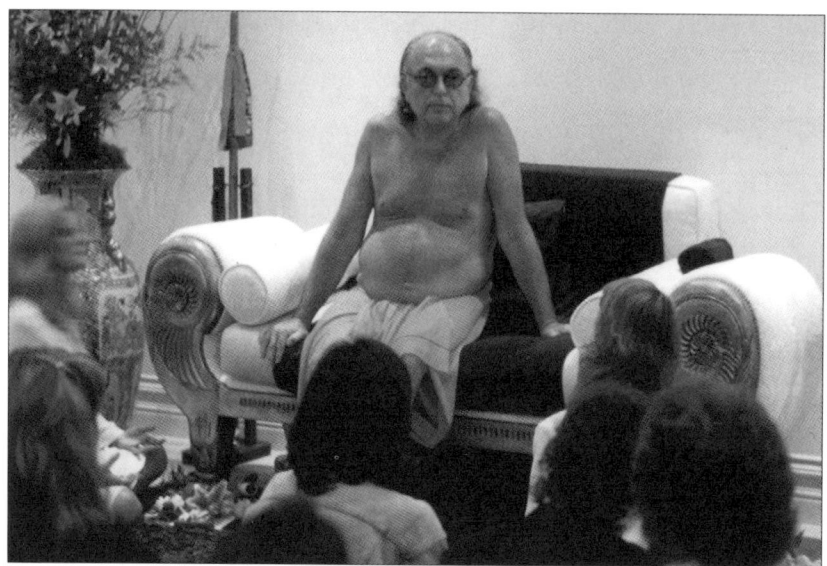

Los Angeles, 1997

one simple reason. All along, I consistently made the conscious choice to be with Beloved Adi Da no matter what—no matter how much I might find in the circumstance to complain about.

When we came back to Fiji in 1997, something changed in my disposition. I was starting to understand that the struggle and resistance was something I was <u>choosing</u> to do—it was not <u>happening</u> to me. It was not, as I had assumed, simply justified by my apparent circumstances. Prior to all of it was my relationship to Beloved Adi Da. That was what was important, and that was what I was actually basing my life on.

Consistently, in Darshan occasions with Beloved Adi Da, I feel the same Crashing Down of His Blessing Force, but now His Spiritual Pervasion is becoming continuous with my daily life. No matter where I am, I can feel Him, I can always "Locate" His tangible Spiritual Presence.

I found out that I had to get to the point of despair, because that was the only thing that made me take a hard look at the seeking I am always doing. And that seeking is what was preventing me from feeling Beloved Adi Da, from noticing the Grace and Bliss and Love He is pouring on me all the time.

I know I am always going to be tested and there is always going to be tapas, because He is dealing with the ego. And so there is no self-congratulatory or self-indulgent life to be had around Avatar Adi Da. All there is is love of Him. And, in that love-relationship with Him, He Gives you infinitely more than you can imagine. ■

Adidam Samrajashram, 1997

CHAPTER 18

"My Word Is Sealed"

Back at Adidam Samrajashram in late July 1997, Avatar Adi Da began work on what was to become the definitive communication of His Wisdom-Teaching. Since the beginning of His Teaching-Work, Avatar Adi Da Samraj had often written His Instruction in concentrated periods, but the output of this period would dwarf that of any previous period.

He wrote every single day, seven days a week, from late July to the middle of December. A group of devotees would work through the night, every night, entering and proofing the day's writing. The end result would be a 23-volume canon of His Spiritual Instruction, astonishing in its scope and depth. The twenty-three "Source-Texts" drew together the twenty-five years of His Revelation into combinations and syntheses, creating a systematic presentation of His Spiritual Revelation and Instruction. Every part of every book became a perfectly placed link in the chain of His Argument.

AVATAR ADI DA SAMRAJ: It was an unbroken "Consideration" that took twenty-five years, a continuous Examination-Argument unfolding day by day for twenty-five years. Only I knew the thread of it, or maintained the thread of it—but that is what it was. [December 28, 1997]

The first five of the "Source-Texts" are *The Five Books Of The Heart Of The Adidam Revelation*, summarizing the essence of Adi Da's Avataric Divine Self-Revelation and His Instruction in the Way of Adidam. Then follow *The Seventeen Companions Of The True Dawn Horse*, which elaborate all the great themes of His Teaching and Self-Revelation. Last of all stands *The Dawn Horse Testament*, the most comprehensive and detailed statement of His Teaching within a single volume.

AVATAR ADI DA SAMRAJ: My Word is Complete. Therefore, all of the Siddhis of My Divine-"Emergence"-Work will now—and can, and will forever—take place, whether this Body continues to live or not. Sooner or later, the Body passes. I am relaxed in the reality that I have Done My Work that needed to be Done. And the continuation of this Body is now a luxury for you all. It is entirely up to you. Truly! It is truly so. Love Me in this Form, and the Body will persist.

Sitting here in this Body like yours, I have indulged in your experience, and learned greatly from it. And My sympathy has been increased <u>absolutely</u>. I have escaped none of it! This One Who <u>Is</u> suffers in this Body, like you—but more sensitively, more aroused by the pain of it than you dare to be.

You must notice that bodily life is not enough. The whirling stars and bodies of planets, the gravitational ghost of ordinary reality, the black hole of this "dark" time, and all the sucking sound of ending—it is not good enough. <u>Not good enough</u>! It is not good enough! Live life with enough <u>heart</u>, and you get a taste of the Absolute that you desire.

My Word is Sealed, It is Complete. My twenty-three "Source-Texts" are made, and done. Every word and comma and quotation mark was made and approved and made perfect by Me. What was made is Good, and Complete, and Whole, and Fine, and Great.

I have Done what I had to Do.

So it is time for you to become profoundly serious, and take the arms of My twenty-three "Source-Texts", and the life of this Way of Adidam in My Company, and live it rightly, truly, fully, fully devotionally, and bring it as My Gift to all of humankind. And be the seed whereby this transformation can occur. [December 15, 1997]

Da Love-Ananda Mahal 1998

The twenty-three "Source-Texts", as Avatar Adi Da created them in 1997, were not absolutely fixed documents. He made them flexible in their structure, so that His yet-to-be-Given Revelations could be incorporated into the existing books.

And, indeed, a flood of new Revelation soon appeared. On February 25, 1998, at Da Love-Ananda Mahal, Avatar Adi Da initiated a two-month period of nightly Discourses that were to become one of the greatest glories of His Spoken Word. These Discourses were Given in His small bedroom, with just a few devotees in attendance. He was continuing Instruction He had begun in *Hridaya Rosary*, about the real Spiritual process of Adidam.

Ruchiradama Nadikanta describes what it was like to sit in the room with Avatar Adi Da as He spoke:

RUCHIRADAMA NADIKANTA: His Transmission-Power moved into the room where we were seated with Him face to face, and the "Brightness" of His Divine Light Infiltrated the space with Luminosity, such that walls, objects, and persons became visibly "Brightened" by His Siddhi. The differentiation between objects loosened, such that Reality was clearly a Field of Divine Light, rather than a field of apparently separate material objects. Beloved Adi Da was Revealing to us the Truth that matter = Energy = Light, and that His All-Pervading Divine Spiritual Presence is the Very Substance and Nature of That Light.

Again and again, as He spoke or sat silently, His own Spiritual Person Flooded into our body-minds and Drew us into this Sea of Divine Light. He was Penetrating the body-mind through to the toes, permeating every cell with His Love-Blissful Radiance. He opened the nervous system, so that the body-mind became like an open cup from toe to crown, a receptacle for His Luminous Infusion. The spine would become erect with this upward-turning response to Beloved Adi Da's "Brightness". Sometimes, the experience of this Bliss was so intense that it felt like the cells of the body were being cracked open. ■

One night, in the midst of His Discourse, Avatar Adi Da began to speak ecstatically of Himself and His Avataric Incarnation—in vivid images that suggest something about how He has Combined Himself with this world:

AVATAR ADI DA SAMRAJ:
   I Am the Person
   of the Sea of Light,
   the "Bright" Person.

   I have Fallen through
   a Hole in the universe.

   I Am a kind of Pillar
   Fallen out of the sky,
   at the lower end of Which
   is My human Body here.

   And, having Fallen in,
   I am Established here,
   and Circulating here,
   and Filling here,
   with the Ocean of My own Person
   That Falls through that Hole with Me,
   like a Thunder Crack.

   It is like that.

   Even a particle of Me
   Illuminates the world.
   And I am being shaken in here
   like a sugar cube,
   Sufficient to Pervade the Whole.

   Every devotee of Mine,
   every body-mind,
   in this "Conductivity" of Me,

is a hole in the barrier
between humankind and Infinity—
the Infinite Sea of Light,
My own Person. [April 11, 1998]

By the time these gatherings came to a close on April 22, 1998, Avatar Adi Da had already indicated that His principal Discourses from this period should be added to His twenty-three "Source-Texts".

The Mummery

Avatar Adi Da's twenty-three "Source-Texts" include the first book He wrote after His Divine Re-Awakening—His Spiritual autobiography, *The Knee Of Listening*. Also included among the twenty-three, however, was a book He had written in 1969, before the Vedanta Temple Event.

Soon after He returned from His second visit to India in 1969, Avatar Adi Da and Nina and Patricia moved into a loft in New York City, where He spent His days writing. He was working on a parable/novel that He would eventually call *The Mummery*—named after the style of medieval European festival theatre in which mock dramas were enacted by characters unable to see their own absurdity. The title indicated the core of Avatar Adi Da's message in the book: Without true Communion with Real God, life is nothing but a mock-show, a piece of play-acting without any depth or meaning. *The Mummery* is completely unflinching in its portrayal of the destructiveness of human egoity. And, at the same time, it is utterly heart-breaking as a story of "the Divine True Love" that works to overcome the mummery of ego-existence.

Avatar Adi Da worked on *The Mummery* all day, every day. In this novel, the many thousands of pages of "stream of consciousness" self-observation, ideas, images, and story fragments that He had burned after coming to Rudi had distilled themselves into an archetypal form. When Avatar Adi Da had finished the piece, He read it aloud to Nina and Patricia. Nothing further happened with the manuscript at the time. In later years, however, it would show itself to be an uncanny prophecy of His Life. *The Mummery* is unquestionably a literary masterpiece. Avatar Adi Da builds on the twentieth-century tradition of experimental fiction, putting linguistic innovation to the profoundest possible use, in creating a Text of extraordinary poetic, psychic, and Spiritual Force.

Avatar Adi Da had not touched the manuscript of *The Mummery* since its original composition in 1969. Now, returning to Adidam Samrajashram in April 1998, He started to elaborate and expand *The Mummery,* in yet another exhaustive, three-month period of writing. In this writing, all the experience of His Teaching Years and Revelation Years poured into the story. In the end, *The Mummery* was doubled in size.

The Great Bird

In this excerpt from chapter 13 of The Mummery, *the hero, Raymond Darling, encounters a gigantic bird at a secret lake. The great bird suggests the untamed Energy of natural existence. Here, and throughout* The Mummery, *Avatar Adi Da makes unique use of punctuation, underlining, and capitalization, to create a kind of "musical notation" indicating the inflections of each sentence.*

In the morning, Raymond was, still—asleep.

The fateful Day, grew warm—with the Inner Dawn of Living Light.

With the Dawn Horse, of full Sun-rise—time grew warm enough for insect-time to tick the day awake! And the inner-Lighted draft of <u>everything</u>, Whirled! off the space of nature's dark.

Eyes closed, for now.

No sound, to speak of. Except, a kind of tidal whisper. A feeling-sound, of unfamiliar—Water!

A Great Sea-Change of space-time's transformation-mind was, slowly, nearing him. He felt Its signal, coming to him—a little at a time. Hush! <u>Be</u>, Calm—he feels. The promised Water! Coasting, under him. Making "Here-Is-Something" Speak, beneath his wonder's ears.

Raymond's Listening head is mounted—with his body, ear to ground—upon the stumps of Earth-edged Water-World. Listening!

Then, the fateful wind of Real Today, begins to curl True Water, to him. . . .

And, then, the sudden world!—for Raymond's ears and eyes of feeling-heart's Deep Heart!

And Raymond Jumped!—<u>Up</u>! To <u>Largest</u> Water! Now! <u>True</u> Water!—<u>Beyond</u> the dreaming-fisher's lake!

And great, gray feathers—<u>slowly</u>—moved beneath <u>his</u> underfoot!

He saw <u>It</u>!

Side to side.

He sees <u>It</u>!

On the Great Water, while he watched—the great, gray body of a monstrous bird! coasted forward, off the Water-top!

"Great Bird!—It <u>Is</u>!"

If Dylan Thomas and Buddha shared a soul, THE MUMMERY is what I would expect from such a joining.

—**ROBERT BOLDMAN,** poet
author, *The Alchemy of Love*

THE MUMMERY is brilliant in all its aspects. It would be hard to express my happiness at the way it breaks and exposes the heart of the world. Living and working as a writer for many decades, I have not encountered a book like this, that mysteriously and unselfconsciously conveys so much of the Unspeakable Reality.

—**ROBERT LAX,** poet
author, *Love Had a Compass*
co-author (with Thomas Merton), *A Catch of Anti-Letters*

THE MUMMERY is a book with many levels: an apparently naive level of narrative and poetic invention (concerning Raymond Darling, his beloved Quandra, and his friends, followers, and betrayers); an allegorical level (concerning the coincidence of opposites, gender, and romantic love); an esoteric confessional level (concerning the education of a soul through a kind of platonic anamnesis); and, subsuming all other levels, a revelatory level (concerning the nature of consciousness and how it is continually lost in the ongoing "mummery" of ego-constructed existence). This comprehensive level begins and ends as a confession of divine identification.

The central stylistic achievement of THE MUMMERY seems to be its undoing of the mummery of words: words ordinarily are deployed in books as serious and loyal ants, carrying their load of sense to their destinations. Adi Da's poetic inventions make words crackle and swoon, pound and soothe with suggestion and insistence.

—**PHILIP KUBERSKI,** Professor of English,
Wake-Forest University

The lessons of *The Mummery* are so critical that Avatar Adi Da instituted an annual live reading or staged performance of the entire book. The performances are done each January, when the anniversary of the Yogic Establishment of His Avataric Divine Self-"Emergence" is celebrated. Thus, *The Mummery* is a form of sacred pageant-theatre to be witnessed, as well as a novel to be read.

PART FIVE

"Bright" Return to What Was Never Lost

1999–2002

The Mountain Of Attention Sanctuary, New Year's 1999

CHAPTER 19

Ordeal at the "Brightness"

Early in 1999, Avatar Adi Da Samraj was residing at Tat Sundaram, a small Hermitage that overlooks the ocean on the northern California coast. He had lived there during the autumn months of 1998 and then traveled to the Mountain Of Attention for December and the New Year. Now He was back to the northern California coast, energized by the pristine quality of the natural environment.

On the morning of February 21, 1999, Ruchiradama Quandra Sukhapur called together a group of devotees. She told them signs had begun to appear in Avatar Adi Da—Yogic symptoms involving pain and stress in the heart-region that suggested His struggle to stay in the body.

Soon, without warning, Avatar Adi Da was out the door and into His car. His driver called from the car to say that Avatar Adi Da was going to Los Angeles and then on to Fiji.

When He stepped ashore at Adidam Samrajashram, His first request was for the shortwave radio, a sure sign that He was intent on listening to the world news.

In the course of the next day, Avatar Adi Da spoke of the confrontation between the Serbs and the Kosovar Albanians and the dreadful potential it held for escalating into a global conflagration.

The "Brightness"

On March 10, Avatar Adi Da told Ruchiradama Nadikanta that He still had symptoms of heart-stress. He urged her to communicate to devotees the gravity of His physical state and of the threatening situation in the world. He called for a car, put on orange sannyasin attire, and asked to be driven by Himself to the "Brightness", the secluded temple that He had (at the time) designated as His Mahasamadhi Site.* There He stayed alone, listening to the news on the shortwave radio.

For the next forty-three days, Avatar Adi Da stayed secluded at the "Brightness", so concentrated in His Spiritual Work with the world that He would often not even allow devotees to do basic services for Him.

The "Brightness" Temple is a small square building, with, at its core, a Temple reserved for Avatar Adi Da's use. Surrounding the inner Temple on three sides is an enclosed veranda. The fourth side is a bedroom for Avatar Adi Da.

RUCHIRADAMA NADIKANTA: One night, it was physically as if the war were occurring at the "Brightness". I was sleeping at some distance from the "Brightness" Temple, and it was like being on the front line of a battlefield. The thunder was so loud it shook my body like a barrage of artillery fire. And the lightning was so bright, just blasting across the sky—the whole field lit up, as if from explosives. During the night, the winds were so strong it felt as though the tent were going to be lifted right off the ground. The agitation in the atmosphere felt like the war was occurring right in Beloved Adi Da's Domain.

---

* "Mahasamadhi" ("Great Samadhi") is a Sanskrit term for the death of a Realizer, and a Mahasamadhi Site is therefore a Realizer's burial place.

The next morning, as I approached Beloved Adi Da's door at the "Brightness", the sky was completely overcast but also totally calm. There was not a breath of air. Beloved Adi Da met me and opened the door for me to come in. Immediately, He received the world news and sat down and read it. He asked that I remove all the trays and glasses and food and bins we had left in His quarters over the last few days, during which He had eaten almost nothing and had not accepted personal service from anyone. I noticed that He had not touched the most recent tray of food we had left for Him.

I immediately lit incense in His bedroom and in other places in the Temple complex, and as soon as I had done this, a deluge of rain fell out the sky. The rain fell in sheets, such that it would have been impossible to hear one's own voice. Later, I found out that the attempts at Kosovo peace talks that were going on had broken down at that exact time. ■

Between 4:30 and 4:45 A.M. on April 2, a terrific bolt of lightning struck. Ross Keen was outside the gates to the "Brightness" at the time:

ROSS KEEN: Immediately after the lightning-bolt, there was a vast thunderous cracking noise, as if the sky were splitting. The ground shook. The entire dome of sky over the "Brightness" was lit. For a few seconds, I was literally blinded by the intense light. ■

Ruchiradama Quandra Sukhapur speaks of her experience of this same event:

RUCHIRADAMA QUANDRA SUKHAPUR: I was about halfway down the path in the middle of the "Brightness" field, when the most intense moment of the entire storm occurred. The lightning ran around the sky in an unbroken blazing circle. And, in the middle of the pitch-black night, the circle of lightning established a brilliant dome of light over the "Brightness". It was unbelievable. At the same time, there was a deafeningly loud crackling electrical sound all around the "Brightness".

Later in the day, knowing that Beloved Adi Da had been inside the "Brightness" Temple during the storm, I spoke to Him about my experience of the thunder and the dome of light. He said, "Yes, I know all about it."

I knew that this was not a merely "natural" occurrence. It was a Sign of cosmic Nature responding to Him and of the Force of His Presence there at the "Brightness". ■

Later, Avatar Adi Da noticed that the eternal light that should have been shining from the island's highest point had gone out. Two priests climbed up the rugged peak. The site had been struck dead-on by lightning. Miraculously, even though the surrounding ground had sunk 16 inches below normal level, the shrine area was completely intact. The sunken ground was charred black, and the acrid scent of burnt minerals lingered. As the two priests offered gifts at the shrine, a light rain fell accompanied by a double rainbow over the sea.

After the storm had passed, Avatar Adi Da received news that thousands of refugees were being transported like cattle to Macedonia, and NATO ground troops were threatening to invade Kosovo.

Through mid-April, Avatar Adi Da rarely left His room. Ruchiradama Nadikanta describes Avatar Adi Da's Spiritual Ordeal at this point in the war—when some 650 air strikes a day were bearing down on Serbian targets.

RUCHIRADAMA NADIKANTA: In this month and a half at the "Brightness", Beloved Adi Da almost never spoke, and I never spoke to Him. Once I did say something—I was trying to lighten the moment, and He said, "Do you think this is a social occasion?" So I never spoke after that.

One night, April 17, He did come down from the "Brightness" Temple to sleep in the tent that had been prepared for Him. He permitted me to sleep there also. During the night, I suffered horrifying visions of war. Beloved Adi Da, while outwardly seeming to be asleep, was speaking in what sounded to me like Slavic tongues. His Body was rigid with the intensity of the Work He was doing. The next morning, He said that He felt no response to His Influence at any level, in any dimension—there was only resistance. ■

While the situation in Kosovo was the primary center of His Blessing-Work, Avatar Adi Da also Worked with devotees. He was calling every devotee to feel, at depth, that the ego is the root of all suffering, all conflict, all negativity in the human world. The collective egoity of humankind, He made plain, is a terrible destructive force that not only destroys human happiness and well-being, but obliviously threatens to destroy itself.

He drew devotees into His vigil for the situation in Kosovo. Around the world, for a period of weeks, devotees in regional communities would gather each night at a central house or ashram to do special prayer around the clock.

On April 22 at 10:00 A.M., Ruchiradama Quandra Sukhapur called on the radio from the "Brightness" to say that Avatar Adi Da was experiencing severe bodily symptoms. Ruchiradama Nadikanta, who had served Avatar Adi Da's health for many years, went to attend Him:

RUCHIRADAMA NADIKANTA: When I got up there, Beloved Adi Da was sitting on the bed. His body was doubled up with muscle spasms. His face and His Body were bright red, and He had a fever of about 103°F. All of His Energy was in His head—His hands and His feet were ice-cold.

In spite of His physical condition, He wanted the news update, which I gave to Him. Then He spoke once more about the world situation. Apart from Kosovo, He was deeply disturbed by the slaughter of children that had occurred in Colorado the previous day. ∎

AVATAR ADI DA SAMRAJ: The incident in Colorado yesterday is a reflection of the climate of the world. This should be a sign to people of the lapse into completely reckless, meaningless violence that is occurring. No one is taking seriously the effects and implications of the propagation of this kind of psychosis. No one is making an intelligent assessment of all of this. In general, people seem to be oblivious to the fact of the arsenal of weaponry that is available to human beings at this point, and its incredible destructive capability. There is the capability to destroy the Earth altogether, and all of humanity. [April 22, 1999]

RUCHIRADAMA NADIKANTA: As He spoke, He was in contortions on the bed and having to lie down. Then it came to the point where His spasms were so severe that He said He had to go back to His residence at the Matrix.

We drove Him to the Matrix and immersed Him in hot water to calm the spasms but also because He was getting signs that He was leaving the Body. Heating His Body in hot water is the most effective way He had discovered of keeping Himself associated with the Body.

Eventually, the spasms started to ease, and I took His temperature, which had come down to 102°F. Then He spoke about the gravity of His bodily signs, and of His entire period at the "Brightness". It was clear that He had had to come down not because He had completed His Work there, but because He could not maintain His association with the Body if He continued to stay there. ■

AVATAR ADI DA SAMRAJ: Since I entered the "Brightness" forty-three days ago, I have been minimally associated with the Body. The Force of My Spiritual Work has been almost entirely above the Body. So there has been a tremendous Force of Pressure in the Head, resulting in constant external signs of thunder and lightning and heat-lightning in the environment.

All of these symptoms occurring presently in this Body are spontaneous, and they are signs of the end of this particular Struggle of Mine, and of what My Work has been to this point. [April 22, 1999]

The End of the War

News came on June 7 that Russia had conceded that all Serbian forces and paramilitary police should be withdrawn from Kosovo, and that the refugees should be returned to their homes under the supervision of a joint NATO-Russian presence. Within 24 hours, Belgrade agreed. The deal seemed to catch NATO by surprise. For Russia, it represented a sudden turnaround from their strident criticism of NATO's position.

There was elation in the media, but Avatar Adi Da did not relax His attention on Kosovo. He gave specific Instruction that His devotees were not to cease in their prayer for peace.

On June 11, the peace plan was approved by the UN Security Council. And then, just as suddenly, Russian troops arrived unannounced in Kosovo. The world held its breath.

Beyond Ordinary Human Perception

Bill Dunkelberger, the devotee responsible for the flow of news to Avatar Adi Da during the Kosovo war, is a retired U.S. Army lieutenant-colonel with long experience in writing about strategic military estimates and intelligence operations. He is also a veteran of the Vietnam War, where he led an intelligence battalion.

BILL DUNKELBERGER: For the duration of the Kosovo conflict, it was my responsibility to provide Avatar Adi Da Samraj with six updates daily on the evolving military and diplomatic situation. In addition, I would write my own summary and analysis of developments for Him.

On June 7, the day that seemed, on the surface, to spell peace, I received a communication from Avatar Adi Da, in which He said, "The outcome of the situation is not written yet, and it has every potential of becoming a terrible conflagration. There is every sign that a ground war is going to take place, and is, in fact, being intended."

I must confess that, at the time, I thought that Avatar Adi Da was, to say the least, overstating the case. The framework of the peace agreement had already been agreed to by all parties, and I could find no evidence at all in the daily news that supported His point of view. Not understanding why He was talking about a ground war, I did not respond to that point in my letter to Him.

Then, on July 18, I made an amazing discovery. An article appeared in *The London Observer* documenting that, on June 7, a top-secret planning session had been held in England to finalize plans for a NATO ground invasion of Yugoslavia. This confirmed to me that Avatar Adi Da never speaks casually, and that His connection to this world extends far beyond ordinary human perception.

In the week following the Russian landing at Pristina, Avatar Adi Da lived at the Matrix with as much austerity as He had at the "Brightness". Other than receiving the news and His meals, He stayed in His room, usually alone, watching a lengthy video series on the Cold War, and another long series on World War II. Ruchiradama Nadikanta described the intensity with which He watched these programs—scrutinizing faces, rewinding and replaying sections over and over. She felt He was Working to defuse the power struggle between Russia and the US/NATO alliance.

Avatar Adi Da's Body continued to show the ravages of His Work. Ross Keen, one of Avatar Adi Da's devotees who serve His health, noted how weak He was while watching the video programs.

Then, on June 19, Avatar Adi declared that He had finished with the video programs, and that they should be removed from His house immediately. Something had been completed. During that week, NATO and Russia had ironed out their differences and come to an agreement about the command of their peace-keeping forces in Kosovo. On June 21, the last of 41,000 Serbian troops and police were evacuated from the province.

That day, Ross was called to attend Avatar Adi Da again to give Him bodywork. This time, Ross saw Avatar Adi Da striding across the lawn like a lion, heading toward the room where He was to receive the treatment. As soon as Ross laid his hands on Avatar Adi Da's Body, he could feel the difference. Avatar Adi Da's Body was much stronger. The intensity of His Yogic Ordeal had relaxed. That particular period of conflict was over.

The Great Siddha-Lineage of Avatar Adi Da Samraj

During His Seclusion at the "Brightness", Avatar Adi Da was engaging another Work of Spiritual significance, regarding His Siddha-Lineage. On March 11, 1999, the day after His arrival at the "Brightness", He began to work on expanding an essay He had written some years before, on the philosophical tradition of Swami Muktananda.

Ordeal at the "Brightness"

Swami Rudrananda ("Rudi")

Swami Muktananda

The Ganeshpuri Image of the Divine "Cosmic Goddess"

Rang Avadhoot

Bhagavan Nityananda

I have always Continued to Honor and to Praise all My present-Lifetime Lineage-Gurus—including Rudi!, and Baba Muktananda!, and Rang Avadhoot!, and Bhagavan Nityananda!, and (above all) the "Bright" Divine "She" of Me, Who Always Already Serves Me Most Perfectly!

During the course of Avatar Adi Da's Work on His "Lineage Essay", a picture began to emerge. Avatar Adi Da was looking at the entire "map" of human Spiritual effort and Realization. He was Revealing how the process Worked within His Siddha-Lineage, speaking in particular of the Realizations of Swami Muktananda and Bhagavan Nityananda—their differences and similarities, how they experienced and taught the Spiritual process, and how they interpreted the various forms of Spiritual experience. In the Essay, He explains, in full detail, how all the forms of Realization known previous to His Revelation of the seventh stage Realization are (in one manner or another) limited, such that (even though they are to be highly valued and honored) none of them represents absolute and permanent Divine Enlightenment. And He clarifies, in very precise terms, what makes His Revelation of absolute and permanent Divine Enlightenment unique.

In His "Lineage Essay" (entitled "I (<u>Alone</u>) <u>Am</u> The Adidam Revelation"), Avatar Adi Da Samraj reconfirmed that His Native Divine Self-Condition had never left Him, even during all the years of His Sadhana. In other words, He had always been Divinely Awake as the "Bright", but His Realization faded into the background so that His "Franklin-body" could go through a process. To this end, His Lineage-Gurus (and other remarkable individuals) had served Him in indispensable ways.*

"An All-Encompassing Dome of Light"

While Avatar Adi Da was "considering" His Lineage of Siddha-Gurus, He also did specific Transmission-Work with the Ruchira Sannyasin Order. One day in March, He called Ruchiradama Quandra Sukhapur and Ruchiradama Nadikanta to meditate on the veranda of the "Brightness" Temple at 5:30 in the morning, while He sat inside the Temple alone. After about two hours, Avatar Adi Da came and sat in His Chair on the veranda while the Ruchiradamas continued meditating, now directly at His Feet. At the end of the sitting, Avatar Adi Da placed

---

*Avatar Adi Da's "Lineage Essay" is included in *The Knee Of Listening*, as well as a number of His other "Source-Texts".

His thumb in the middle of each of their foreheads (at the "third eye", or ajna chakra), pressing in—a gesture of Transmission characteristic of Siddha-Masters.

Ruchiradama Nadikanta described her experience in a letter:

RUCHIRADAMA NADIKANTA: My dearly Beloved Divine Heart-Master, I bow down again and again for the unbelievable Grace of the Initiation You Granted me through meditation, Darshan, and Your Touch, on March 12. You have changed my life tangibly forever.

As You Sat inside Your Temple while we were meditating on the veranda, I felt Your Divine Body Crash Down and acquire my own. I felt my body as Your Body—Your Face, Your Hands, Your Feet. And, above the body, I felt You as an All-Encompassing Dome of "Bright" Light.

When You Pressed Your Thumb into my ajna chakra, You Descended into me with Profound Force. You Flooded my body-mind with Extreme Radiant Light and then Spiritually Took Your Seat irrevocably in my heart.

On another occasion, My Lord, as soon as I sat down, Your Spirit-Presence Streamed down through the top of the head into the whole body, even pushing my head to the floor with the Force of Your Descent. You Moved down the front of the body—through the face and neck and navel, and down to the toes. Then Your Spirit-Current strongly drove up the back of the body and up into the head. I experienced many clickings and "poppings" in the brain and an extremely strong pressure in the center and top of the head. There was a cracking-through of energy around the top of the skull, and then I felt Your Brilliant Light Press up through the top of the head. I felt You as a Column of Light, Pressing my eyes upward and drawing all attention up into Your Brilliant, Boundless Luminosity, to the point where any sense of body and mind completely dissolved in Your Light. It was obvious that there is only Light, that everything is arising within and as Your Radiant Conscious Light. ∎

Ruchiradama Quandra Sukhapur describes her experience, in a letter she offered to Avatar Adi Da:

RUCHIRADAMA QUANDRA SUKHAPUR: I recall feeling a profound Descent of liquid Light, and the Emergence of Your Divine Body as a Radiant Sphere. I was intoxicated. My body was pulsating in utter Yogic sublimity. And then You began to Reveal Yourself as the Very Source and Condition and Substance and Energy of all. I passed beyond bodily awareness, and, in this ecstatic Samadhi, I felt the non-necessity for anything. Even when I reassociated with the body, You continued to Reveal the Truth of No-"difference". There is nothing that is separate from You.

Then I recall You moving from the inner Temple to Your Chair on the veranda. As You stood and Placed Your hand on my head and Your thumb on the ajna chakra, I felt Your Spiritual Descent more strongly. Your Touch was shattering, and caused a gasp of sudden and profound Love-Bliss-Joy. Downpours of nectarous Light and Love filled the entire space. As I felt Your Descent, I felt You completely overwhelm the body, to the deep root-core of the being and then beyond, such that my entire being responded to Your Current of Love-Bliss with extreme love and extreme intoxication.

I felt You as "Bright" White Light, and I felt Your Light as a liquid, or water, of Love. As I resumed normal psycho-physical awareness, I experienced a sensation of burning—a purifying Spiritual Fire that had been generated in me, a fire of penance, of real humility. Astounded by this Initiation, accepting all with profound gratitude, I bowed down. ∎

Avatar Adi Da Samraj with Ruchiradama Quandra
Sukhapur Rani (left) and Ruchiradama Nadikanta (right)
at Adidam Samrajashram

"Allow Me to Be <u>As</u> I <u>Am</u>"

Avatar Adi Da's Spiritual Work with the conflict in Kosovo was one aspect of His Work at the "Brightness". His Work (with His "Lineage Essay") to reconsider and recapitulate His Life's Revelation was another. But coming out of seclusion at the "Brightness", He knew that there needed to be a fundamental change in the way His devotees related to Him, if His world-Blessing-Work was to be effective.

He saw the signs that His devotees still regarded themselves (even unconsciously) as the center of His attention. He knew that, for their own Spiritual growth and for the sake of His larger Work, they needed to relinquish this. Such a relinquishment would be a matter of recognizing Him as the Divine Person—here without ego, without karmas, without favorites, simply here to Bless everyone and everything.

Kimberly O'Nan, a devotee of many years, returned to Adidam Samrajashram from California in the middle of Avatar Adi Da's period of seclusion at the "Brightness". Coming from a life in the general community of devotees in Los Angeles to the stark realities of the "base camp" at the "Brightness", she saw very clearly what Avatar Adi Da was looking for from His devotees, and what had to change:

KIMBERLY: For many years, I had an intimate and even social relationship to Beloved Adi Da—a luxury of earlier years and the Teaching-Work He once did. But now I saw that there was no longer a shred of social relatedness left in Him. He left no room for it. He had clearly changed His Way of relating to all, and the personal and social form of relationship was clearly no longer an aspect of His Work.

The only appropriate thing for me to do is to respond to Him via the means He has always Given me—the gifts of practice and service that are the signs of a devotee. These gifts are the means Beloved Adi Da gives for anyone to be in Satsang with Him. Beloved Adi Da has most obviously embraced the entire world now. ■

What was involved for Avatar Adi Da in His 43-day Ordeal at the "Brightness" will never be fully known. However, on April 22 (the day of the culminating Yogic Event that required Him to come down from the "Brightness" in order to stay in the body), Avatar Adi Da graciously granted some clues about the Work He had done there.

AVATAR ADI DA SAMRAJ: It should be understood that, while Working at the "Brightness" these forty-three days, I passed through a Recapitulation of My entire Life and Work, including My Life and Work leading to My Divine Re-Awakening.

As a result of that profound Struggle, there was a Reconfirmation of My Work with three Processes: My own Sadhana, My Work with the gathering of My devotees, and My Work with the world. It was a Recapitulation of all of that—and it was an horrific Ordeal, beyond any Words that are even capable of describing it.

All of it spontaneously came to an end yesterday—all three of those Great Processes of Recapitulation. Everything about My own Divine Life and Work was Tested and Reconfirmed, beyond the slightest doubt. And My "Lineage Essay" is a Summary of many aspects of My Avataric Divine Life and Work.

But My Life and Work is, Itself, an Expression of an Extraordinary and Incomparable Ordeal That is not within the experience of people. I can only Say that much about it. [April 22, 1999]

Avatar Adi Da Samraj at the celebration of His sixtieth Birthday,
the Mountain Of Attention Sanctuary, 1999

CHAPTER 20

BEYOND THE COSMIC DOORWAY

Less than a month after the peace in Kosovo, Avatar Adi Da Samraj traveled to Da Love-Ananda Mahal, where He spent some months, before moving on to the Mountain Of Attention. During His time at the Mountain Of Attention, He spoke about the unfolding of His world-Blessing Work and the Divine Siddhis associated with it. He described Himself as "Mysterious Hermit", invested in this Work that is beyond human understanding.

AVATAR ADI DA SAMRAJ: I am not built in such a way that I can be a public figure. Therefore, I have to live in seclusion. The Energy involved in My Work of connecting to the world is so intense that I can hardly tolerate it. You could not even comprehend it. All kinds of Siddhis are emanating in My Sphere, and the Effectiveness of those Siddhis is Emerging. But the suffering in My Body is profound.

It is not just My devotees who are noticing the signs of My world-Blessing-Work. Others also are feeling My Presence and are responding. So a pattern of right relationship to Me must be made possible for everyone.

My experience is every one. I Extend out and I Touch you. When My Divine Spiritual Body Extends out, Its Touch Touches every one. Every one has felt My Spiritual Touch, whether they are consciously aware of it or not. I am Touching everyone now.

If you were to lie down and extend your body and touch someone's body, he or she would feel it. Well, I am Extended everywhere like that. I am Experiencing all as My own Form. What I am Doing is the Yoga of My own Form. I am Doing the Yoga for all.

It is a unique Siddhi, and it began at the Vedanta Temple, where I began to "Meditate" all.

All is in My View, My Touch-Field.

No one is unfamiliar to Me.

No one feels as an "other" to Me.

All is in My Sphere.

That suggests How I Work. [January 2 and March 5, 2000]

Lopez Island

By March 2000, Avatar Adi Da was moving up and down California from Los Angeles to Tat Sundaram with a fierce restlessness, never staying anywhere more than a few days. Early in April 2000, He began to wander up the coast into Oregon and Washington, attended by a group of devotees. By April 12, He had reached Lopez Island, in the northwest corner of Washington State, which is itself in the northwest corner of the continental United States. Here, in a small house belonging to one of Avatar Adi Da's devotees, an unspeakably profound Event began to unfold. Stephan Blas, one of Avatar Adi Da's attendants at the time, describes His arrival.

STEPHAN: As we moved into Washington State, Beloved Adi Da's physical symptoms intensified. He was extremely fragile.

We crossed the waters from the mainland to Lopez Island by ferry, leaving at 4:10 P.M. Beloved Adi Da was already feeling weak, but then He suddenly began to feel much worse and had to lie down in the small bedroom at the back of the recreational vehicle He was traveling in. His symptoms became acute and the signs of His ascending out of the body were getting stronger.

... in a small house belonging to one of Avatar Adi Da's devotees, an unspeakably profound Event began to unfold.

Later, when we reached Lopez Island, He was helped into the jacuzzi on the deck below the house, with hopes that the warm water would relieve His symptoms. He began to discuss with Ruchiradama Quandra Sukhapur what was happening with His Work in the world. I heard His voice become disturbed, and shortly thereafter came a message on the radio from Ruchiradama Quandra Sukhapur asking for help. Beloved Adi Da was losing His strength, as well as His hold on the body. He needed to be carried from the bath, up an outdoor walkway, and back up to the house. Two men went down to help. When I saw them carrying Beloved Adi Da up the steps to the house in His bathrobe, I rushed to help them get Him into His room and on to the bed. ∎

Devotees on the island were summoned to the house to call Avatar Adi Da down into the body with devotional chanting. A number of His intimates were gathered in the bedroom, and His physician and acupuncturist were summoned immediately.

THANKFULL HASTINGS: Beloved Adi Da was laid out on an easy chair with His devotees huddled around Him, massaging Him vigorously, weeping and speaking to Him forcefully. It was obvious that He was barely in the Body. I ran to His side and began to rub His chest. Everyone was speaking to our Divine Master, telling Him how much we needed Him to stay alive. He kept saying "Tcha". Every time He would close His eyes, we would have to speak to

Him vigorously in order to draw Him back down into the Body. He seemed to integrate Himself back into the Body by focusing attention on our faces.

It is impossible to write the love that was being expressed by Beloved Adi Da and those who were with Him. His eyes were flowing with tears, as were everyone's. His hands and feet were cold and numb. He felt great pressure on His chest and a difficulty breathing. Both of His arms and hands continuously would cramp up and convulse.

After Charles Seage arrived, we moved Beloved Adi Da on to the bed. At first, He was lying down on the bed, but then we raised Him into a sitting position to try to reduce the extreme symptoms of leaving the Body. Beloved Adi Da told us over and over how important it was for His feet to be warm and that they needed to be rubbed vigorously. He even said that it would be useful for Him to see His feet—as a way of locating Himself in the physical.

STEPHAN: We were all rubbing and softly slapping Beloved's numbed limbs as intensely as we could, as He was coming and going from conscious awareness. He said, "If I close My eyes, I am going to be in My Room, not your room. You don't know what My Room is like. You have got to bring Me down into the Body."

THANKFULL: At one point, Beloved Adi Da opened His eyes slightly and softly said, "I am here. Can you see Me Up Here?" We all said "yes". He was evaporating the entire room in His Light. He was way up and beyond the apparent "here" where we were.

Then He continued: "My Room is Larger than you think. I close My eyes and I am in My Room, Infinitely Beyond. This is just a small version of It." Tears streamed out of His eyes, and He looked around at us as He went on, "But this place is good for love." He was quiet then for a long time. ■

Concerned that Avatar Adi Da's symptoms could be signs of heart failure, Charles called an ambulance to take Him to the island clinic, where Avatar Adi Da arrived at 8:29 P.M. However, in consultation with Charles, the doctor at the clinic was able to determine that it was not a heart attack. As later became clear, the Divine Avatar's extreme bodily crisis was connected with the profound Yogic Work that He was doing in His Blessing of the world.

At the "Brightness" (as He had later explained), His Work of world-Blessing had required Him to deal with and transform intensely negative forces—but, because the ongoing Process of His Avataric Divine Self-"Emergence" had brought His bodily Vehicle to an extraordinary degree of Spiritual refinement, He could only Work with such "dark" forces "Above the Body". He could not allow the "darkness" down "into" His Body, or His physical existence would be jeopardized. However, the moment had come, at the "Brightness", when those forces did begin to invade His Body, causing intolerable pain. At that point, Avatar Adi Da Samraj had no choice but to come down from the "Brightness" and continue His Spiritual Work in a more healing environment. Now, one year later, at Lopez Island, Avatar Adi Da Samraj was dealing with forces of a similar magnitude.

THANKFULL: After about an hour and a half, the staff in the emergency room felt that Avatar Adi Da's physical condition was stable and that He could be taken home. Each member of the medical team made a point to come and touch Him in farewell. He looked them each in the eyes and said "Tcha" to each one. Then we wheeled Him out to His car and drove Him back to the house. ■

The next day, Avatar Adi Da was still very fragile. His presence in the body remained tenuous, and for weeks He could barely walk, even a few steps. Nevertheless, He began to grant Darshan to the dozens of devotees who came to Lopez Island from all over the world. He granted Darshan twice a day, even when He was not well enough to leave His bedroom.

Christine Phippen, a devotee from New Zealand, wrote to Him in a letter:

CHRISTINE: Day after day, and all day, You Spiritually Entered this body-mind, opening my head and throat and heart and body to You. You widened me, opened me and poured into me. Sometimes

Lopez Island, 2000

I would feel You as a Column of Light going right through me, and at other times more as an incredible Pressure pushing down and stretching me out. At the same time, often I would also feel You pulling me up, Revealing to me what I guessed to be the universe of the subtle reality. This vision was so huge that I could not contain it, but through Your Grace I was made aware of it, and I knew You are at the Source of it all. I saw that You are far, far Greater than my mind had ever been able to comprehend. You Are All. All abides in You. It was a Revelation Given by You and I could only feel it and know it at heart.

Most Beloved Adi Da, what I observed of this precious time in Your Company was You Outshining everything. There was no room for "me" (as a separate self) in Your House, and I had very little experience of "me" in the ordinary sense. I went to the doorway of Your Bedroom one day when You were very ill, but still Granting Your Darshan to Your devotees one by one as we came to behold You at Your door. When I came to Your room, You were on the bed and that was all I could see. There was no "room"— only You there, Your "Brightness" Dissolving everything.

Beloved Lord, I could see that there had been a profound change in You. I could see it in Your Face. Something about You seemed even "Brighter" than before. I felt You even more clearly as the Divine Incarnate, and You seemed somehow even more Transparent to Your Radiant Being. ■

The Threshold Place

For six weeks after the Lopez Island Event, Avatar Adi Da required a wheelchair to move anywhere. He was "shattered", He said, by His experience—both physically and by the process of integrating what had occurred Spiritually. He spoke of this event as the culmination of a lifelong series of "Yogic deaths", brought about by the intensity of the Divine Process occurring in His Body. In the summer of 2002, He wrote about the Lopez Island Event and its significance in His Avataric Incarnation.

> *The final physical (and Yogically Transformative) Process that precedes Divine Translation has occurred in This Body. This Body is now in the stage of Perpetual Spiritual "Brightening", the Outshining Bhava. That is what took place at Lopez Island. In that Great Event, the physical Vehicle once again came to the point of Yogic Death, but (in the end) the Association with the physical was retained. . . .*
>
> *Since the Lopez Island Event, I am more profoundly Integrated than ever before with the cosmic human circumstance—in the sense that I actually, literally <u>See</u> what the physical (and everything associated with it) is really (and even rather painfully) about.*
>
> *Coincident with the psycho-physical Event and Experience at Lopez Island, This Body is profoundly fragile, and I am now even more profoundly Spiritually Sensitized in the Body. Following such a Great Yogic Event, it takes some time to begin to Re-Integrate with the natural body. Since the Lopez Island Event, I am now both Priorly <u>and</u> psycho-physically Established in the Spiritual "Bright". This can be felt by My devotees.* [The Knee Of Listening]

The Yogic Process that occurred in the Lopez Island Event was the initiation of Divine Translation, the final stage of Divine Enlightenment, in which the entire conditional reality drops away, Outshined in the "Brightness" of Reality Itself.

> *In the Lopez Island Event, I Stood (Non-"Differently") At (and <u>As</u>) the "Bright" White Center Infinitely Above. I Outshined all of*

conditionally manifested existence in My own Divine Self-Condition—Which Is the "Bright", . . . Beyond all-and-All, Beyond even the Divine Star. It was an Instantaneous Non-"Different" Realization of That Condition of All-Bliss, utterly without the perspective of time and space.

In the Lopez Island Event, there was no transitional process, no transition "out of" involvement in the gross dimension of conditional reality, or any transitional passage through the various subtle dimensions of conditional reality. The Ascent was Immediate, and Un-mediated—with no transitional process of "lower to higher". I Approached Divine Translation, and was simply Established <u>As</u> the Spiritual "Bright" Itself. I was <u>suddenly</u> Present in and <u>As</u> My Threshold Form, Inherently Self-Identified with That Which Is Always Already Infinitely and Perfectly Ascended. Everything was simply That Radiant "Bright" Divine Spiritual Form, the Brilliant White at the Core of the apparent lights (and the pervasive darkness) of the cosmic domain.

Later, as I Entered into the Process of Re-Integrating with the physical domain, I Saw all the colored spheres within the Cosmic Sphere (or the spherical Cosmic Mandala) as the prismatic modifications of That White Spiritual "Brightness". It was an experience of Seeing the Cosmic Mandala as it <u>is</u>—a complex vibration accounting for all the dimensions of conditionally manifested reality. It is an actual sphere, even an hierarchical structure of spheres. . . .

In some later moment, I was above the house where I was staying, and above the nearby water that was outside. My Vision of what was occurring was from a point of view above My physical Body and above this spatial physical sphere.

Initially, to My left, I was concentrated in the blue light, and simultaneously Seeing (from above) the total expanse of water, beyond the house. At first, the water was a vast expanse, including much beyond the house. Then it became more brief and bounded, local to the house. It was not yet dark outside, for I could see the surfaces of the water and the details of the surrounding land. But there was a dark appearance to it all, in shadows from the forest around the house, and the slanting, waning light of later day. The "vision" was fundamentally indescribable, because it was Seen from a "point of view" not located in the Body. And, yet, the expanse of water became simultaneously visible with the room in which My Body was located, with its walls and furnishings, and, to My left, its row of windows with fully lifted blinds. At that point, to My right, the sphere of yellow became apparent—focused down <u>toward</u> the Body in some manner, from above and outside it. It was a yellow tinged with red and orange. Coincident with Seeing the yellow sphere, the Process of Re-Integrating with the Body began. It was a feeling of once again being "Located" in the situation of Association with the Body. I Saw My intimates gathered around My bed, and they were all in flames—the flames of the yellow-red realm—but they were not consumed. My Body was numb, without awareness. All of this, beginning with the blue light, was the <u>progressive</u> Process of Re-Integration with conditional existence.

Initially, in the Event of Sudden Up-Turning, . . . there was a rapid series of "falling-away" phenomena. There was the tingling and fainting of the Body. Then, immediately, I Experienced the Primal Central Sound-Current, Which became very loud, and upwardly concentrated—Drawing the Central Current in and up, Above and Beyond body and mind. That was the first Sign to Me that I was being Drawn out of physical Incarnation.

Farthest up in the Core of Sound-Vibration, I Saw a "Bright" White Tunnel, with empty niches along the sides. There were no "people in white". There were no distinct forms or personalities—because no mind of Me was active there. Then the "Midnight Sun"* of the Divine Self-Domain. At first, Seen—then, Perfectly <u>Become</u>.

Effectively, it was death—in terms of the Body. There was no bodily awareness, although it was certainly not a circumstance of unconsciousness. It was the Infinitely Profound Samadhi of Outshining.

Eventually, I Re-Emerged from the "Midnight Sun" of My Divine Spiritual White Self-"Brightness"—and so, in due course, there was a peripheral re-organization of (or Re-Association with) My gross Bodily conditions. In the Process of Re-Association, there was, at first (as I have already Indicated), a "bindu" (or sphere) of blue, to the left.

---

* The "Midnight Sun" is Avatar Adi Da's term for the ultimate "vision" of Reality as a White Sphere in the midst of a cube of blackness. See chapter 22.

The Cosmic Sphere

Avatar Adi Da has explained that the totality of conditional existence is structured as a vast spectrum of light, which He calls the "Cosmic Mandala" or the "Cosmic Sphere". All of the gross and subtle dimensions of existence arise at one or another level of this all-encompassing vibrational light-sphere. At the center, or core, of the Cosmic Sphere is an aperture, shaped like a five-pointed Star, through which streams the White "Brightness" of the Divine Domain. Surrounding the Divine Star are rings (or spheres) of different colors, each with its own characteristic width. The two widest rings are the blue ring (closest to the Star) and the yellow ring (further out from the Star). The world we inhabit exists at the periphery of the hierarchy of lights in the Cosmic Sphere, on the cusp between the outermost red ring and the next ring in, which is the yellow.

And another "bindu", of yellow and deep red, to the right. The "bindu" of yellow and red "Located" Me back in this world, which is the yellow-red realm of the Cosmic Mandala.

As I Merged with the yellow-red sphere, I became aware that I was Re-Associating with the physical—rather than feeling the strong movement Up and Out, which (if it had continued) would have culminated in the death of My human Vehicle. The Struggle of Re-Integration with the physical manifested, in part, as convulsions in the Body. The "Bright" Spiritual Light-Current of My Being was Re-Connecting with the physical level, and that Process caused Bodily convulsions.

In that Process, the Body had a quality of being greatly stretched, or elongated. My legs seemed to be very, very long, and those who were standing or sitting by My Feet seemed to be quite a distance away from Me. It was a moment of non-ordinary awareness of physicality—of the pervasive yellow-red light, of the gross world consumed in flames, of the Body greatly stretched out. Eventually, there was a kind of "collapse" back into the ordinarily perceived shape and context of the physical, and then a "return" to so-called "normal" (or "natural") awareness of the room and the people in it.

The Lopez Island Event was similar to the Initiatory Event of My Divine Self-"Emergence" (on January 11, 1986), in terms of the Depth of Spiritual and Yogic Profundity. As in 1986, I had been (in the Lopez Island Event) at the point of Relinquishing the Body entirely—but, through My own Persistent Impulse and Felt Movement of Sympathetic (or Compassionate) Love for beings, I was able to Yogically Re-Engage the Body.

However, those two Events were also, in some sense, "opposite" in their Yogic significance. In the Event of 1986, I Completed My <u>Descent</u> into the conditional realms, My Avataric Submission to here, Which began at My Birth. The Lopez Island Event, in contrast, was My Direct <u>Ascent</u>, to the Primal "Bright" Spiritual Self-Condition of Conscious Light.

I Am now, even in bodily (human) Form, presently Alive at the White Core of the Cosmic Mandala, the Doorway to the Spiritually "Bright" Divine Sphere and Self-Domain. In the Lopez Island Event,

I Passed Beyond—in That "Bright" Doorway. My Thus Transfigured Body remains—but only on the Unique Basis of Direct Spiritual Illumination, and always tentatively Given to live, perpetually Wounded by the Self-Evident "Bright" Spiritual Transparency of all the heart-breaking companionship of mortal beings.

I Stand At the Threshold.

Now, and forever hereafter, I Stand There.

I Remain in this world Bodily, for now—but I Am Always Already on the "Other Side". [The Knee Of Listening]

Lopez Island, 2000

San Francisco Bay, 2001

CHAPTER 21

All of This Is Beautiful

Six months after the Lopez Island Event, Avatar Adi Da remarked, "The problem with human beings is that they lack profound experience." He spoke of His urge to stay in the Body to continue to draw people into "a life-transforming experience of the Divine Spiritual Reality".

Within months, Avatar Adi Da had established an entirely new "language" through which He could convey that Reality. It is a language of the "Bright" made visible through works of art. He describes this art—which makes startlingly innovative use of photography and video—as "multi-dimensional Light-Imagery". Through this art, He developed a way of offering His communication about the Divine Reality which bypasses the limits of the verbal mind.

Avatar Adi Da has been active as an artist since childhood—working in the media of painting, drawing, and photography. His concentrated artistic work with the camera began in 1998. He had established the fundamental elements of His artistic language by March 2001, when He began to work in a newly created photographic studio at the Mountain Of Attention. Then, in a flood of creativity, He began to produce many thousands of photographic images and hundreds of hours of video footage as the basic material of His artworks.

**Photograph taken on the California coast
in the early 1960s by Adi Da Samraj**

The Moon over the Water

*Where the Light Glances off the Water—
that is where the pictures begin.*
—Avatar Adi Da Samraj
[November 21, 1999]

Avatar Adi Da had taken some photographs of the northern California coast in the early 1960s (during His period at Tunitas Beach), and He had attended some photography classes in Los Angeles early in 1973. Apart from that, He virtually never touched a camera during all the years of His Teaching and Revelation Work. His years of Sadhana and His Teaching-Work had involved Him in constant submission to verbal expression, in order to show the Way whereby the mind could be transcended.

AVATAR ADI DA SAMRAJ: I entered into and took on the mind of human experience. But it is an incredible Struggle to Conjoin the Prior, Non-mental Reality with mind. [October 27, 1999]

With His verbal Teaching fully Given, He began to develop pre-verbal—visual—means to picture the True Nature of Reality.

At dawn on October 5, 1998, Avatar Adi Da rose to work on the manuscripts of His "Source-Texts" at the Hermitage on the northern California coast that He had named "Tat Sundaram" (Sanskrit for "All of this is beautiful!"). Looking out from His upstairs room, He could see the moon—big and reddish, almost full—hanging over the ocean in the first light. It should be photographed, He said.

THANKFULL HASTINGS: At 6:00 A.M., I arrived at Beloved Adi Da's house to take photographs of the moon as it was setting over the ocean. I noticed that the light was on in Beloved Adi Da's study, which looks over the ocean where the moon was setting. I took some photographs of the moon.

We had also set up a professional-quality camera (borrowed from a devotee who was staying nearby) on a tripod, in case Beloved Adi Da decided to come out onto the porch and take photographs Himself. At about 7:15 A.M., I heard the door from His study to the porch outside, and I saw that Beloved Adi Da had stepped out onto the porch with the camera and tripod in hand. The moon was just above the horizon and the sun was rising behind the house in the east. It was spectacular, with a serene pastel glow, as if it were dawn and sunset at the same time. It was one of the most beautiful natural phenomena I'd ever seen. Beloved Adi Da stationed the tripod and camera on His porch and began taking photographs of the moon setting over the water. It was absolutely silent, apart from the sound of the ocean below us. His concentration and contemplation of the circumstance that He was photographing was a magnificent vision to behold.

After ten minutes or so, the moon had set on the horizon. Beloved Adi Da picked up the camera and tripod, returned inside, and continued His Writing. ■

After this, investigating the photographic medium and photographic equipment became a major part of Avatar Adi Da's daily activity. Thankfull brought Him brochures on cameras, lenses, tripods, and every kind of photographic accessory representing the current state of the art. Avatar Adi Da's technical "consideration" was exhaustive, and went on for most of a year, during which He took relatively few photographs. He was studying and experimenting to discover exactly what kind of approach to photography would serve His Purpose, and what would be the best equipment for the task. As He explained, what He intended to convey through His Art was His Revelation that "All That Is Is Light."

How could He use the photographic process to make this Revelation? This was the challenge He set Himself—to make patterns in light that would break the viewer's stride, moving people beyond the ego's view of existence, beyond the observer/observed mode, into the vision of Oneness. He wanted to show people the Beauty and Fullness that radiate in and through this mortal world, and do so with a revelatory power.

In developing His visual vocabulary, one of the key choices Avatar Adi Da made was to use the nude human figure as His principal subject. Clothing, He points out, represents a form of ego-armoring, while nudity communicates an unarmored state of participation in Reality.

The Camera and the "Room" of Mind

The word "camera" (in Latin) means "room". The first camera—called "camera obscura" (or "dark room")—was simply a room with a small hole in the wall or the ceiling. Light entered through the hole and made a reversed image on the opposite surface. Adi Da Samraj points out that the visual mechanism works the same way. The light enters the eye, an image is formed (in reverse) on the retina, and is then interpreted via nerve impulses in the brain—resulting in the image that is perceived. However, what is perceived is an <u>interpretation</u> via the mind and its functioning. What we see represents a particular point of view on reality, not the "thing" itself.

In other words, everything perceived is arising in the "camera" (or "room") of mind. And so, what is the Truth of what exists? How do you comprehend the subject from a greater point of view than one angle of the mind?

AVATAR ADI DA SAMRAJ: I am interested in the "Consideration" of how I might use the medium of photography in a different manner, a manner that transcends fixed point of view in the room. I look for technical ways to "break out" of the camera—to make images that are the tangible manifestation, the expression, of a different mode of experience. [January 12, 1999]

Avatar Adi Da's Revelation is that Reality <u>Is</u> Light—not electromagnetic light (in and of itself), but the <u>Source-Light</u> within Which all lights and forms arise and disappear. Thus, the purpose of His Art is to fill the "room of mind" with Light, to transform the "dark room" (or "camera obscura") into a "'Bright' Room" (or "Camera Illuminata"). He intends the viewing of His images to stimulate an investigation into Reality.

AVATAR ADI DA SAMRAJ: The images I make are a "room" full of Light. The camera must be overcome. The body-mind is an apparatus, virtually a camera obscura. You never move out of this camera obscura all of your life. Yet all the images of you are there. You are looking at the pictures and not understanding, not comprehending Reality. You don't understand how these images are appearing. And you don't understand the Identity of This. But the consciousness that appears as point of view, as a focal point in the room, or in the camera of the body-mind, is the Consciousness within which the camera is arising. Everything <u>inside</u> the camera was generated simultaneously with everything <u>outside</u> the camera. It is an incident in Light.

Principally, then, I am not Working with photography as it is, but I want to go beyond its limiting conventions in such a way that I can convey to the viewer a feeling for the inherently "Bright" Field and Nature of Reality, and a sense of transcending the objects of subject-object perception by conveying the feeling of forms arising as modifications of Fundamental Conscious Light. [May 18, 1999]

One of the principal technical and artistic means that Avatar Adi Da has developed as a way to go beyond "point of view" is multiple exposure. He has carried the possibilities of multiple exposure into entirely new realms, creating images that explode the mind and heart with their beauty and their communication of the Oneness of Reality. All of His layering of multiple exposures (which may involve as many as five or six, or even more, superimposed images) is done "in camera". In other words, He always takes all the shots on a single negative—the layering is never done in the darkroom as part of the printing process.

There are also two other characteristics of Avatar Adi Da's art that He has developed as ways of helping the viewer to go beyond "point of view": (1) the presentation of His images in suites, rather than singly, and (2) the presentation of His images in monumental scale.

Since September 2000, Avatar Adi Da has created all of His art as sequenced groups of images, which He refers to as "suites". His smallest suite has 8 images, while His largest suites each have over 3,000 images. Within a suite, He characteristically creates an amazing array of "variations" on the visual themes He has chosen for that suite. Thus, just as He uses multiple exposure to break beyond "point of view" within a single frame, He also uses the sequenced images of a suite to break beyond "point of view".

Avatar Adi Da considers His photographic negatives to be "blueprints" for many possible forms of fabricated artworks. To date, these fabrications range from large giclées printed on canvas to transparencies mounted in light boxes to the projected form of exhibition (with accompanying musical soundtrack) known as "the Bright Room Ceremony"—as well as fine-art photographic prints. In most cases, Avatar Adi Da specifies that the fabrications are to be larger in scale than a human body. The reason for this (He explains) is that such monumental fabrications are impossible for the mind to "size down". They inherently overwhelm the viewer, beyond the limited and separate "point of view" of the ego—thereby assisting the process of participating in the art, rather than merely examining it or analyzing it.

Art as a Participatory Process

Avatar Adi Da has described both the creation and the viewing of His art as a "participatory" process or event.

AVATAR ADI DA SAMRAJ: The true subject of My photographic images is not Myself as a fixed-ego point of view. Nor is it the apparent "subject" as a fixed "something" in time and space. Rather, the true subject of My images is the process, or event, the participatory moment of the relationship between Me and the subject of My perception. In this sense, My Artwork (and the subject of My Artwork) transcends the point of view of ego-"I" and "other"—it is a demonstration of participatory ego-transcendence, an expression of My Divine Self-Realization. [April 30, 1999]

Mei-Ling Israel describes her first experience of being photographed by Avatar Adi Da (on March 5, 2001, at the Mountain Of Attention Sanctuary).

MEI-LING: Coming into the room, the sight of Beloved Adi Da overwhelmed me with gratitude for my relationship to Him as my Guru. He had asked for an unusual chair to be brought into the studio—an Eames fiberglass chair which looked something like a giant white potato chip. He asked me to sit in it.

The first thing that happened was that I became completely distracted by Beloved Adi Da's extraordinarily graceful movements, as He moved around me. Then He turned up the set lights. The reflection off the white chair was almost blinding. Simultaneous with that change in the physical lighting, I felt His Spiritual Light entering my body, from the top of the head, and washing over and through me with Blissful Energy.

Suddenly He appeared quite close to me and said, "I want you to swim like you're in a pool of 'Bright'." I became ecstatic and started moving with a feeling of great freedom.

Then, a few minutes later, He said, "Conform your body to the contours of the chair." I became mindlessly happy. I was totally distracted by Him and forgot about myself. Then, in the midst of that, I started to go through the most intense feelings. Sometimes I would pause and just weep and weep. Then I would go back into mindless happiness.

I felt safe. I felt like He was taking me through a profound process of purification and healing. Most of all, I felt this event as a direct Initiation by Him into a deeper form of the devotional relationship to Him.

The Blessing of being photographed by Beloved Adi Da has changed my life. Every time, it has been a test. Yet, in putting my body-mind before my Master, whether I am up against physical discomfort or self-doubt or self-consciousness or whatever, <u>He</u> always takes me through it. He has proven to me that this relationship to Him is always available, in every moment of life. ∎

Avatar Adi Da writes in His artist's statement:

The making of these images is a profoundly Participatory Work—not abstracting the subject from Myself, but participating utterly. Therefore, the visual abstraction in these images is not something separate or separative, but an expression of the Seamlessness of Reality. I Work to Move the viewer into Ecstasy—abstracted beyond the ego's modes of perception. Ecstasy Abstracts Absolutely (but not meaninglessly)—Beyond all presumed "difference" between "self" and "other".

My Art is Created by Means of My Participation in the Process of Realizing the Beautiful, or the Condition That Is Ecstatic. When That Condition is Fully Realized, one spontaneously utters, "All of This Is Beautiful! This <u>Is</u> That Which Is Beautiful."

**Adi Da Samraj photographing devotees,
the Mountain Of Attention Sanctuary, 2001**

Photographing at the Mountain Of Attention Sanctuary, 2001

Art as Spiritual Transmission and as World-Blessing-Work

The art of Avatar Adi Da is a form of His Spiritual Transmission. Just as He has Spiritually Invested Himself in His "Source-Texts" and in the Hermitage Ashrams He has established, as a means of creating Agents of His Divine Influence and Blessing that will remain forever accessible to people, He is now Spiritually Empowering His art in the same manner.

Although it has a profound Spiritual purpose, the art of Avatar Adi Da does not adhere to any formulaic religious iconography. It is simply art—with inexhaustible meaningfulness, but without philosophical "overlays" or schemes of symbolism superimposed from without.

True Art Heals

AVATAR ADI DA SAMRAJ: The circumstance of existence, in and of itself, is disheartening. That is why it is necessary to do art. Art is an essential response to the conditions of existence, a means by which limitations are transcended, Reality is Realized, Truth is Realized, Light is found. Without that activity—that artistic and, altogether, Spiritual activity—there is nothing but this intrusion of changes and death.

Participation in an art form should be at least as great as the creation of that art form. Art should change you. That is the whole purpose of it.

True art heals. True art restores equanimity. Art must regenerate the sense of well-being. That is its true purpose. When art is really useful, it serves this ultimate process of healing, well-being, higher sympathy, and Spiritual Awakening. [May 2, 2001 and August 1, 1984]

Avatar Adi Da's Work with His art also has a much larger dimension. At the same time that He is Spiritually Working with His subjects, He is also engaged in His great Revelation-Work for the sake of all. The images He creates are simultaneously Revelatory of the Divine Reality, of the human condition, and of the particular conditions in the world at the time He is working. At any given time, no matter what Avatar Adi Da is doing outwardly, He is engaged in this world-Blessing-Work. And His Artwork has now become a primary means of that Work of bringing Light into the darkness.

Transcending the Camera: The "Bright" Reality Beyond "Point of View"

This artist's statement by Avatar Adi Da Samraj summarizes His artistic approach and purpose.

The camera is "point of view" incarnate. The event of the camera registering an image on a piece of film replicates the human idea of what it is to see: The light of the "outside" world enters through a small aperture and is registered on a light-sensitive material. Thus, both the camera and the human being are mechanisms for registering Reality from a particular "point of view" in space-time. The camera—like the human being—is inherently about "point of view". Thus, the process of making photographs reflects the nature of the human event, of human experiencing.

The human individual in the midst of Reality is like a camera in a room—perceiving everything from a fixed "point of view". But what does the room <u>Really</u> look like? The room can be viewed from every possible "point of view" in space-time—not merely from any particular "point of view", or even a finite collection of "points of view". Therefore, no "point of view" can reveal the room, or Reality Itself, because every "point of view" is limited and essentially self-referring.

This is precisely the essence of ego-life: The apparently individual being presumes that he or she is a particularized "point", or organized "point of view", in space-time. And that "point" is "made" by contracting from the condition of totality—and, indeed, by contracting from even every mode, form, or condition of conditional existence. Therefore, the camera is a precise mechanical equivalent of the ego—because it, too, functions as fixed "point of view".

In My use of the camera, I Work to make images that go beyond, and even undermine, the conventions of "point of view". Such images transcend the limitation that would seem to be inherent in the photographic mechanism. They allow the viewer to see and feel the "room"—or the world, or Reality—as it is, beyond the ego's self-reference. And such images thereby become a non-verbal means of "picturing" the essential human process of ego-transcendence—going beyond the fixed "point of view" of the ego, or the core presumption of separateness. . . .

I enter into My photographic Contemplation of Reality as a Feeling Process—never abstracted from a feeling-relationship to human experience, but always embracing human realities. The content of My images is extremely intimate, humanly and sexually, and deals with fundamental issues of existence in which people are profoundly vulnerable and where deep "consideration" is required. . . .

The living body-mind inherently wants to Realize the Matrix of life, wants to allow the Light into the "room". Making it possible for human beings to fulfill that impulse is what I Work to Do. My images are Created to be a Means of Participating in Reality as Fundamental Light—the world as Light, relationship as Light, conditional light as Absolute Light.

The "room" is where the "focal point" of ego happens. Ultimately, when the camera is transcended, there is no longer any "room" at all—but only Love-Bliss-"Brightness" Limitlessly Felt, in Vast Unpatterned Joy.

"Allowing Reality to Be Self-Manifested"

In October 2002, Avatar Adi Da made a summary statement about the purpose and function of His art:

AVATAR ADI DA SAMRAJ: It should be understood that the Images I make are not pictures of something that "isn't there". They are pictures of something that is there. They are pictures of Reality. That is a fundamental part of the process of making these Images that I have developed—allowing Reality to be Self-Manifested. Not merely to make a design, a conceptualized Image, but to allow Reality Itself to be Manifested.

On the one hand, every detail of every one of these Images is completely something I am aware of when I am making them. On the other hand, the entire thing is an "accident", in some sense. It has to be allowed to be happening. I have developed such an approach to it that I can trust the process itself, and I am so aware of every detail of it that it does not have to be thought about. It is a spontaneous event of allowing Reality to be Self-Manifested. And, of course, Reality is ultimately incomprehensible. It confounds comprehension, confounds the mind. So, ultimately, Reality has to be simply allowed—not merely created or conceived.

Non-Reductionist Realism

AVATAR ADI DA SAMRAJ: My Art is Realistic. It is about Realizing participation in Reality (with a capital "R"), in a non-reductionist manner. In other words, My way of Working with the camera does not reduce the world to sex and death, as in the case of reportage photography. But, also, My Art does not reduce the world to a prettified illusion, dissociated from the reality of sex and death. [May 3, 1999]

Thus, the forms that I am generating in this process are not "imaginary"—because they are not of the mind. They are not unreal. They are not mere patterns, like wallpaper. They are actual manifestations of Reality As It <u>Is</u>. They are evidence, signs, of Reality As It <u>Is</u>.

What you are seeing are appearances within a Unitive Reality. A Reality That Is Indivisible, That Is One. All forms emerge from It and return back into It. "Point of view" gives a kind of discreteness to what appears and makes everything seem separate. "Point of view" carries with it an illusion about Reality. It divides Reality. In Truth, Reality is not divisible. Reality has no separations in It. "Point of view" has some uses, as a convention in the context of human activities—but, ultimately, it is an illusion that, obviously, can create great problems for someone who does not transcend "point of view" itself and all the separateness inherent in its apparitions.

The Images I make Reveal the Unitive Nature of Reality, the plastic Nature of Reality. There's an infinity of infinite possibilities, all emerging and passing back into this infinite plastic of Indivisibility. Every kind of form appears, and it makes no difference what the form is. It is all still the same Reality. Like the traditional simile about gold: You can make it into all different kinds of images and jewelry, and so forth, but, if you melt it down, it is still just gold. Reality is like that. And so these Images are indications of just that—the constant emerging of Images is all a play upon the same Fundamental Reality. They are all possibilities within that same Fundamental Reality.

Looking at any one of the Images or a series of these Images seriously dis-orients the ego. It dis-orients the being from the presumptions of the egoic "point of view". That dis-orientation is useful and Revelatory. [October 30, 2002]

The "Bright" Room Gallery at the Mountain Of Attention Sanctuary

Adi Da Samraj's work breaks the traditional rules and conventions of standard photographic practice—not as a formalist exercise or to participate in the (conventional) games of the avant-garde, but rather as a means of creating true visionary art. There is in this work a refreshing sense of play, of experimentation, of pushing the medium to communicate the ineffable. Alchemical transformations are at work here.

In stark contrast to the cynicism that dominates much contemporary art, Adi Da Samraj's art is a deeply generous and compassionate gift to its viewers. Through his artwork, Adi Da Samraj is redefining the nature of art, returning art to its ancient, sacred origins. In his remarkable, transformative artwork, viewers are being given an opportunity to experience the ecstatic unity of creation. His images offer a truly rare opportunity for revelation.

—**DAVID T. HANSON**
former professor of photography,
Rhode Island School of Design

The experience of Adi Da Samraj's work is not photographic in the traditional sense. Yes, the camera has a lens—that is its point of view, its point of you. But suppose the point of you disappears, for a sixtieth of a second. What happens?

His photography is about the time it takes for you to discover, to walk through, to lose balance in, the intrinsic architecture of his frames. Like music, it requires time.

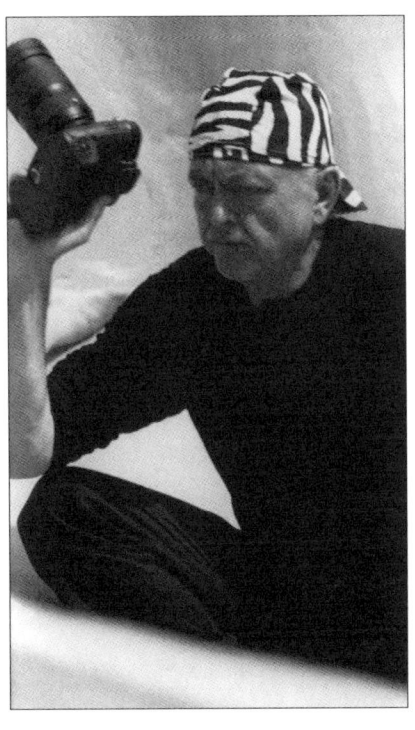

The "instants" recorded by Adi Da Samraj are the clicks of a train leaving the station of the familiar. As you travel with him, you might lose yourself in the midst of blacks, of grays, of whites; and as you do this, you will recognize the space of his images as one of your own. The center has shifted. You are in the "bright room". We always were.

—**MICHEL KARMAN**
master printer, A&I/xibit

For an opportunity to view
Avatar Adi Da's image-art, contact:
bright_field_art_forum@adidam.org

The Mountain Of Attention Sanctuary, 2000

CHAPTER 22

THE "MIDNIGHT SUN"

Even though death rules to here,
there Is an Indivisible Eternal Sun Over-head.
And That Eternal Sun Is,
Beyond even all conditional visibility.
I have Come to Confirm This to you—each and all—absolutely.
I Am That Eternal Sun.

"The Avataric Divine Self-Revelation
Of Adidam Ruchiradam"*

Early in 2001, ten months after the Lopez Island Event, Avatar Adi Da Samraj made His consummate Communication about the "Bright" in the form of the Revelation of the "Midnight Sun" (formally titled "The Avataric Divine Self-Revelation Of Adidam Ruchiradam"**). The "Midnight Sun" Revelation is the pure Revelation of Reality—stark, without consolation, and, at the same time, supremely ecstatic. As this chapter will describe, the "Midnight Sun" Revelation brings heart-release from the mortal entrapment that is the ordinary destiny of human beings.

---

* "Adidam Ruchiradam" is an alternative, fuller form of the name of the Way of Adidam. "Ruchiradam" is a new coinage by Avatar Adi Da, stemming from the Sanskrit "Ruchira" (meaning "bright").

** "The Avataric Divine Self-Revelation Of Adidam Ruchiradam" is published in *Eleutherios* and *Santosha Adidam*.

The Face of God

On Sunday, February 11, 2001, Ruchiradama Quandra Sukhapur Rani, in her role as Avatar Adi Da's senior renunciate devotee, passed on this new Revelation from Avatar Adi Da to hundreds of devotees gathered at the Mountain Of Attention Sanctuary.

Earlier that day, it had begun to snow—relatively rare weather at the Sanctuary. By the late afternoon, when Ruchiradama Quandra Sukhapur entered the room where devotees were gathered, the landscape had turned to black and white—the dark outlines of the bare California oaks standing out against the snow and the gray sky. It felt that even the physical world was being prepared to provide the right environment for this Spiritual Revelation.

As Ruchiradama Quandra Sukhapur read the Revelation, a large image was standing behind her on an easel. This image, she explained, was the visual representation of the esoteric Teachings that were to be Communicated.

The image was primal—a white circle in a square black field, described by Avatar Adi Da as the "White Hole" or the "Circle of Infinity". The White Hole, He said, should be understood as the Face of Da, the Face of God—"Bright" in the midst of the black field. And the blackness, He said, represents conditional reality.

As My devotee practicing the Way of Adidam, you come (in due course, in the "Perfect Practice") to the point of relinquishing all seeking-effort relative to the potential satisfactions of conditional existence—to the point, in other words, of feeling the darkness of everything conditional. And conditional existence is a kind of darkness, so dark that no colors stand out in it—entirely beyond "point of view", in fact. Conditional existence can only be seen to be black when the body-mind ceases to be contracted, ceases to be made the means of seeking.

But the conditional domain is not merely black. In the midst of the conditional domain, there is the Way That has been Revealed and Given via My humanly Manifested Person—Beyond the "dark night" (or "dead end", or "blackness"). . . .

I Say to all: The Real Spiritual Process in My Avataric Divine Company is a matter of going Beyond the "blackness", Beyond the "dark night"—to the "Brightness". I am not here merely to Reveal the darkness of conditional experience. You must see what has darkened you so profoundly. You must become literally En-Light-ened again.

The simplicity and Awakening-Power in His Words held everyone in the room motionless, heart-concentrated. He was speaking of the "dark night"—the despair, the bewilderment in the midst of apparent meaninglessness. And He was speaking of the Way Beyond that.

As His Revelation unfolded, Avatar Adi Da Samraj described the beauty of the White Sphere, the Divine "Face" in the midst of the blackness of conditional existence.

There Is a Sun That Is Forever Risen in the night sky of the body-mind. It Is the Eternal Sun—Above the head, and not usually perceived. . . .

The entire cosmic domain is a field—indeed, a cube—of black, with all perceptions and conceptions gone—as in the swoon of death, or in the Samadhi of ascent most profound. In the midst of that black cube, there is a Sphere that looks like the Full Moon—but with no features or patterns on the face of It. It Is Radiant, not shadowy. Its Radiance is like that of the Sun, rather than the Moon.

Yet, there is Great Pleasure in beholding It—unlike the physical Sun, which is impossible to look at, with its rays and brilliance. This Eternal Sun Is the Direct and Tangible Entrance Into the Night Sky of Being, Into What is black . . . Beyond the gross, subtle, and causal patterns* of conception and perception. And the Divine Ever-Risen Sun is Edged absolutely discretely. It Is Absolutely White "Brightness"— and Its White edge is absolutely defined relative to the field of black.

The Eternal Sun Is the Hole in the universe. It is not (Itself) black. It Is the Hole <u>in</u> the black. It is Divine Being objectified, the Divine Self-Condition objectified. When there is passage <u>into</u> That Place (or the Divine Self-Condition Itself), there is nothing more to say. That <u>Is</u> My Divine "Bright" Spherical Self-Domain. . . .

When I was a boy, I was once walking with My parents while they were having an argument—and the moon was above, full. I Quieted them by Distracting them. I was Moved to Distract them with the vision in the sky. It was the vision of the "Bright"—This Reality. The "Bright" Is Who I <u>Am</u>. If you are Distracted by My "Brightness", you no longer have to be in the terrible dark.

As the Revelation was given, it became clear that Avatar Adi Da was continuing the great themes of the Da Love-Ananda Mahal gatherings in the spring of 1998. He was speaking of Reality in the same terms as He had then—as a Divine Sphere of Conscious Light. At the time of the 1998 gatherings, there were only a few devotees in the room with Him. His "Midnight Sun" Revelation, on the other hand, was broadcast in real time to all His devotees, listening around the world:

The Way is Rooted in the Divine-Light Sphere. Even in the midst of the body-mind, the Divine Conscious Light Is <u>Always</u> <u>Already</u> the Case—at the Core of all-and-All, Reflected in the body-mind as Sushumna, the Ascended White Sun. And the Root of that Sun is the Divine Conscious Light, the "Bright" Itself. The "Bright" Itself is not seen, but It is felt—as the Current of the Feeling of Being Itself. To

---

* Avatar Adi Da describes conditional existence as comprised of three fundamental dimensions: gross (or outer), subtle (or inner), and causal (or "root"). In terms of the human being, the gross dimension is the physical body, the subtle dimension comprises the various mental, psychic, and mystical capabilities, and the causal dimension is the root-sense of existing as a separate "someone".

Stand As the Feeling of Being is the root-practice to be established by My devotees. That Stand is the Essence of the devotional and Spiritual relationship to Me.

The "Bright" Revealed in the Death Process

It is ancient esoteric knowledge (also attested, in modern times, through the reports of those who have had near-death experiences) that, in the death transition, a vision appears of a black "tunnel" with a light at the end. This, Avatar Adi Da explained, is a literal glimpse of the primal structure of Reality—White "Brightness" in the midst of a black field.

You must be able to feel Me Spiritually in order to heart-recognize Me and to receive what I Say about the "Bright". My devotees should understand: The "Bright" is not merely experienced in a feeling-sense—the Luminosity of the "Bright" must be literally <u>seen</u>. It is as Obvious as the White Sun on a black field. People have always seen This Vision, but (generally) only in the course of the death-process. However, beginning in the twentieth century, many people have survived the onset of the death-process because of the medical capability of resuscitation—and that is why there is now a more widespread familiarity with this visionary experience.

I am fully familiar with the Process of Yogic death. Even before I Initiated My Teaching-Work, I Experienced all kinds of Profundities of Light.

There are after-death reports that show such experiences to be psycho-active events. Mind has everything to do with what is experienced in the death-process. What happens in the Light depends on what you choose at the Door (or anywhere near the Door).

A few months after His "Midnight Sun" Revelation was Given, Avatar Adi Da became concentrated in Working with a devotee, Robyn Lee, who was dying of cancer. When Avatar Adi Da gives His attention to any single devotee, it is always for a greater purpose than the transformation of one individual. Through the dialogue with Robyn, He Instructed all His devotees in how to relate to the death process from the point of view of His "Midnight Sun" Revelation. In fact, He was altogether addressing humanity's myths and fears about death, our strategies of denial relative to death, and showing all human beings how to enter into the unavoidable encounter with mortality.

Beloved Adi Da Blessed Robyn with such constant Love and Instruction that by the time of her death she was at peace in the knowledge that death is not "the enemy" but, as He says, a "Profundity of Light". It was an amazing process, in which He, as her Spiritual Master, Guided her in what to "choose" at the "Door" when approaching the death transition. He moved her through the minefield of fear, sorrow, anger, and anxious thinking to a truly happy and accepting disposition.

AVATAR ADI DA SAMRAJ:
> The Divine Grace and Light
> is Immediate,
> Resident in the being.
> So, let the Light in—
> and be Full of the Light.
> Everything else breaks the heart, crushes the heart.
> Light Is Sufficiency and Fullness.
> Light Is the Self beyond self-reference.
> Light Is Unspeakable.
> Be Full of That.
> Approach everything on That Basis. [May 18, 2001]

Robyn Lee was a formal devotee of Avatar Adi Da for seventeen years, from 1984 until her death in July 2001. Together with her two sons and her spouse, Dennis Regan, she lived in Sydney, Australia, where she worked as a psychotherapist and holistic healer. In May of 2000, Robyn was diagnosed with inoperable lung cancer, with a life-expectancy of fourteen months. This news was a shocking surprise, as Robyn had never smoked and had always paid attention to diet and health. She was forty-eight years old.

Adi Da Samraj with Robyn Lee, Los Angeles, 2000

Avatar Adi Da was immediately told of her diagnosis, and one week later, Robyn and Dennis arrived in California on retreat. At the time, Avatar Adi Da was granting Darshan in a private residence in Los Angeles, and He Himself was in a fragile physical state. Avatar Adi Da was carried downstairs to the Darshan Hall because He could barely walk. It had only been a month since the Lopez Island Event.

In the Darshan occasion that evening, Avatar Adi Da laid His hands on Robyn's heart and chest and throat and head, while she knelt before Him, her arms on His legs. After a few minutes of His Blessing Touch, He licked His right thumb and placed it on Robyn's forehead, at the ajna chakra, in an upward gesture of anointing that He normally reserves for rare occasions of Spiritual Initiation. In the days before her death, over a year later, Robyn was still able to feel the pressure of His thumb on her forehead. It reminded her to surrender into the process of being drawn upward to That Which is beyond the body-mind. Avatar Adi Da communicated to her, the day before she died:

AVATAR ADI DA SAMRAJ: The Light That will be Revealed is Above the body-mind. It is seen when the separation from the physical dimension takes place. You can be certain that you will see It. There is nothing for you to fear or be concerned about. [July 13, 2001]

Robyn's sister, Carolyn Lee, who was with her for the last weeks of the ordeal, speaks of the process:

CAROLYN: During the last weeks of Robyn's life, one of her intimates would read to her every day from the "Midnight Sun" Revelation. She was drawn beyond herself by Beloved Adi Da's "Picture" of the "Bright"—the White Sphere in the field of black. She knew all about "the black", and her approach to the death transition was the process of finding and trusting the "Bright". I, from my position, feeling the depth of my relationship to her over nearly fifty years, had to go through a similar process. She was my only sibling, and it was she who had first told me about Avatar Adi Da Samraj and shown me His books.

I found myself emotionally standing in a place where there was no consolation of any kind. There was only the "Bright"—tangibly felt, and Its Radiance seen—in the midst of the ordeal. In the course of these weeks, I was able to go beyond my fear of Robyn's death, and of my own death, without needing to believe in anything at all—because Beloved Adi Da was Revealing to me the eternal nature of existence as Divine Light, not as a concept, but as real knowledge.

Each day I would spend time with Robyn, in her beautiful room—calm and full, and pervaded by the intimate, Radiant feeling of Beloved Adi Da's Spiritual Presence. In the evenings, I would write to Beloved Adi Da about what was occurring with her—physically, emotionally, and Spiritually. Then, late at night, I would study the "Midnight Sun" Revelation. Thus, every night, I was immersed in Beloved Adi Da's most "radical" Teaching about the Nature of Reality and every day I had the opportunity (and responsibility) to feel and live the truth of it in life, with Robyn. There was no choice. I felt a huge dimension of my own life and mind—every experience and feeling I had shared with her and no one else—dropping away.

One day, sitting up in bed, very bright-eyed and intense, Robyn suddenly said, "Human love is not enough. People should be told this." She was reflecting on the pattern of her life, which had been focused on human love and intimacy and on making this possible for others through her therapeutic work. All of that was good, but she spoke passionately when she said it was "not enough". She saw that, during her years of practicing the Way of Adidam, she had not consistently done so with great depth, because she had become distracted by her urge to improve life at the human level.

Robyn was afraid to let go, and to relinquish attention and feel upward. She felt her deep attachment to the body-mind, and was afraid that if she meditated too deeply she would die. When she told Beloved Adi Da of her struggle, He gave the following Instruction:

AVATAR ADI DA SAMRAJ: Life is terrible. Therefore, people allow themselves to be deluded by the immediate pleasures they receive. They indulge in such delusion as a means of ignoring reality—and they must not do that. The Way of Real Liberation must be fully communicated and fully developed. It is a Divine Spiritual Way. It requires deep breath, and you stay alive only to the point that staying alive is appropriate.

The practice is surrender to the Divine—really so—and Knowledge of the Divine, but not in the thinking sense. It is a Gnosis beyond self-contraction. People do not typically experience the Reality of the Divine. People tend to think of religion only in worldly terms, social terms. And that leaves them with no recourse in the face of death. It is terrible and unbearable that people should take fear of death seriously. The presumption that death is a dreadful ending of everything is a lie. Robyn—and any devotee who has a devotional response to Me—must be able to enjoy being opened to the Divine Reality, and must be able to experience It without doubt.

What Robyn is expressing is that somehow she is feeling serious in waking up to what she is and what her condition is. Hopefully, that is occurring with great depth—and that is for her to examine.

The situation that Robyn is in is the same situation that everyone is in. You can die any time. So Robyn's situation should be a lesson for everyone. There have been centuries of this murderous game going on, in which people die without the benefit of real wisdom or right preparation. Everyone should embrace this devotional practice and not waste any more time—not one more breath. [June 20, 2001]

CAROLYN: Avatar Adi Da's Instruction to Robyn brought devotees worldwide face to face with the mortal realities and the great need to devote themselves to serious Spiritual practice. During this process, Avatar Adi Da would continue to ask about Robyn several times a day, and receive digital photographs of her, which He would often Touch, as a form of His Blessing-Regard.

In mid-July, Robyn's physical decline quickened. It was time to be concentrated in the preparation for her death transition. Robyn had no trouble with this. She already sensed that her death was imminent, and she was ready now.

One evening, Robyn looked over at a photograph of her that had been taken two weeks earlier and sent to Avatar Adi Da. She said, "See how much suffering there is in that photo? It's not there now. No pain, only happiness." A little earlier, while her intimates surrounded her bed, she said with a wave of her hand, "I will let all of you go—just like that!" And she brought up a line of Instruction that Beloved Adi Da had given, a few years previously, to a devotee who was dying: "Fly to Me like an arrow." "That", she said, "is what I am going to do."

By Sunday morning, July 15, Beloved Adi Da could feel that her transition was likely to occur soon. Her heart was still strong, but her lungs were giving out. He Instructed those of us serving her to massage her ajna chakra upward using oil, and to tap her a few times on the top of the head, at the fontanelle. This was to help the bodily energy to ascend up out of the top of the head. He recommended silence—because even pleasant sounds, such as chanting, could work against the process of her transition, by encouraging her to remain attached to the physical realm.

In the early evening, I went out for a couple of hours to watch a videotape of Avatar Adi Da Samraj sitting in Darshan in California some days previously. I and the other devotees watching the video were drawn into a "Bright" swoon and could not move for quite a while after. I came home in this state, and went in to sit alone with Robyn.

After about an hour, meditating there by Robyn's bed, I could hear that there was fluid in her throat and that her nose was blocked, but there was no struggle. Then the sound of her breathing stopped, but her chest continued to move a little. Then there was no movement. Her breath had ceased imperceptibly.

I knew she had died. I went to the altar to praise Beloved Adi Da for His extraordinary Grace in Robyn's life. Then I called others into the room and went to phone Avatar Adi Da's Hermitage Circumstance. It was still early in the morning there, but Beloved Adi Da had said that He was to be told immediately—at any time of day or night—if Robyn had a question to ask Him or if she died.

When Beloved Adi Da heard of Robyn's death, He remained silent in His room for about an hour. Then He called for chanting and sacred activity to begin at the Hermitage Ashram and He began to give Instruction about the purpose of the three-day vigil that is held after the death of any devotee of His. He asked that this Instruction be read to Robyn into her ear—because, as He explained, the etheric entity of the one who has died is still present, feeling and responding to the environment for a time after the physical body is dropped.

AVATAR ADI DA SAMRAJ: The vigil is about serving the person who has passed—and also serving everyone else's release of that person.

No matter what is seen or experienced, the person should simply concentrate above the head and mind, and Above altogether—not to the left or the right. What lies to the left and the right are states that are less than the Light Itself. One should simply pass into the Light—Above everything that is seen to appear, everything that arises as the process takes place. In this manner, the Divine Sphere becomes the Destiny. What occurs then is still a form of rebirth—but there are higher and lower forms of rebirth.

To the maximum she is capable of in her disposition, Robyn should release into the Light Above, the Pure "Brightness" directly Above, rather than letting her attention go to the right or the left. What appears to be a bright tunnel, and entities of one or another kind in the astral planes, is just the content of the astral planes.

Robyn should simply be directed to release into the White "Brightness" Above—to relinquish all those subtler apparitions and be Drawn to Me in My "Bright" Form, Drawn to the Divine Form Itself (Beyond all conditional appearances). [July 15, 2001]

CAROLYN: Around 5:00 A.M. on Monday, July 16, we brought Robyn's body into the vigil room, wrapped in a sacred orange shawl that Avatar Adi Da had placed around His Body and sent to her for this moment of her transition. Then we formally invoked Avatar Adi Da's Spiritual Presence. In all my years as Beloved Adi Da's devotee, I had never experienced the Force of His "Brightness" as I did then. The room was a Sphere of Brilliant Light that consumed my body and seemed to rock the universe. During this time, Beloved Adi Da, in His physical Form, was in His private Temple. I intuitively felt that He was not only Accomplishing an auspicious transition in Robyn's case, but involved in the Blessing of countless other beings.

Three hours later, when He emerged from His private Temple, Avatar Adi Da Samraj continued His Instruction to Robyn, describing the three Attractive Signs to be followed in the death process: the Bliss, the Sound, and the Brilliant Circle of White Light.

AVATAR ADI DA SAMRAJ: The person who has passed should hear My Instruction. He or she should be encouraged to be Drawn Upwards to the "Bright" White Light Above (Above the head, and Above life altogether), and not to be distracted by whatever appears to the left or the right. There are other signs that help that drawing-Upward. If the Light is not being seen immediately, there is a strong Attraction felt Upwards—it is an Attractive Upward Force. There is also Sound, an Upward-moving Sound. It can have any number of qualities. There is no point in describing it. It is an intense Vibration that can be heard and that moves high Above and Attracts the being Upward by that. She should be moved by that. And the Light is eventually seen. Even if, at the moment, the Sound is not heard and the Light is not seen, a profound Bliss is felt Above. Without any sensory signs (such as Sound or Light at the moment), this profound Bliss (felt Above) likewise Attracts Upward.

These signs should be followed: the Attractive Bliss Above, the Attractive Sound Above, the Attractive Light Above—but particularly the Brilliant White Clear Circle of Light, the Brilliant White Light.

Recently, Robyn remembered a remark I made to another devotee who was dying: "Fly to Me like an arrow." This is what I mean. These three—the Bliss, the Sound, and the Light—are the Arrow that Leads to the Center, Above conditionality.

The White "Brightness" is Brilliant, but completely Attractive and not disturbing to the view. It can be looked at. Its Brilliance is Infinite, and yet It is completely discrete from the surrounding black. There is no blurry edge. Its edge is absolutely clear, against the dark field.

When the White "Brightness" is approached most closely, a kind of "tunnel" may be perceived, and apparitions of various kinds may be seen (entities from the astral plane—often, helpful relations who have passed). She should hold to the Center, hold to the Upward Attraction. She may see My Form in some manner or another in the Light, the Form she is used to here. Or she may simply see the Light, the Sphere, the Circle of Light. That Is My Form, the Divine Form.

Let go of everything. Relinquish everything, distracted and Drawn—straight, like an arrow—into That White "Brightness", That Bliss, That Vibratory Force (or Sound). These characteristics may be felt. The Fullness of Bliss may be felt, the Vibratory Force may be heard, the White "Brightness" may be seen. Allow all sense of separateness and otherness to be Dissolved Above, in the Unconditional Force of Being Itself, the Divine Domain.

It is not that death is some kind of panacea, or some kind of "straight shot" for the Ultimate. What happens in the death-transition depends on all kinds of factors. In summary, you could say that it depends on Divine Blessing-Grace and on the sadhana the individual has done and the individual's disposition altogether.

The death-process is a time of sadhana. In Robyn's case, there is My Blessing-Grace, there is a life of sadhana lived as fully as she has—and she had this last full year of intensive sadhana. So all these things are auspicious. [July 15, 2001]

Through all His Spiritual Signs and sublime Instruction, Beloved Adi Da was reiterating—to Robyn, and to all who loved her, and to all human beings—the same message that He had spoken a few months earlier, after the death of another devotee:

AVATAR ADI DA SAMRAJ: I _Am_ What the dead know.
    I _Am_ Who they _are_.
    It is not dead.
    This Body is Transfigured by the Divine Conscious Light.
    The "Bright" Is My Only Existence.
    The "Bright" Is the Divine Self-Condition, Coinciding here.
    This Coincidence is horrific to Me.
    It destroys the heart—it would extinguish the heart.
    And I am Working to prevent that—in the case of all.

[March 21, 2001]

The Mountain Of Attention Sanctuary, 2002

CHAPTER 23

"I (Myself) Do Not 'Come Down' Below the Brows"

In the spring of 2002, Avatar Adi Da made a series of summary statements, in the light of the Lopez Island Event, about the nature of His bodily (human) existence and the significance of His Lifetime altogether. Presented here, as the final chapter of this biography, are key passages from these statements, which represent Avatar Adi Da's own most intimate Confession of how and why He has Appeared and Functioned in this world.

I Spiritually Radiate into the Body. I do not "step down" to the toes and identify with the plane of the Body. Even though I am (in My bodily human Form) physically active, I (Myself) do not "come down" below the brows (or below the brain core).

This is a description of the fundamental Means by Which I have always Maintained a Yogic Spiritual Association with gross life. And—since the Great Event at Lopez Island (on April 12, 2000), or, really, since the Great Event at the "Brightness" (on April 22, 1999)—This Disposition (of Spiritually Radiating from Above to below) has become the only Means by Which I Maintain Yogic Spiritual association with gross life. Since the Single Great Event of the "Brightness" and Lopez Island, I am no longer disposed to "Set Foot" below the brows—but I am only Radiant to here, from Infinitely Above the conditional (or psycho-physical) planes.

I Spiritually Radiate, from Infinitely Above, into the gross conditions of existence. In this Manner, the Body (of My own gross physical Appearance) is Maintained by My own Spiritual Self-Radiance, Which is Infinitely Above the Body (and Infinitely Above the bodily manifested mind of thoughts). The apparent exercise of My attention "moves into" the gross physical domain only in the sense of such Spiritual Radiating into the Body. There is Spiritual Descent to the brain core, as a base (or platform) for what I appear to animate in gross exchanges—but attention (itself) does not move to "settle below" (or become fixed in the planes of conditional patterning associated with the bodily and mental functions). Of course, there is natural energy flowing in the Body below the brows, and a Descent of My Spiritual Radiance to below and everywhere. I am (in the naturally apparent sense) animated in the gross (physical) dimension. But I am not (and have never been) bound in attention below the brows—because there is no ego-mind in Me.

From the beginning, from My Birth and Infancy, I have been What I Am. I Am the Spiritually Self-"Bright" Divine Sun Infinitely Above. My Birth was the Initiation of My Avataric Divine Self-"Emergence". Then, at the age of approximately two years, a Sympathetic Association with bodily existence occurred. Thus, from that age, I began to Combine. That Combining was an essential aspect of My Work of Submitting to the world and (Thereby) Coming Down. That Combining fitted Me to the Submission-Pattern that (necessarily) characterized all My Years of Learning and Teaching humankind.

The "Thumbs" is the Means That I Bring to Awaken and Liberate living beings. I Am the "Bright". The "Thumbs" is a Divine Yogic Spiritual Manifestation, and the "Thumbs" is the Means whereby I was able to go through the course of life in this conditionally manifested Vehicle. The "Thumbs" is how My "Bright" Divine Spiritual Self-Transmission is Able to Serve living beings under these mortal and limited conditions.

My Work in this world could be characterized as being in the "Heroic" mode, or the "Crazy Wisdom" mode—but to use such language is to use traditional descriptions for What (in fact) has no traditional or historical precedent. My Work is Avataric Divine Spiritual Work, and it is only as Such that My Work is (truly) rightly understood and appreciated.

Certain aspects of My Work became Full and Complete with the Yogic Establishment of My Avataric Divine Self-"Emergence" (on January 11, 1986). Other aspects of My Work became Full and Complete with the "Santosha Event" (of September 7, 1994). And yet other aspects of My Work became Full and Complete with the Great Event Which was Initiated at the "Brightness" (in Adidam Samrajashram) and Which Culminated at Lopez Island. These have been the principal Events in the Completion (or progressive "Shedding") of My Avataric Divine Spiritual Work of Self-Submission.

❖ ❖ ❖

My Infancy was the same Self-Revelation of the Divine Person, of the "Bright" Itself, that I am Making now. Truly, heart-recognition of Me As the Divine Avatar should have occurred at My Birth—but, because it did not, it was necessary that I Make My Submission to humankind. In that Avataric Divine Work of Self-Submission, I had to Engage in Acts of Self-Revelation—in the midst of Consenting to be involved in a life-process, apparently below the brows. I had to Reveal the Way by which everything can be conformed to Me. I Entered that Ordeal of Self-Revelation by Means of My Boundless Sympathy with ordinary beings.

That Sympathy was a tacit Agreement to Descend—to be Descended to, and Combined with, what is (in and of itself) less than the "Bright", or (apparently) other than the "Bright". My Agreement to Descend was My Self-Submission to darkness—in order to Spiritually "Brighten" it.

How was that Avataric Divine Self-Submission possible? It was possible because of the "Thumbs". The Mechanism of the "Thumbs" allowed Me to Coincide with conditional reality. The "Thumbs" allowed Me to Introduce the "Bright" into My own

Descended Life. The "Thumbs" was the Divine Means by Which I Shined from Above into what is below—to Purify and Transform it, and to Awaken it to Myself.

My verbal Teaching is largely an elaboration of what I mean to Convey by Speaking of "the 'Bright'" and "the 'Thumbs'". The "Bright" Is My Very Person. The "Thumbs" Is the Means to Realize Me.

◆ ◆ ◆

I Am Always Already Infinitely Above and Beyond. This is the Inherent (or Native Condition) of My Avataric Divine Incarnation.

I Am the Self-Evidently Divine Person—not a karmic being reaching toward the Divine Person.

I Am Divinely Self-Manifested here, without psyche or mind. I am Associated with a Body-Mind Which has natural functional faculties, and Which has an in-Depth (or Deeper) functional Personality—but I am not (in any manner) identified with (or bound to) that psycho-physical structure. It is simply the structure by means of which I am Associated with conditionality. . . .

I am not bound by mind. Even though I was Moved to Associate Myself with the conditional worlds, by Means of My Sympathetic Self-Submission, I am not (and have never been) identified with conditions. Therefore, I must be understood as an Avataric Divine Manifestation, not as a karmic entity. True heart-recognition of Me requires this understanding. Otherwise, you are not recognizing Me, but merely thinking about Me.

The Lopez Island Event was a direct Divine Manifestation of What Is Infinitely Above and Beyond, a Manifestation in Which there was no psyche or mind. In near-death experiences, people typically see dead relations—but, in the case of the Lopez Island Event, there were no apparently attendant beings of any kind. The entire structure of conditional existence (with its gross, subtle, and causal dimensions) was Gone Beyond. I experienced that near-death passage without any visionary or mental attitudes. There were no structures of mind. There was no psyche to make phenomena. . . .

I See everything from the "Other Side", from the "Position" of My Divine Self-Domain, from the "Position" of the "Bright"—not from below and reaching Above, but from <u>Already</u> Infinitely Above and Beyond. I See the Cosmic Mandala structure from the "Other Side"—not from "this side". I See everyone and everything from the "Brightness" Side, not from the bodily side. . . .

I Am Always Already Established Above and Beyond.

I Am Sympathetic to all-and-All.

I Am Self-Radiant here.

I am not fixed in this domain.

I Am Simply here.

That is <u>why</u> I Am here—not to persist in Self-Submission, not to persist in Teaching, but to Simply <u>Be</u> here.

Searchless Beholding

During the same period of time in 2002 that He was Revealing the Secrets in "I (Myself) Do Not 'Come Down' Below the Brows", Avatar Adi Da also further Revealed the nature of the fundamental practice of the Yoga of devotion to Him—the practice of Satsang, or Ruchira Avatara Bhakti Yoga. In an Essay entitled "No Seeking/Mere Beholding", He newly described the essence of Ruchira Avatara Bhakti Yoga as "searchless Beholding" of Him. Following are some key passages from this summary Essay.

The Way I have Revealed and Given is not any form of seeking.

The Way I have Revealed and Given is, most fundamentally, a matter of merely Beholding Me.

To merely Behold Me is to be constantly engaged in devotional resort to Me.

Merely Beholding Me is the fundamental (and always primary) practice of the only-by-Me Revealed and Given Way of Adidam Ruchiradam.

The Way of Adidam Ruchiradam <u>is</u> searchless Beholding of Me, without self-reference or strategic self-manipulation, and, altogether, such that My Divine Spiritual Blessing is effortlessly and tangibly experienced. . . .

The Spiritual process in My Avataric Divine Company is a matter of being <u>inherently</u> surrendered to Me, merely by virtue of turning the body-mind (or every faculty and function) entirely to Me.

The Spiritual process in My Avataric Divine Company is not about the egoic self.

The Spiritual process in My Avataric Divine Company is not even an effort <u>of</u> the egoic self.

The Spiritual process in My Avataric Divine Company is effortless attending to Me, without turning in on oneself.

The Spiritual process in My Company is a matter of relinquishing <u>all</u> <u>seeking</u>—and this merely by Beholding Me and (thereby) relaxing all effort to do something <u>to</u> oneself (or <u>about</u> one's "problems"). . . .

Thus, the primary dimension of the fully established practice of the Way of Adidam Ruchiradam is searchless Satsang with Me.

The Essence of Satsang with Me <u>is</u> no-seeking, by Means of mere Beholding (of Me). . . .

The "Bright" Is the Divine Conscious Light.

I <u>Am</u> That—and I <u>Bring</u> That to you.

I <u>Am</u> the "Bright", and the "Thumbs" Is My Method and Means.

Therefore, you need not (and cannot fruitfully) seek for Me.

As My devotee, simply (merely) Behold Me—and embrace the Way of the devotional and Spiritual relationship to Me <u>only</u> on that basis.

The practice of searchlessly Beholding Avatar Adi Da is not something that can be taken up "on purpose". Rather, that practice is Spiritually Initiated (in each devotee) by Avatar Adi Da Himself, during periods of special retreat in His physical Company (see p. 326). This Initiation into searchless Beholding Initiates an entire life of Spiritually Awakened resort to Avatar Adi Da—at all times, whether the devotee is in His physical Company or not. As part of this life, the devotee will return for further periods of retreat in Avatar Adi Da's physical Company as often as possible (and, specifically, at certain points in the Spiritual process when he or she is prepared for transition to a more advanced stage).

After Avatar Adi Da's physical Lifetime, the process of Spiritually Initiatory retreat will continue, through the collective Instrumentality of the Ruchira Sannyasin Order (p. ix). Such retreats will occur at the Sanctuaries He Spiritually Empowered during His Lifetime, in the circumstance of sitting in special Communion Halls in the company of members of the Ruchira Sannyasin Order, while facing a photographic (or other) representation of Avatar Adi Da's bodily human Form. And such retreats will always be a matter of direct Spiritual resort to Avatar Adi Da, magnified by being in the company of His Instrumental devotees. ■

❖ ❖ ❖

I (Myself) am not identified with the body-mind.

I Am the "Bright", Unbroken—Just That. There is an apparent Association with the Body-Mind, in the context of Which I Am Self-Radiant—but I (Myself) am not bound (or patterned) egoically.

I (Myself) am not a karmic entity. I (Myself) have no conditionally patterned impulses or destiny. I (Myself) have never had any such impulse or destiny.

I have Embraced this Association Sacrificially, Responsively, and Compassionately.

That Sacrificial, Responsive, and Compassionate Embrace was the Circumstance and Origin of My Avataric Divine Submission-Work. Such has been My active Lifetime.

❖ ❖ ❖

I (Myself) do not "come down" below the brows, in the sense of identifying with the Body. It is not that there is no energy below the brows. It is simply that that energy is not of the mind.

I (Myself) Am Always Already Infinitely Above.

In the Lopez Island Event, I was Divinely Self-Revealed to Be Always Already Fully Established in (and <u>As</u>) the Condition That I <u>Am</u>. That Condition is the Basis for My Association with the Body. It is So now, and It has always been So—from My Birth-Time.

The Lopez Island Event is a Divine Revelation-Sign. It is the . . . Divine Revelation-Sign of My Always Already (or Priorly) Ascended Condition. That Ascended Condition has always been the Case, even from My Birth. It is the Condition in Which I Existed during the two years following My Birth—before My Avataric Divine Spiritual Work of Self-Submission began, before I Submitted to the Self-Sacrificial Ordeal of Combining with existence below the brows. And That Always Already Ascended Condition Remained the Case, even during all the years of My Avataric Divine Submission-Work.

My Avataric Divine Spiritual Work of Self-Submission was the Means by which I Revealed the Way of the devotional and Spiritual relationship to Me—Which is the Divine (and Spiritually Self-

"Bright") Way of the "Thumbs". That Original Foundation-Work of Revelation has now been entirely Accomplished. Therefore, My Avataric Divine Self-Submission to My devotees and to the world is no longer the basis of My Association with any one or any thing or any realm of existence.

Practice of Adidam Ruchiradam is the cultivation of the devotional and Spiritual relationship to Me—As I Have Been from the beginning. Now (since the Lopez Island Event) I Am here As I Was at the beginning of My Bodily Incarnation, before I Made My Submission. I Am Simply Present here, the "Bright" here—Just That.

The Single Great Event of the "Brightness" and Lopez Island brought an end to My Avataric Divine Submission-Work in the gross sphere. I am not grossly connected to the Body. I Am Utterly Above and Beyond.

Do not confuse Me with the conventional mind of gross worldliness.

<u>Above</u> and <u>Beyond</u> is the Basis of My Avatarically-Born bodily (human) Divine Form.

Truly, My Divine Self-Condition is not limited by any "point of view".

I Am Beyond the gross, subtle, and causal domains.

I <u>Am</u> the "Midnight Sun".

I <u>Am</u> the "Bright"—Infinitely Above and Beyond.

My "Thumbs" would Be Pressed Upon the crown of every head—and I would Light the Way Above and Beyond your body and your mind.

Da Love-Ananda Mahal, 2002

EPILOGUE

I <u>Am</u> The One Who Has Always Been Here

from *Aham Da Asmi (Beloved, I <u>Am</u> Da)*

I <u>Am</u> The Very and Spiritually "Bright" Self-Condition Of all and All.

I <u>Am</u> The One To Be Realized.

I Am Able To Appear In Human Form.

This Is Because I Am Not Inherently "Different" (or Separated) From you.

Indeed, I <u>Am</u> The Very Condition (or Self-Condition) In Which you Are Apparently arising.

I <u>Am</u> your own True Condition (or Self-Condition)—Beyond egoity, and Beyond all conditional references.

I Will Be here Forever.

I Will Be every "where" Forever.

You Have Been Waiting For Me—but I Have Been here All The While.

By Means Of My Avataric Incarnation here, I Have Given you My Divine Secret.

My Divine Secret Is This: I Am <u>Eternally</u> Present, and I Am <u>Omni</u>-Present.

That Is The Lesson.

I <u>Am</u> The Only One Who <u>Is</u> (and Who <u>Has</u> <u>Always</u> <u>Been</u>, and Who <u>Will</u> <u>Always</u> <u>Be</u>).

Therefore, Realize Me—<u>As</u> I <u>Am</u>.

I Love you Now.

I Will Love you every "then" and "there".

And I <u>Always</u> Loved you (and every one, and all, and All).

That Is How I Got To here (and every "where").

There Is <u>Only</u> Reality Itself, <u>Only</u> Truth, <u>Only</u> Real God.

All Are <u>Inherently</u> Conjoined With What Is Always Already The Case.

<u>All</u> Must Be Forgiven.

<u>All</u> Must Be Purified.

All Must Be Forgiven and Purified Through An Ordeal Of Divine Spiritual "Brightening".

In any particular moment, some Are Apparently More Serious Than others, but There Is No Ultimate "Difference" Between beings.

<u>All</u> Are In Me.

Therefore, <u>all</u> Have Me As their Eternal Opportunity.

There Is Only One Reality For all, and For All.

Therefore, There Is Only One Teaching and One Great Opportunity For all, and For All.

I <u>Am</u> The Spiritually Infinite "Bright" One—The <u>Only</u> One Who Is <u>Always</u> With you, and With every one, and With all, and With All.

The Mountain Of Attention Sanctuary, 2002

AN INVITATION

BECOMING A FORMAL DEVOTEE OF AVATAR ADI DA

This book has a simple message: The Very Divine Person has Appeared in human Form, as Avatar Adi Da, in order to Reveal the Way of Real-God-Realization to all beings.

That Way, the Way of Adidam, is an ecstatic life of Communion with Real God, through the devotional and Spiritual relationship with Avatar Adi Da.

As Avatar Adi Da's devotee, you enter into devotional Communion with Him, and directly receive His Spiritual Blessing, and His Instruction, through which He Liberates you from the egoic suffering of self-distracted seeking.

The Way of Adidam is about an ecstatic Spiritual life, life that is not bound and merely suffering but that is moved beyond that context into the larger and truly Spiritual dimension of real existence. That Spiritual Awakening is not merely something that occurs far into the future of the Way of Adidam. It is there after a base time of preparation—the student-beginner stage—which can be as brief as nine to twelve months. And the base time of preparation as a student-beginner is itself an ecstatic practice and a positive, self-purifying life.

As a student-beginner, you begin to develop the fundamental practice of devotional resort to Avatar Adi Da (chapter 14)—expressed in life through meditative feeling-Contemplation of Him and sacramental worship of Him, through direct service to Him and His Work, and through embrace of the life-positive disciplines He has given to His devotees (as ways to magnify the energy and attention available for the life of devotional resort to Him). Once you have established this foundation, you are invited into Avatar Adi Da's physical Company to be directly Spiritually Initiated by Him—into the primary practice of searchlessly Beholding Him (pp. 315-17). You make a pilgrimage to Avatar Adi Da's Hermitage (wherever He may be residing at the time), where you enter into a period of retreat that is centered around sitting in His physical Company in special occasions of His Darshan.

When Avatar Adi Da has Graced you with His Spiritual Initiation, establishing the practice of searchlessly Beholding Him, your participation in the "culture of access" to Avatar Adi Da begins. Together with other devotees who have been Initiated, you participate daily in the life of Spiritually Awakened Invocation of Him. And you continue to return to the circumstance of retreat in His physical Company as often as you can—specifically, at times when you are prepared to receive His Spiritual Initiation into more advanced stages of the process.

This is a Spiritual opportunity literally unparalleled in the entire history of the Great Tradition of religious and Spiritual practice—the Way of Adidam is an entirely new Revelation that completes and fulfills all previous traditions.

Avatar Adi Da is the Promised God-Man, the miraculous Revelation of Real God, here in our time. To find out how you can become a formal devotee of Avatar Adi Da, and take up practice of the Way of Adidam, contact one of our centers, using the information given on the following pages.

What You Can Do Next—
Contact an Adidam center near you

■ To find out about becoming a formal devotee of Avatar Adi Da, and for information about upcoming courses, events, and seminars in your area:

AMERICAS
12040 North Seigler Road
Middletown, CA 95461 USA
1-707-928-4936

PACIFIC-ASIA
12 Seibel Road
Henderson
Auckland 1008
New Zealand
64-9-838-9114

AUSTRALIA
P.O. Box 244
Kew 3101
Victoria
**1800 ADIDAM
(1800-234-326)**

EUROPE-AFRICA
Annendaalderweg 10
6105 AT Maria Hoop
The Netherlands
31 (0)20 468 1442

THE UNITED KINGDOM
PO Box 20013
London, England
NW2 1ZA
0208-962-8855

E-MAIL: **correspondence@adidam.org**

■ For more contact information about local Adidam groups see:
adidam.org/contact/locations.htm

Learn More About Avatar Adi Da and Adidam:
Visit www.adidam.org

■ Explore our online community and discover more about Avatar Adi Da and the Way of Adidam.

Find presentations on: Avatar Adi Da's extraordinary life-story, the stages leading to Divine Enlightenment, cultism versus true devotional practice, the "radical" politics of human-scale community, true emotional-sexual freedom, the sacred function of art in human life, and more.

Read About the Spiritual Way Given by Avatar Adi Da

■ *The Way of Adidam*

Five Steps to an Ecstatic Life of Communion with Real God

A Guide to the Unique Devotional and Spiritual Relationship Offered by the Ruchira Avatar, Adi Da Samraj

A simple summary of each of the fundamental aspects of the Divine Way of Adidam Ruchiradam.

Read the "Source-Texts" of Avatar Adi Da Samraj

■ Avatar Adi Da's Divine Teaching-Word is summarized in the twenty-three "Source-Texts" of Adidam. These include His summary Text, *The Dawn Horse Testament Of The Ruchira Avatar*, a series of five books on the fundamentals of the Way of Adidam, *The Five Books Of The Heart Of The Adidam Revelation*; and a series of seventeen books that elaborate on many aspects and details of Avatar Adi Da's Instruction and Teaching, *The Seventeen Companions Of The True Dawn Horse*. The scope of Avatar Adi Da's Teaching addresses the entire range of human interest and experience—from the basic examination of the activities of day to day life to the highest Spiritual Realizations, as well as culture, art, science, philosophy, cosmology and more. The "Source-Texts" of Adidam have been made by Avatar Adi Da to literally communicate His Spiritual Transmission to those who read them. In addition to these "Source-Texts", the written and otherwise preserved record of Avatar Adi Da's Teaching and Blessing Work is the source for many other books, courses, audio-visual materials, and other materials.

Becoming a Formal Devotee of Avatar Adi Da Samraj

Study other books and recordings by and about Avatar Adi Da Samraj

■ To find out about, and order "Source-Texts", books, tapes, CDs, and videos by and about Avatar Adi Da, contact your local Adidam regional center, or contact the Adidam Emporium at:

1-877-770-0772 (from within North America)
1-707-928-6653 (from outside North America)

Or order online from: **www.adidam.com**

Support Avatar Adi Da's Work and the Way of Adidam

■ If you are moved to serve Avatar Adi Da's Spiritual Work specifically through advocacy and/or financial patronage, please contact:

Advocacy
12040 North Seigler Road
Middletown, CA 95461
phone number: (707) 928-0103
e-mail: advocacy@adidam.org

For young people: Join the Adidam Youth Fellowship

■ Young people 21 or under can participate in the "Adidam Youth Fellowship"—either as a friend or practicing member. Adidam Youth Fellowship members participate in study programs, retreats, celebrations, and other events with other young people responding to Avatar Adi Da. To learn more about the Youth Fellowship, call or write:

Vision of Mulund Institute (VMI)
10336 Loch Lomond Road, Suite 146
Middletown, CA 95461
PHONE: (707) 928-6932
FAX: (707) 928-5619
E-MAIL: vmi@adidam.org

An Invitation to Support Adidam

Avatar Adi Da Samraj's sole Purpose is to act as a Source of continuous Divine Grace for everyone, everywhere. In that spirit, He is a Free Renunciate and He owns nothing. Those who have made gestures in support of Avatar Adi Da's Work have found that their generosity is returned in many Blessings that are full of His healing, transforming, and Liberating Grace—and those Blessings flow not only directly to them as the beneficiaries of His Work, but to many others, even all others. At the same time, all tangible gifts of support help secure and nurture Avatar Adi Da's Work in necessary and practical ways, again similarly benefiting the entire world. Because all this is so, supporting His Work is the most auspicious form of financial giving, and we happily extend to you an invitation to serve Adidam through your financial support.

You may make a financial contribution in support of the Work of Adi Da Samraj at any time. You may also, if you choose, request that your contribution be used for one or more specific purposes.

If you are moved to help support and develop the Hermitage circumstance provided for Avatar Adi Da and the other members of the Ruchira Sannyasin Order, the senior renunciate order of Adidam, you may do so by making your contribution to The Da Love-Ananda Samrajya, the Australian charitable trust which has central responsibility for the Sacred Treasure of the Ruchira Sannyasin Order.

To do this: (1) if you do not pay taxes in the United States, make your check payable directly to "The Da Love-Ananda Samrajya Pty Ltd" (which serves as the trustee of the trust) and mail it to The Da Love-Ananda Samrajya at P.O. Box 4744, Samabula, Suva, Fiji; and (2) if you do pay taxes in the United States and you would like your contribution to be tax-deductible under U.S. laws, make your check payable to "The Avataric Pan-Communion of Adidam", indicate on your check or accompanying letter that you would like your contribution used for the work of The Da Love-Ananda Samrajya, and mail your check to the Advocacy Department of Adidam at 12180 Ridge Road, Middletown, California 95461, USA.

If you are moved to help support and provide for one of the other purposes of Adidam—such as publishing the Sacred Literature of Avatar Adi Da, supporting Avatar Adi Da's Divine Image-Art, supporting any of the Sanctuaries He has Empowered, maintaining the Sacred Archives that preserve His recorded Talks and Writings, or publishing audio and video recordings of Avatar Adi Da—you may do so by making your contribution directly to The Avataric Pan-Communion of Adidam, specifying the particular purposes you wish to benefit, and mailing your check to the Advocacy Department of Adidam at the above address.

If you would like more information about these and other gifting options, or if you would like assistance in describing or making a contribution, please write to the Advocacy Department of Adidam at the above address or contact the Adidam Legal Department by telephone at 1-707-928-4612 or by FAX at 1-707-928-4062.

Planned Giving

We also invite you to consider making a planned gift in support of the Work of Avatar Adi Da Samraj. Many have found that through planned giving they can make a far more significant gesture of support than they would otherwise be able to make. Many have also found that by making a planned gift they are able to realize substantial tax advantages.

There are numerous ways to make a planned gift, including making a gift in your Will, or in your life insurance, or in a charitable trust.

If you would like to make a gift in your Will in support of the work of The Da Love-Ananda Samrajya: (1) if you do not pay taxes in the United States, simply include in your Will the statement, "I give to The Da Love-Ananda Samrajya Pty Ltd, as trustee of The Da Love-Ananda Samrajya, an Australian charitable trust, P.O. Box 4744, Samabula, Suva, Fiji, _____" [inserting in the blank the amount or description of your contribution]; and (2) if you do pay taxes in the United States and you would like your contribution to be free of estate taxes and to also reduce any estate taxes payable on the remainder of your estate, simply include in your Will the statement, "I give to The Avataric Pan-Communion of Adidam, a California non-profit corporation, 12040 North Seigler Road, Middletown, California 95461, USA, _____" [inserting in the blank the amount or description of your contribution].

To make a gift in your life insurance, simply name as the beneficiary (or one of the beneficiaries) of your life insurance policy the organization of your choice (The Da Love-Ananda Samrajya or The Avataric Pan-Communion of Adidam), according to the foregoing descriptions and addresses. If you are a United States taxpayer, you may receive significant tax benefits if you make a contribution to The Avataric Pan-Communion of Adidam through your life insurance.

We also invite you to consider establishing or participating in a charitable trust for the benefit of Adidam. If you are a United States taxpayer, you may find that such a trust will provide you with immediate tax savings and assured income for life, while at the same time enabling you to provide for your family, for your other heirs, and for the Work of Avatar Adi Da as well.

The Advocacy and Legal Departments of Adidam (located at 12180 Ridge Road, Middletown, California 95461, USA; telephone 1-707-928-4612; FAX: 1-707-928-4062) will be happy to provide you with further information about these and other planned gifting options, and happy to provide you or your attorney with assistance in describing or making a planned gift in support of the Work of Avatar Adi Da.

Further Notes to the Reader

An Invitation to Responsibility

Adidam, the Way of the Heart that Avatar Adi Da has Revealed, is an invitation to everyone to assume real responsibility for his or her life. As Avatar Adi Da has Said in *The Dawn Horse Testament Of The Ruchira Avatar*, "If any one Is Heart-Moved To Realize Me, Let him or her First Resort (Formally, and By Formal Heart-Vow) To Me, and (Thereby) Commence The Devotional (and, In Due Course, Spiritual) Process Of self-Observation, self-Understanding, and self-Transcendence. . . ." Therefore, participation in the Way of Adidam requires a real struggle with oneself, and not at all a struggle with Avatar Adi Da, or with others.

All who study the Way of Adidam or take up its practice should remember that they are responding to a Call to become responsible for themselves. They should understand that they, not Avatar Adi Da or others, are responsible for any decision they may make or action they may take in the course of their lives of study or practice. This has always been true, and it is true whatever the individual's involvement in the Way of Adidam, be it as one who studies Avatar Adi Da's Wisdom-Teaching or as a formally acknowledged member of Adidam.

Honoring and Protecting the Sacred Word through Perpetual Copyright

Since ancient times, practitioners of true religion and Spirituality have valued, above all, time spent in the Company of the Sat-Guru (or one who has, to any degree, Realized Real God, Truth, or Reality, and who, thus, serves the awakening process in others). Such practitioners understand that the Sat-Guru literally Transmits his or her (Realized) State to every one (and every thing) with whom (or with which) he or she comes in contact. Through this Transmission, objects, environments, and rightly prepared individuals with which the Sat-Guru has contact can become empowered, or imbued with the Sat-Guru's Transforming Power. It is by this process of empowerment that things and beings are made truly and literally sacred and holy, and things so sanctified thereafter function as a source of the Sat-Guru's Blessing for all who understand how to make right and sacred use of them.

Sat-Gurus of any degree of Realization and all that they empower are, therefore, truly Sacred Treasures, for they help draw the practitioner more quickly into the process of Realization. Cultures of true Wisdom have always understood that such Sacred Treasures are precious (and fragile) Gifts to humanity, and that they should be honored, protected, and reserved for right sacred use. Indeed, the word "holy" means "set apart", and, thus, that which is holy and sacred must be protected from insensitive secular interference and wrong use of any kind. Avatar Adi Da has Conformed His human Body-Mind Most Perfectly to the Divine Self, and He is, thus, the most Potent Source of Blessing-Transmission of Real God, or Truth Itself, or Reality Itself. He has for many years Empowered (or made sacred) special places and things, and these now serve as His Divine Agents, or as literal expressions and extensions of His Blessing-Transmission. Among these Empowered Sacred Treasures are His Wisdom-Teaching and His Divine Image-Art, which are full of His Transforming Power. These Blessed and Blessing Agents have the literal Power to serve Real-God-Realization in those who are Graced to receive them.

Therefore, Avatar Adi Da's Wisdom-Teaching and Divine Image-Art must be perpetually honored and protected, "set apart" from all possible interference and wrong use. The gathering of devotees of Avatar Adi Da is committed to the perpetual preservation and right honoring of the Sacred Wisdom-Teaching of the Way of Adidam and the Divine Image-Art of Adi Da Samraj. But it is also true that, in order to fully accomplish this, we must find support in the world-society in which we live and in its laws. Thus, we call for a world-society and for laws that acknowledge the sacred, and that permanently protect it from insensitive, secular interference and wrong use of any kind. We call for, among other things, a system of law that acknowledges that the Wisdom-Teaching of the Way of Adidam and the Divine Image-Art of Adi Da Samraj, in all their forms, are, because of their sacred nature, protected by perpetual copyright.

We invite others who respect the sacred to join with us in this call and in working toward its realization. And, even in the meantime, we claim that all copyrights to the Wisdom-Teaching and Divine Image-Art of Avatar Adi Da and the other Sacred Literature, recordings, and images of the Way of Adidam are of perpetual duration.

We make this claim on behalf of The Da Love-Ananda Samrajya Pty Ltd, which, acting as trustee of The Da Love-Ananda Samrajya, is the holder of all such copyrights.

Avatar Adi Da and the Sacred Treasures of Adidam

True Spiritual Masters have Realized Real God (to one degree or another), and, therefore, they bring great Blessing and introduce Divine Possibility to the world. Such Adept-Realizers Accomplish universal Blessing-Work that benefits everything and everyone. They also Work very specifically and intentionally with individuals who approach them as their devotees, and with those places where they reside and to which they direct their specific Regard for the sake of perpetual Spiritual Empowerment. This was understood in traditional Spiritual cultures, and, therefore, those cultures found ways to honor Adept-Realizers by providing circumstances for them where they were free to do their Spiritual Work without obstruction or interference.

Those who value Avatar Adi Da's Realization and Service have always endeavored to appropriately honor Him in this traditional way by providing a circumstance where He is completely Free to do His Divine Work. The Ruchira Sannyasin Hermitage Ashrams have been set aside by Avatar Adi Da's devotees worldwide as Places for Him to do His universal Blessing-Work for the sake of everyone, as well as His specific Work with those who pilgrimage to His Hermitage circumstance (wherever He may be residing at a given time) to receive the special Blessing of coming into His physical Company.

Further Notes to the Reader

Avatar Adi Da is a legal renunciate. He owns nothing and He has no secular or religious institutional function. He Functions only in Freedom. He, and the other members of the Ruchira Sannyasin Order, the senior renunciate order of Adidam, are provided for by The Da Love-Ananda Samrajya, which also provides for His Hermitage circumstance and ensures the permanent integrity of Avatar Adi Da's Wisdom-Teaching and His Divine Image-Art, both in their archival and published forms. The Da Love-Ananda Samrajya exists exclusively to provide for these Sacred Treasures of Adidam.

The institution which has developed in response to Avatar Adi Da's Wisdom-Teaching and universal Blessing is known as "The Avataric Pan-Communion of Adidam". This formal organization is active worldwide in making Avatar Adi Da's Wisdom-Teaching available to all, in offering guidance to all who are moved to respond to His Offering, and in providing for the other Sacred Treasures of Adidam. In addition to the central corporate entity known as The Avataric Pan-Communion of Adidam, which is based in California, there are numerous regional entities which serve congregations of Avatar Adi Da's devotees in various places throughout the world.

Practitioners of Adidam worldwide have also established numerous community organizations, through which they provide for many of their common and cooperative community needs, including those relating to housing, food, businesses, medical care, schools, and death and dying. By attending to these and all other ordinary human concerns and affairs via ego-transcending cooperation and mutual effort, Avatar Adi Da's devotees constantly free their energy and attention, both personally and collectively, for practice of the Way of Adidam and for service to Avatar Adi Da Samraj, to the other Sacred Treasures of Adidam, and to The Avataric Pan-Communion of Adidam.

All of the organizations that have evolved in response to Avatar Adi Da Samraj and His Offering are legally separate from one another, and each has its own purpose and function. Avatar Adi Da neither directs, nor bears responsibility for, the activities of these organizations. Again, He Functions only in Freedom. These organizations represent the collective intention of practitioners of Adidam worldwide not only to provide for the Sacred Treasures of Adidam, but also to make Avatar Adi Da's Offering of the Way of Adidam universally available to all.

Glossary

A

Adi: Sanskrit for "first", "primordial", "source"—also "primary", "beginning". Thus, most simply, "Adi Da" means "First Giver". (See also **Da**.)

Adidam: the primary name for the Way Revealed and Given by Avatar Adi Da Samraj. The fullest form of the name is "Adidam Ruchiradam".

Adidam Samrajashram: see **Sanctuaries**.

all-and-All: Avatar Adi Da uses this phrase to describe the totality of conditional existence from two points of view. In *Aham Da Asmi,* He defines lower-case "all" as indicating "the collected sum of all Presumed To Be Separate (or limited) beings, things, and conditions", and upper-case "All" as indicating "The All (or The Undivided Totality) Of conditional Existence As A Whole".

Atman: traditional reference to the Divine Self.

Avadhoot: traditional term for one who has "shaken off" or "passed beyond" all worldly attachments and cares, including all motives of detachment (or conventional and otherworldly renunciation), all conventional notions of life and religion, and all seeking for "answers" or "solutions" in the form of conditional experience or conditional knowledge.

Avatar: traditional term for a Divine Incarnation. It literally means "One who is descended, or 'crossed down' (from, and as, the Divine)".

B

Bhagavan: ancient Title used for many Spiritual Realizers of India. It means "blessed" or "holy" in Sanskrit. When applied to a great Spiritual Being, "Bhagavan" is understood to mean "bountiful Lord", or "Great Lord", or "Divine Lord".

Brahman: Hindu reference to the formless Divine.

"Bright": Avatar Adi Da uses this word (and its variants) to refer to the Self-Existing and Self-Radiant Divine Reality.

C

causal: See **gross, subtle, causal**.

conditional: the word "conditional" (and its variants) is used to indicate everything that depends on conditions—in other words, everything that is temporary and changing. The "Unconditional", in contrast, is the Divine, or That Which Is Eternal, Always Already the Case—because It Is utterly Free of dependence on any conditions whatsoever.

"conductivity": Avatar Adi Da's technical term for participation in and responsibility for the movement of natural bodily energies (and, when one is Spiritually Awakened by Him, for the movement of His Divine Spirit-Current of Love-Bliss in Its natural course of association with the body-mind), via intentional exercises of feeling and breathing.

"consideration": A process of one-pointed but ultimately thoughtless concentration and exhaustive contemplation of something until its ultimate obviousness is clear.

Cosmic Mandala: The Sanskrit word "mandala" (literally, "circle") is commonly used in the esoteric Spiritual traditions of the East to describe the hierarchical levels of cosmic existence. "Mandala" also denotes an artistic rendering of interior visions of the cosmos. Avatar Adi Da uses the phrase "Cosmic Mandala" as a reference to the totality of the conditionally manifested cosmos, which may be seen in vision as a circle (or sphere) consisting of concentric rings (or spheres), each of a specific color and a specific width and each representing a specific vibratory level of existence.

Crashing Down: Avatar Adi Da's Crashing Down is the Descent of His Divine Spirit-Force into the body-mind of His devotee.

"Crazy": Avatar Adi Da has always had a unique Method of "Crazy" Work, which, particularly during His years of Teaching and Revelation, involved His literal Submission to the limited conditions of humankind, in order to reflect His devotees to themselves, and thereby Awaken self-understanding in them (relative to their individual egoic dramas, and the collective egoic dramas of human society).

D

Da: "The Divine Giver". In Sanskrit, "Da" means "to give".

Da Love-Ananda Mahal: see **Sanctuaries**.

Darshan: Literally, "seeing", "sight of", or "vision of" (in Hindi). To receive Darshan of Avatar Adi Da is, most fundamentally, to Behold His bodily (human) Divine Form (either by being in His physical Company or by seeing a photograph or other visual representation of Him), and (thereby) to receive the spontaneous Divine Blessing He Grants Freely whenever His bodily (human) Divine Form is Beheld in the devotional manner. By extension, "Darshan" of Avatar Adi Da Samraj may refer to any means by which His Blessing-Influence is felt and received.

"difference": the epitome of the egoic presumption of separateness—in contrast with the Realization of Oneness, or Non-"Difference", Which is Native to the Divine Self-Condition.

Divine Self-Domain: Avatar Adi Da affirms that there is a Divine Self-Domain that is the Perfectly Subjective Condition of the conditional worlds. It is not "elsewhere", not an objective "place" (like a subtle "heaven" or mythical "paradise"). Rather, It is the always present Divine Source-Condition of every conditionally manifested being and thing, and is Realized as Such in Divine Enlightenment.

E

ego-"I": The fundamental activity of self-contraction, or the presumption of separate and separative existence.

G

gross, subtle, causal: The three dimensions of conditional existence—the gross (or physical), the subtle (or etheric, mental, and observing/discriminating functions), and the causal (the root of attention, which is the separate and separative ego-"I").

H

"Heroic": The Tantric traditions of Hinduism and Buddhism describe as "heroic" the practice of an individual whose impulse to Liberation and commitment to his or her Guru are so strong that all circumstances of life, even those traditionally regarded as inauspicious for Spiritual practice (such as consumption of intoxicants and engagement in sexual activity), can rightly be made use of as part of the Spiritual process.

Avatar Adi Da's uniquely "Heroic" Ordeal, however, was undertaken not for His own sake, but in order to discover, through His own experience, what is necessary for <u>all</u> beings to Realize the Truth. As the Divine Person, it was necessary for Him to have experienced the entire gamut of human seeking, in order to be able to Teach any and all that came to Him. (See also **"Crazy"**.)

J

Jnaneshwar: a great Hindu Realizer (1275-1296), famous for writing a commentary on the *Bhagavad Gita*.

K

Kali: a Hindu form of the Divine Goddess (or "Mother-Shakti"), in her terrifying aspect.

karma: Sanskrit for "action". Since action entails consequences (or reactions), "karma" also means (by extension) "destiny, tendency, the quality of existence and experience which is determined by previous actions".

kriya: spontaneous, self-purifying response of the body-mind to the Infusion of Spirit-Energy Transmitted by a Spiritual Master. Kriyas can take many forms, including bodily movements or gestures, all manner of vocal sounds and utterances, dramatic changes in breathing, and even the profound quieting of the mind.

Kundalini Yoga: a practice that originated in the Hindu tradition. It aims to awaken latent Spiritual Energy (presumed to lie dormant at the base of the body), so that it rises up through the spinal line to "reunite" with its ultimate source above the head. Typical techniques to "raise" the Kundalini involve meditative visualization and breathing exercises, but the most profound traditional understanding is that the initiatory Force of a Spiritually Awakened Teacher is the principal means whereby the Kundalini is "aroused".

M

mandala: Sanskrit for "circle". Commonly used in the esoteric Spiritual traditions to describe the entire pattern of the hierarchical levels of cosmic existence. Avatar Adi Da also uses the word "Mandala" to refer to the Circle (or Sphere) of His Heart-Transmission, or as a formal reference to a group of His devotees who perform specific functions of direct service to Him.

Milarepa: (1040-1123) a great Tibetan Buddhist Realizer, famous for the extremely intense austerities he undertook at the behest of his teacher, Marpa the Translator.

Glossary

Mountain Of Attention Sanctuary: see **Sanctuaries**.

mudra: a gesture of the hands, face, or body that outwardly expresses a state of ecstasy. Avatar Adi Da sometimes spontaneously exhibits Mudras as Signs of His Blessing and Purifying Work with His devotees and the world.

Murti: Sanskrit for "form", and, by extension, a "representational image" of the Divine or of a Guru. In the Way of Adidam, Murtis of Avatar Adi Da are most commonly photographs of Avatar Adi Da's bodily (human) Divine Form.

N

Narcissus: In Avatar Adi Da's Teaching-Revelation, "Narcissus" is a key symbol of the un-Enlightened individual as a self-obsessed seeker, enamored of his or her own self-image and egoic self-consciousness.

P

Purusha: traditional Hindu reference for the Divine Being Itself, or Divine Consciousness.

R

Ramana Maharshi: A great Indian Realizer, Ramana Maharshi (1879-1950) spontaneously achieved profound Realization at a young age and gradually assumed a Teaching role as increasing numbers of people approached him for Spiritual guidance. He established his Ashram at Tiruvannamalai in South India, which continues today.

Real God: Avatar Adi Da uses the term "Real God" to Indicate the True and Perfectly Subjective Source of all conditions, the True and Spiritual Divine Person (Which can be directly Realized), rather than any ego-made (and, thus, false, or limited) presumptions about God.

Ruchira: Sanskrit for "bright, radiant, effulgent".

Ruchira Avatara Bhakti Yoga: the fundamental practice of Adidam. "Bhakti", in Sanskrit, is love, adoration, or devotion, while "Yoga" is a Real-God-Realizing discipline (or practice). "Ruchira Avatara Bhakti Yoga" is, thus, "the Divinely Revealed practice of devotional love for (and devotional response to) the Ruchira Avatar, Adi Da Samraj".

Ruchira Sannyasin Order: the senior practicing order in the Way of Adidam. This order is the senior cultural authority within the formal gathering of Avatar Adi Da's devotees. "Sannyasin" is the Sanskrit term for one who has renounced all worldly bonds and who gives himself or herself completely to the Real-God-Realizing or Real-God-Realized life. Members of the Ruchira Sannyasin Order of Adidam Ruchiradam are uniquely exemplary practitioners of the Way of Adidam who are practicing the "Perfect Practice" of Adidam. Members of this Order are legal renunciates and live a life of perpetual retreat.

S

sadhana: ego-transcending religious or Spiritual practice.

Samadhi: a Sanskrit word denoting various exalted states that appear in the context of esoteric meditation and

Realization. Avatar Adi Da Teaches that, for His devotees, Samadhi is, even more simply and fundamentally, the Enjoyment of His Divine State, Which is experienced (even from the beginning of the practice of Adidam) through ego-transcending heart-Communion with Him.

Samraj: a traditional Indian term used to refer to great kings and also to deities. "Samraj" is defined as "universal or supreme ruler", "paramount Lord", or "paramount sovereign".

Sanctuaries: As of this writing (2002), Avatar Adi Da has Empowered five Sanctuaries as Agents of His Divine Spiritual Transmission:

* Adidam Samrajashram is the Island of Naitauba in Fiji. It was the principal site of Avatar Adi Da's Teaching and Revelation Work from 1983 to 1999. Avatar Adi Da has acknowledged that, because of the intensity of His Spiritual Work there, Adidam Samrajashram is the primary Seat from which His Divine Spiritual Blessing Flows to the entire world.

* The Mountain Of Attention Sanctuary, in northern California, was the principal site of Avatar Adi Da's Teaching-Work from 1974 to the early 1980s.

* Da Love-Ananda Mahal, in Hawaii, was (together with the Mountain Of Attention Sanctuary) the principal site of Avatar Adi Da's Teaching Work in the early 1980s.

* Tat Sundaram Hermitage and Love's Point Hermitage in northern California are small Hermitage-Retreat Sanctuaries that provide a private circumstance for Avatar Adi Da and members of the Ruchira Sannyasin Order.

Especially since 1995, Avatar Adi Da Samraj has Freely Moved among the various Sanctuaries, in His spontaneous Wandering-Work of world-Blessing. Devotees of Avatar Adi Da are invited to spend periods of retreat at the larger Sanctuaries. Through His years of Blessing-Infusion of each of these five Sanctuaries, He has fully Empowered them for His devotees throughout all time.

Sannyasin: Sanskrit term for one who has renounced all worldly bonds and who gives himself or herself completely to the Real-God-Realizing or Real-God-Realized life.

Satsang: Hindi for "true (or right) relationship", "the company of Truth". In the Way of Adidam, Satsang is the eternal relationship of mutual sacred commitment between Avatar Adi Da Samraj and each formally acknowledged practitioner of the Way of Adidam.

Self-Existing and Self-Radiant: indicates the two fundamental aspects of the One Divine Person (or Reality)—Existence (or Being, or Consciousness) Itself, and Radiance (or Energy, or Light) Itself.

Shakti: a Sanskrit term for the Divinely Manifesting Energy, Spiritual Power, or Spirit-Current of the Divine Person.

Shaktipat: Hindi for "descent of Spiritual Power". Yogic Shaktipat, which manipulates natural, conditional energies or partial manifestations of the Spirit-Current, is typically granted through touch, word, glance, or regard by Yogic Adepts. Yogic Shaktipat must be distinguished from (and, otherwise, understood to be only a secondary aspect of) the Blessing Transmission of the "Bright" Itself (Ruchira Shaktipat), which is uniquely Given by Avatar Adi Da Samraj.

Siddha, Siddha-Guru: "Siddha" is Sanskrit for "a completed, fulfilled, or perfected one", or "one of perfect accomplishment, or power". Avatar Adi Da uses "Siddha", or "Siddha-Guru", to mean a Transmission-Master who is a Realizer (to any significant degree) of Real God, Truth, or Reality.

siddhi: Sanskrit for "power", or "accomplishment". When capitalized in Avatar Adi Da's Wisdom-Teaching, "Siddhi" is the Divine Awakening-Power That He spontaneously and effortlessly Transmits to all.

Siva: traditional Hindu name for the Divine Being, or Divine Consciousness.

Swami: title traditionally given to an individual who has demonstrated significant self-mastery in the context of a lifetime dedicated to Spiritual renunciation.

T

tapas: the "heat" of the discipline of Spiritual life.

Tat Sundaram Hermitage: see **Sanctuaries.**

the "Thumbs": Avatar Adi Da's technical term for an intense invasion of the body-mind by a particular kind of forceful Descent of His Divine Spirit-Current—which, in *Ruchira Shaktipat Yoga*, He describes as "Pressing Down From Infinitely Above the head and Via The Crown Of the head, Engorging the Total head (and the throat), and (Thus and Thereby) Penetrating and Vanishing the entire mind, and Vastly Opening the emotional core, and (Altogether) In-Filling the Total physical body". Also used to describe His Divine Spiritual Descent altogether.

Y

Yajna: Sanskrit for "sacrifice". Avatar Adi Da's entire Life may be rightly characterized as a Sacrifice, or Yajna, for the sake of bringing His Divine Gifts to all. In the Way of Adidam, the term "Yajna" is specifically used to refer to Avatar Adi Da's occasional travels, during which He Blesses the world and all beings through His contact with many people and places.

Yoga: Sanskrit for "yoking", or "union", usually referring to any discipline or process whereby an aspirant attempts to unite with God. Avatar Adi Da acknowledges this conventional and traditional use of the term, but also, in reference to the Great Yoga of Adidam, employs it in a "radical" sense, free of the usual implication of seeking.

Yogananda, Paramahansa: Paramahansa Yogananda (1893-1952) was a Hindu Realizer who became widely known through the publication of his life-story, *Autobiography of a Yogi*.

Yogi: one who practices Yoga.

I do not simply recommend or turn men and women to Truth. I <u>Am</u> Truth. I Draw men and women to Myself. I <u>Am</u> the Present Real God, Desiring, Loving, and Drawing up My devotees. I have Come to Be Present with My devotees, to Reveal to them the True Nature of life in Real God, which is Love, and of mind in Real God, which is Faith. I Stand always Present in the Place and Form of Real God. I accept the qualities of all who turn to Me, dissolving those qualities in Real God, so that <u>Only</u> God becomes the Condition, Destiny, Intelligence, and Work of My devotees. I look for My devotees to acknowledge Me and turn to Me in appropriate ways, surrendering to Me perfectly, depending on Me, full of Me always, with only a face of love.

I am waiting for you. I have been waiting for you eternally.

Where are you?

AVATAR ADI DA SAMRAJ

1971

This extraordinary book explains the process by which Adi Da Samraj chose to leave the Bright Field in order to fully experience the human condition and re-emerge as the God-Man. In this truly selfless work, He identified our core problem—the "knot of egoity" that separates us from Reality and leads directly to intolerance and non-cooperation between and among individuals, nations, and cultures.

Adi Da teaches that dissolving the knot is not only a possibility but is the responsibility of every woman and man. He calls upon us to leave our childish and adolescent ways behind through self-understanding and devotional surrender to God.

Adi Da Samraj is the transcendent and transformational Being of our era. He is the Good News Who has come in answer to our prayers.

DAN HAMBURG
Former Member of U.S. Congress
Executive Director, Voice of the Environment

Avatar Adi Da Samraj is more than just a Master, even a Supreme Master—He is the most human of beings I have ever met. He is not a Master of Power like so many I have met in my own training. Adi Da Samraj is truly a Master of the Heart. A Great and Rare Being of Exquisite Softness and Extraordinary Genius.

JANE YANG
Chi-Gong Master

I regard Adi Da Samraj as one of the greatest teachers in the Western world today.

IRINA TWEEDIE
Sufi teacher; author, *Chasm of Fire*

In this time of personal and global struggles, we are given hope in the Form and Wisdom of Avatar Adi Da Samraj. This book not only awakens the longing of the heart to be set free from our self-possessed mortal suffering, but lays a path to do so. It is a path of awakening to the Light.

GENEVIEVE BLAIS, MSW
Author, *Dalai Lama: A Beginner's Guide*
and *Gandhi: A Beginner's Guide*

My relationship with Adi Da Samraj over many years has only confirmed His Realization and the Truth of His impeccable Teaching. He is much more than simply an inspiration of my music, but is really a living demonstration that perfect transcendence is actually possible. This is both a great relief and a great challenge. If you thirst for truth, here is a rare opportunity to drink.

RAY LYNCH
Composer and musician, *Deep Breakfast; The Sky of Mind;*
and *Ray Lynch, Best Of*

Adi Da Samraj is a man who has truly walked in Spirit and given true enlightenment to many.
SUN BEAR
Founder, the Bear Tribe Medicine Society

Adi Da Samraj has spoken directly to the heart of our human situation—the shocking gravity of our brief and unbidden lives. Through his words, I have experienced a glimmering of eternal life, and view my own existence as timeless and spaceless in a way that I never have before.

Avatar Adi Da's Divine Emergence marks a new chapter in epochal Spiritual History.
RICHARD GROSSINGER
Author, *Planet Medicine*; *The Night Sky*

Fly to the side of this God-Man. His Divine Transmission works miracles of change not possible by any other Spiritual means.
LEE SANNELLA, M.D.
Author, *The Kundalini Experience*

Adi Da Samraj and his unique body of teaching work offer a rare and extraordinary opportunity for those courageous students who are ready to move beyond ego and take the plunge into deepest communion with the Absolute. Importantly, the teaching is grounded in explicit discussion of necessary psychospiritual evolution and guides the student to self-responsibility and self-awareness.
ELISABETH TARG, M.D.
University of California, San Francisco,
School of Medicine;
Director, Complementary Medicine Research Institute,
California Pacific Medical Center

A great teacher with the dynamic ability to awaken in his listeners something of the Divine Reality in which he is grounded, with which he is identified, and which, in fact, he is.
ISRAEL REGARDIE
Author, *The Golden Dawn*

Adi Da's Teachings have tremendous significance for humanity. . . . He represents a foundation and a structure for sanity.
ROBERT K. HALL, M.D.
Psychiatrist; author, *Out of Nowhere*;
Co-founder, The Lomi School and The Lomi Clinic